THE SCANDALOUS RISE OF INEQUALITY IN CANADA

Advance Praise for *The Scandalous Rise of Inequality in Canada*

"Lars Osberg eloquently reminds us that inequality persists in Canada no matter now we measure it. In the absence of collective action, it is likely to increase further in the coming years owing to the joint influences of AI, global warming, and the concentration of the returns to technological innovation . . .

As Osberg forcefully argues, inequality both deprives much of the population from sharing in the benefits of GDP growth and empowers the wealthy to control the political agenda that resists addressing inequality. Like Lars's previous books on inequality, this one relies heavily on published data to make the case. It is a very readable account of the multi-dimensional problem of inequality and what should be done to address it. It should be read by scholars, policy makers and interested citizens."

— Robin Boadway, David Chadwick Smith Chair in Economics Emeritus, Queen's University

"Lars Osberg has once again set the standard for understanding inequality in Canada. His book provides both a detailed map of the extent of inequality and incisive discussions of policy options to respond to it. Most importantly, the book includes compelling new evidence on the extent of wealth inequality and its relationship to true equality of opportunity in Canada. Everyone interested in inequality in the Canadian context should have this book on their shelf."

— David Green, Professor, Vancouver School of Economics (UBC)and Fellow at the Institute for Fiscal Studies, London, UK

"In an age of ever-increasing economic inequality, we can thank Lars Osberg for charting the changing Canadian specifics and thoroughly updating his earlier book. At the national and international level, the case for anti-inequality policies has been buttressed by the sound analysis and prescription of progressive scholars like Osberg."

— Andrew Jackson, *The Globe and Mail* columnist and Senior Policy Advisor, Broadbent Institute

"In the long list of social and economic issues facing Canadians, income and wealth inequality should always be prominent. Lars Osberg's enduring attention to this issue, and the insights and expertise he lends to the task, deserve a wide audience in this turbulent era of climate change, the pandemic, and unbalanced economic growth. Understanding the general discontent among Canadians facing inflation and an affordability challenge depends on it.

Osberg provides the background and current status of income inequality as well as some thoughtful suggestions to arrest or even reverse the trend toward greater inequality in our times."

— Wayne Simpson, Professor, Department of Economics, University of Manitoba

THE SCANDALOUS RISE OF INEQUALITY IN CANADA

LARS OSBERG

JAMES LORIMER & COMPANY LTD., PUBLISHERS
TORONTO

James Lorimer & Company Ltd., Publishers acknowledges funding support from the Ontario Arts Council (OAC), an agency of the Government of Ontario. We acknowledge the support of the Canada Council for the Arts. This project has been made possible in part by the Government of Canada and with the support of Ontario Creates.

Cover design: Tyler Cleroux
Cover image: Shutterstock

Library and Archives Canada Cataloguing in Publication

Title: The scandalous rise of inequality in Canada / Lars Osberg.
Names: Osberg, Lars, 1946- author.
Description: Includes bibliographical references and index.
Identifiers: Canadiana (print) 20240408608 | Canadiana (ebook) 20240408616 | ISBN 9781459419629 (softcover) | ISBN 9781459419636 (EPUB)
Subjects: LCSH: Income distribution—Canada. | LCSH: Equality—Canada. | LCSH: Wealth—Canada.
Classification: LCC HC120.I5 O796 2024 | DDC 339.20971—dc23

Published by:
James Lorimer & Company Ltd., Publishers
117 Peter Street, Suite 304
Toronto, ON, Canada
M5V 0M3
www.lorimer.ca

Distributed in Canada by:
Formac Lorimer Books
5502 Atlantic Street
Halifax, NS, Canada
B3H 1G4
www.formaclorimerbooks.ca

Printed and bound in Canada.

Contents

Charts and Tables

Figures

Tables

Dedicated to the memory of

Zella Crowe Spencer
1884–1977
Henry Elvins Spencer
1882–1972

Partners in the endeavour to make a fairer society —
and my Grandparents

ACKNOWLEDGEMENTS

Thanks particularly to Molly Hurd, whose comments over the years have noticeably improved both this book and its author. Thanks also to Jim Lorimer for making a crucial observation about what I had forgotten to say while there was still time to do something about it. Many, many professional colleagues have commented and criticized over the years — too many to try to list here. Specific acknowledgements are listed in the articles referenced in the bibliography.

INTRODUCTION

When my information changes, I alter my conclusions. What do you do, sir?

— John Maynard Keynes

This book about economic inequality in Canada was written in early 2024. But I wrote my first book about economic inequality in Canada in 1981 and another in 2018; it is an issue that has always existed and always been important. So why write another book about it? What was new in 2024? What was different from 2018 and what was very much the same as it always has been? In 2024 it was "very much the same" to say that the inequality of market incomes in Canada was much greater than in 1981 and that many more people were writing about it. In 2024, as in 2018, the international academic literature on economic inequality was expanding at warp speed.

However, "something very new" about 2024 was the recent lived experience of Canadians that governments can, if they have to, quite quickly do big stuff which affects inequality — which makes inaction a bit of a scandal. In March of 2020, the Covid-19 pandemic morphed from a global health emergency into a global economic catastrophe historically unprecedented in speed, severity and global synchronization.[1] In Canada, a suite of brand-new multi-billion-dollar programs were rolled out within weeks — Canada Emergency Wage Subsidy (CEWS), Canada Emergency Response Benefit (CERB), Canada Emergency Student

Benefit (CESB) and Canada Emergency Business Account (CEBA). (Their direct fiscal support to aggregate demand added up to 13.8 per cent of GDP.[2]) Combined with massive monetary stimulus from ultra-low interest rates, these programs offset the collapse in employment activity and enabled a relatively rapid recovery of the Canadian economy. It was a remarkable public policy response to an extreme situation.

Although there would have been less need for drastic measures and urgent new programs if a more adequate social safety net had already been in place, nonetheless the speed of implementation and size of these programs constituted important "possibility proofs" that dramatic social policy changes can happen rapidly. The Covid-19 pandemic has been the formative experience of the under-25 generation, who have witnessed rapid, substantial social policy changes that made a significant difference to poverty and inequality — both the Gini index of income inequality and the poverty rate fell sharply during the pandemic. As well as spotlighting the failings of Canada's public health system, the pandemic shock revealed the inadequacy of Canada's social safety net and the importance for the well-being of Canadians of both the public health system and the social safety net — as well as demonstrating that the barriers to a better social safety net are political, not economic. There was also a period of months when public discourse was dominated by a rhetoric that "we're all in this together" and there seemed for a while to be a recognition that effective response to collective challenges requires social cohesion, which increasing inequality destroys. However, as Covid-19 cases declined, with remarkable rapidity the business press returned to old themes of balancing budgets and the unaffordability of ever doing anything to appreciably reduce poverty and inequality. Government listened. Covid transfers were wound down and poverty and inequality started to tick back up.

Climate change has many, many impacts and other people will probably have their own lists of the most personally significant impacts but for me, the severity of the summer wildfire season in Canada in 2023 was a particular shock. Although the climate change literature had always said that wildfire severity will increase as the planet warms, I had mentally filed that prediction under "other impacts." Then in 2023 wildfires burned 17.9 million hectares of Canadian forests — significantly more than the area of Denmark, Belgium, Luxemburg and Holland combined (11.9 million hectares).[3] It was shocking to me that in summertime-Canada the atmospheric concentration of wildfire smoke could now make outdoor exertion a health hazard in all major Canadian cities. But that immediacy of climate change impacts, and the knowledge that these and many other impacts will only get worse if nothing is done about climate change, clashed totally with the ability of Canadians to actually do something about it.

My 2018 book argued:

> Effective policy to limit greenhouse gas emissions in Canada is now paralyzed by economic inequality, specifically by the distributional implications of carbon pricing. Because . . . middle-class earnings have stagnated in Canada, when the Harper government framed carbon pricing as a "job-killing tax" whose implementation would "hurt the economy," that fed on the very real insecurities and financial anxieties of low- and middle-income households in Canada.[4] When many Canadians feel pressured financially, promises that a carbon price, which visibly adds to the day-to-day cost of living, will be somehow offset by benefits sometime far in the future require a lot of trust to be believed. . . . Mistrust of big government, resentments of taxation and fears that carbon pricing will be a job-killing attack on hard-working Canadian families are narratives that have been assiduously cultivated for many years by right-wing politicians. Because carbon pricing has therefore been framed to imply costs (potentially large) for ordinary families and as having only uncertain and distant benefits, a new frame of reference is needed.

Most economists (including me[5]) have long argued that "putting a price on carbon" is the most efficient policy to use for reducing carbon emissions. Back in 2018, I was hopeful that returning all the revenue from carbon pricing to Canadians as a rebate would change the frame of reference for carbon pricing because a per capita rebate would more than offset the carbon tax cost for well over 80 per cent of families. However, the administration of the federal government's actual Carbon Tax Rebate was a mess. Differing by province, mysteriously only rebating some carbon tax revenues and delivered invisibly by anonymous direct deposit, it could not compete politically with climate change denialism and the mistrust of government driven by decades of increasing inequality. By 2024, "Axe the Tax" rhetoric had swept the country. Regulatory attempts to force decarbonization were also unpopular, so the question became whether Canada could "get it together" at all to do the necessary and decarbonize.

Back in 2018, like almost everyone else, I was also not aware that a pandemic was possible, much less likely. By 2024 I had, like many other people, learned a lot about pandemics. I now think it likely that ongoing virus mutation makes it probable that new infectious virus variants will emerge periodically in the future, so periodic pandemics will be a recurring problem for Canadian society. The Covid-19 experience should have taught us that an adequate social safety net is an essential part of dealing effectively with a pandemic. However, at the time of writing, there was no sign of official recognition of that in Canada.

Both climate change and periodic pandemics are existential threats to humanity. Both are collective problems which require collective responses. They have vastly different time scales of impact — Covid-19 shut down the global economy in a matter of weeks and has wound down over months while CO_2 concentrations have built up over many decades and will take many centuries to wind down, even after decarbonization. But in both cases economic causes and costs are central to the policy debates and in both cases what economists call "externalities" — the direct adverse impacts of individual behaviour on everybody else's well-being (through transmission of virus infection or burning of carbon-based fuels) — are central to the problem.

However, finding and agreeing on effective solutions to collective action problems requires some level of social cohesion, which requires a shared perception that the individual costs and benefits of action are being fairly distributed, which increasing economic inequality destroys. For decades the dominant intellectual paradigm informing public policy formation in Canada has been a belief that social and political stability can be taken for granted, that self-interested individual decisions in competitive markets will always produce an efficient allocation of resources and that the inequality and the unfairness of rewards generated by the market is of secondary importance. As a consequence, Canada became a place of increasing economic inequality and rising social instability. Big collective problems like climate change are collateral damage.

A crucial long-term question for Canada in the post-Covid-19 world therefore is whether public policy tries to pivot back to the Zombie Neo-Liberalism[6] of 2011 to 2019. Trends in economic inequality are central to this question. In addition to addressing the Covid-19 shock, a 2024 book on inequality trends also has to recognize the accelerating speed of the arrival of artificial intelligence and the potential size of its impact on the inequality of labour incomes and on capital's share of national income. In Canada, a surge of population growth since 2018 also suddenly ramped up demand for housing. The resultant housing crisis has had major impacts on the wealth of homeowners, the cost of living of renters and the well-being of the homeless. New data and new academic articles are also always adding to our understanding — in particular, new data on the distribution of wealth in Canada became available in 2020.

Since 2018, there have been, therefore, multiple "information changes" about economic inequality that need to be recognized in a 2024 book but economic inequality is also, in important ways, a timeless issue. The social and political importance of fair sharing of the benefits of economic growth does not change. From 1950 to 1980, the income share of the top 20 per cent of Canadian family units was roughly ten times the share of the bottom 20 per cent, so the level of income inequality was, as it always has been, a significant social issue, but the general conclusion then was that "economic inequality has remained roughly constant since the Second World War."[7] Back then, the study of economic inequality was often disparaged as boring — a bit like "watching grass grow"[8] — since changes in inequality in the post-war period had been so small. Nobody then fully realized how important the lack of change in post-war economic inequality in Canada really was.

Interest in economic inequality has dramatically increased since the 1980s, in my view because the facts of economic inequality changed. Unbalanced growth in many countries produced increasing inequality, and ordinary people, politicians and academics all want to know where this new reality will lead. During the thirty-five years from 1946 to 1981, it was at least plausible to argue that economic inequality was the price which Canadian society paid for vigorous increases in everyone's absolute living standards. Inequality in Canada was higher than in many European countries, but it was stable. Balanced growth meant that, even when adjusted for inflation, incomes increased every year from top to bottom of the income distribution. However, since then unbalanced growth has become the new normal: incomes at the top of the distribution have grown much faster than those at the bottom or in the middle.

When income growth is unbalanced and the incomes of those at the top grow faster than those of everyone else, economic inequality necessarily increases over time. However, ongoing increases in inequality within a given society, if such trends can be expected to continue, raise fundamentally different issues from a one-time change in the level of inequality. It is one thing to say, "Canada is more unequal now than it was in 1981" but quite another to say, "Canada is more unequal now than it was in 1981 and Canadians can expect it to become even more unequal each year into the indefinite future."

So what reality of economic inequality can Canadians expect for the next forty years? If income growth for the middle classes continues to be much slower than income growth for the top 1 per cent, income gaps will inevitably widen over time, with ever-greater implications for political economy and economic well-being. But what could halt the trend to more inequality? And is it really as simple as that? In 2024 there were more than forty million Canadians, who differed in many ways — "inequality" is just a single word, but there are many inequalities among individuals.

A general definition of economic inequality is "differences among people in their command over economic resources."[9] But there are many different types of economic resources, both financial (like shares or bonds or pension entitlements) and real (like housing, land, cars and consumer durables). In these and many other dimensions, Canadians differ in both what they have today and what they can expect for the future. To answer the seemingly simple question: "Has economic inequality increased or decreased in Canada?" we have to somehow add up all these differences across all these people. In order to say with confidence that inequality now is "greater than" or "less than" it used to be, a single number has to be calculated to summarize all the many kinds of economic differences among all the many types of Canadians.

However, boiling everything down to a single number can sometimes obscure important trends. The Gini index[10] is, for example, the most popular single summary index number for measuring overall inequality in a population, but it is quite insensitive to changes in the income share of the very rich. The Gini index can remain completely unchanged even when the income share of the top 1 per cent is as low as 1.8 per cent or as high as 32.7 per cent, depending on what changes simultaneously also occur among the incomes of the 99 per cent.[11]

The plan of this book therefore is to look separately at trends at the top, in the middle and at the bottom of Canada's income distribution. After Chapter 1 provides a general overview, Chapter 2 discusses the stagnation of middle-class incomes, Chapter 3 examines the implications of strong income growth at the very top and Chapter 4 looks at the erosion of incomes at the bottom.

Looking separately at inequality trends in the middle, at the top and at the bottom of the income distribution is partly motivated by the fact there are several good reasons to care about economic inequality. Some people worry about inequality trends because they think the well-being and the size of the middle class are crucial to our common shared experiences and our identity and social cohesion as Canadians. They worry that a "hollowing out" of Canada's middle class may be undermining the political stability and the social inclusiveness of Canadian society. Many middle-class Canadians have seen their incomes stagnate in recent decades. Worries about future technological change in robotics and artificial intelligence have deepened anxieties about middle-class jobs disappearing and what this might do to Canada's economic and social fabric. If too many people are hurt by economic change and feel their concerns have been ignored while they watch a fortunate few get vastly richer, what solutions will Canada's "left behinds" turn to? Will Canadians be immune to culture wars, authoritarian demagoguery and minority scapegoating?

For many others, the main reason to care about economic inequality is the income share of Canada's most deprived citizens. Concern about the gap between the poor and the middle class may be motivated by ethical or religious values. The Christian social gospel, for example, argues that "Thou shalt love thy neighbour as thyself."[12]

Human empathy and altruism may motivate concern for the well-being of the poor — but even very self-centred people may sometimes consider the possibility that they themselves could someday become poor. Most Canadians do not have the security that comes with big family money. If an accident or a serious illness meant they could no longer work, many would end up having no alternative but dependence on social assistance. "Enlightened self-interest" can imply that people who are currently in the middle class would prefer that poor people not be too deprived because, in an uncertain world, they too could someday become poor. And a final reason for concern about poverty is its social costs, clearly demonstrated in health care costs and in the social inefficiency of the unequal opportunities of the children of the disadvantaged. But whatever one's reason for emphasizing the well-being of Canada's most disadvantaged, a focus on poverty implies that the important issue in inequality analysis is the gaps between the living standards of the poor and the middle class.

For still other people, the most important issue is the income gap between the economic elite and ordinary Canadians. The income share of the top 1 per cent — and, even more, the top 1 per cent of the top 1 per cent — is the aspect of inequality that has changed the most in recent years. When incomes are growing more rapidly at the very top, the gaps between the middle class and the economic elite are, year after year, growing larger. A continuing shift to greater production of luxury goods requires ever more aspirational advertising to create the demand for such goods — advertising which increases both sales, among those who have the money to buy, and resentments and unhappiness among those who cannot remotely afford to buy but are increasingly often being told about luxuries that they cannot have. The increasing concentration of income and wealth at the very top also heightens the importance of the inheritance of wealth and of unequal socio-economic status. Trends to greater top-income shares and a greater concentration of economic power also lead to a greater concentration of political power, undermining democracy in Canada. At the same time as social discontent rises, economic instabilities also increase because the macroeconomic imbalance of saving and lending produces recurrent financial crises.

These are all important reasons why economic inequality matters, but elite concentration or middle-class inclusion or the income share of the disadvantaged are all somewhat different reasons why inequality matters. They are very much linked, but they do not always coincide. Since they have somewhat distinct causes and different implications, they require different policy solutions. Chapters 2, 3 and 4 therefore look separately at what is going on in the middle, at the top and at the bottom of Canada's distribution of annual household income.

Talking about the "top," "middle" and "bottom" is already simplifying. The top 1 per cent of Canadian incomes started at just under $350,000 in 2021,[13] but there is a huge range, from heart surgeons and corporate lawyers to superstar CEOs and billionaires. In 2022, for example, J. Patrick Doyle, CEO of Restaurant Brands International, Inc., was paid $152,000,000 — far above the $350,000 starting point of the top 1 per cent[14] but also a long, long way below the $1.8 billion annual income of the Thomson family from 2021 to 2023.[15] There are also big differences in the "middle." Over 90 per cent of Canadian taxpayers declared total incomes under $120,000 in 2021. The "middle 80 per cent" of Canadian households includes a huge range of occupations: factory managers, engineers, accountants, university professors, carpenters, teachers, nurses, salesclerks and truck drivers — with widely varying levels of economic security and prospects for advancement. There are also big differences among the 20 per cent of households with the lowest incomes, which include some people who are "long-term poor," such as families dependent on provincial disability benefits and the minimum-wage working poor. However, in any given year, the low-income population also includes many people who have hit a patch of recent bad luck (like a divorce, a major illness, a long layoff or some combination of the above) and who hope soon to be back in the middle class. In Canada, the top, middle and bottom differ hugely from each other, but there is also a wide range of experiences within each of these broad segments of Canadian society.

Furthermore, income, wealth and economic security are all important aspects of economic advantage, but they are different dimensions — correlated and linked, but not quite the same. Substantial assets and high annual incomes do not always coincide. One of my oldest friends is now a retired high school teacher who was able, in the late 1960s, to buy a house near the subway in downtown Toronto.[16] Buying a house in his neighbourhood on one high school teacher's salary is now inconceivable, but as things have turned out, he and his wife now have an asset that is worth millions, even if his monthly pension is what they have available to spend. A hockey player who has just been called up to the NHL will have a pay package that puts him firmly in the top 1 per cent of annual money incomes, but he will probably not be in the top 1 per cent of wealth until he has had some years to save part of his income — and he has very little job security.

Income, wealth and security do not always align. However, at the very bottom, the homeless do not have income or wealth or security and at the very top, the children of the great family fortunes of Canada — the Weston, Thomson, Irving, Desmarais, Rogers, Shaw, Sobey and other dynasties — have it all: great wealth, high annual incomes and rock-solid economic security.

Although the statistics used in Chapters 1 to 4 refer to annual money income, Chapter 5 takes a step back to question what statistics on inequalities in annual money income can really tell us about unequal economic well-being. Threaded throughout all these chapters is the theme that the method by which data on income inequality are collected — by sample surveys, in Census questions or via income tax returns — can make a significant difference to perceptions of inequality. Seemingly small differences in how the data are collected and treated can sometimes have surprisingly important implications. Since each data source has strengths and weaknesses at different parts of the income distribution, no single data source is "always best."

Canadians have multiple data sources with which to examine the inequalities of annual income in the country, but income inequality is only one piece of the puzzle. Our economic well-being today depends on both what we can consume now out of our current income, and what the wealth we have accumulated in the past and the security of our life situations enables us to expect for tomorrow. Chapter 6 presents the data on inequalities of wealth before Covid-19, how those inequalities increased during the Covid-19 pandemic and the associated inequalities of economic power.

The homeless on the sidewalk and the wealthy in their penthouses differ dramatically in the economic outcomes they experience daily, but Chapter

7 asks whether we should worry about those inequalities of outcome or about inequalities of opportunity. Would ending discrimination in the determination of who will be a corporate executive and who will be homeless solve Canada's inequality problems, or would it just reallocate mansions and homelessness? Is it race or ethnicity or gender that matters in the allocation of advantages, or is it class? And even if labour market discrimination were eliminated, does a market economy like Canada's trend toward increasing inequalities of opportunity over time, as the inequalities of income and wealth among parents determine the opportunities available to their children (which then get passed on to the grandchildren, and then to the great-grandchildren)?

Assessing the nature, extent, causes and implications of economic inequality and poverty is crucial to any judgement about the equity or fairness of the world we live in — hence I think these issues constitute some of the most important, and complex, problems of social science. The range and depth of the issues involved is huge. Back in 1981, it was possible to summarize the international literature on economic inequality and all the available data on Canadian inequality in a little over 200 pages of text.[17] Today, a single book cannot hope to summarize the international literature. So this book tries to address some key dimensions of our Canadian reality, with the full realization that every week brings new books and articles which document changes in poverty and inequality and changes in our understandings of these issues.

Most of the tables and figures in each chapter are taken from Statistics Canada's database and are freely available online at statcan.gc.ca. Unless otherwise explicitly noted, all dollar numbers presented in this book have been converted to 2022 dollars using the Consumer Price Index. Data in the text are the most recent available at the time of writing in early 2024.

In the academic literature, many articles about economic inequality present scores of tables and graphs to show explicitly how "bullet-proof" their conclusions are to every possible different definition and measurement choice. This pedantry is important to show the robustness of results, and it is essential for publication in peer-reviewed academic journals. However, even the most diehard subject specialist sometimes can admit that this is also often fairly boring stuff, so this book tries to save the minutiae and the references for the endnotes. The economics literature is also often made more complex by obscure mathematical notation, and the occupational hazard of people (like me) who lecture for a living is that they sometimes may not notice when other people are bored silly. In an attempt to avoid all that, the mathematics here is kept to a minimum and is also stored in the endnotes.

As well, it seems to me that although economists love their statistics and their econometric results, these numbers are sometimes very imperfect ways of getting at what is really going on. Often, a real-life example communicates much more effectively. Sometimes readers also want to know who the author is and a bit about why they came to a particular perspective, so this book contains some real stories from my own life and the lives of people I have known. The identities of people other than myself are obscured, but they may recognize themselves. I apologize in advance if I have misinterpreted events.

In thinking about economic inequalities and how they have been increasing in recent decades, it is natural to ask what policies could make a difference — but the prior question to ask is why and how economic inequalities matter for human well-being. So before Chapter 9 analyzes a few specific policies, Chapter 8 asks why economic inequalities might matter in early twenty-first-century Canada.

One of the biggest challenges in writing a book on economic inequality is defining the focus of the book. An immense number of issues are relevant to economic inequality, but a book of 100,000 words or so can only address a limited selection of them. Omissions are inevitable. Unlike my 1981 book, this book does not discuss global inequality and poverty. The inequalities we observe in Canada are small compared to the vast gulfs in living standards in places like Mumbai or Dar es Salaam, and the poorest of the world's eight billion people experience much more extreme deprivation than that felt by Canada's disadvantaged. The measurement,[18] causes and implications of trends in global inequality and poverty raise many complex issues that are not necessarily directly relevant to inequality and poverty trends within Canada.

An adequate discussion of global issues would need another book. This book's focus on Canada is driven by the fact that although the borders which divide humanity into separate nations are accidents of history, Canadians do now share a national identity — an "imagined community"[19] that defines the set of people whom we think share common rights of citizenship. Canadians also share a political system which could, as clearly demonstrated in 2020, change economic inequality fairly quickly. A different government could change the framework of laws, social programs, taxes and transfers in ways that would reduce the level of economic inequality and poverty in Canada. There is no global counterpart, so this book focuses on Canada.

However, this book does not address the complexities of Canadian and First Nations inequalities. Indigenous people are overrepresented in the poverty discussed in Chapter 4 and as Indigenous people, racialized minorities, and women all know all too well, a greater likelihood of encountering discrimination in the labour market means individuals from disadvantaged groups often face lower-than-average incomes (sometimes much lower) and a greater probability of poverty. Chapter 7 discusses inequalities of opportunity and their relationship to inequalities of outcome. However, the issues raised by economic inequality go far deeper for Canada's Indigenous people. They require solutions more complex and encompassing than eliminating discrimination in the labour market.

The unequal money incomes of individuals are, of course, an important part of the problem — but only a part. For First Nations people who are living off-reserve and working in the Canadian public and private sectors, part of the injustice of Canadian society is discrimination and inequality of individual opportunity. The lower incomes and inadequate inclusion in Canadian society that discrimination causes are things which individuals from other disadvantaged groups also experience — but eliminating discrimination and inequality of individual opportunity would not be nearly enough to "fix things" for Indigenous people. The issues raised by First Nations people go far deeper.

One way to see that is to ask yourself: Would it "solve the problem" if all Canadians, including all Indigenous people, made $250,000 per year and everyone lived in Toronto? If all Canadians made $250,000 per year and lived in Toronto, that would definitely eliminate both income inequality and material poverty, for both Indigenous and non-Indigenous people alike. If the only issue for Indigenous people was inequality of the money income of individuals, that would indeed "solve the problem." But this scenario would also mean that First Nations people would be assimilated into Canada's urban population and would lose contact with the land of their ancestors. Collective identity — knowing that, for example, the Mi'kmaq language and culture will continue into the future — is vital for many Indigenous people. Connection with the land — more precisely, connection with the particular piece of land where generations of one's ancestors have lived and generations of descendants will live — is central to that identity.[20] The collective inheritance of ancestral traditions and rights raises very different issues from the individual inheritance of private property in a market economy. Adequately discussing the tensions between individual and collective rights, and Indigenous and non-Indigenous identities and outcomes, would require another book[21] so despite their importance, these issues are not addressed here.

As well, I should be explicit about my biases. I have sometimes wondered if I acquired some of my basic perspectives rather young. When I was seven, I was appointed "milk monitor" for my Grade Two class. In those days in Ontario, primary school students could get milk for a mid-morning snack at a weekly cost of 25 cents. As milk monitor, it was my job to collect the money weekly, keep track of who had paid and who had not, pick up the correct number of cartons of milk from the school office every day and then distribute them to the desks of those classmates of mine whose parents had paid, being sure to skip the kids whose parents had not paid, because otherwise, the milk supply would run short. I found it a lot of work to keep track of who got milk that week and who did not — and I also thought it was a total waste of time. I thought then,[22] and I think now, that every seven-year-old needs a glass of milk in the morning and that if they all want it, they should all get it — my preference for equal treatment started early.

While doing the initial research for my 2018 book, I learned that, Ontario in 2017 still had a school milk program, although not at all schools. The program's website then suggested a price of 60 cents per carton of milk. By 2024, that had been changed to a recommendation that schools sell the milk at "not more than $0.05 above the distributor cost, but ultimately it is their decision." It is a sign of the times that today's inadequate and unequal funding of public education means that, as the website notes, "the program is also a great opportunity to fund raise."[23] However, each child's milk still has to be paid for individually, which means there still are "milk monitors" in Ontario, whose job every day still is to make sure that some little kids do not get any milk.

When I was getting my PhD in economics, I learned that in the terminology of economics, the hassle of keeping track of who gets milk is called the "administrative cost of program delivery." It was typically mentioned briefly but then assumed, for convenience of modelling, to be zero. The stigma of being left out and the moral case for equal treatment of all seven-year-olds was also usually ignored. In the eyes of academic economists, the big issue was "incentive effects," and the possibility that charging a price for milk would somehow improve economic efficiency in the allocation of resources. Even back in graduate school, I understood that whether economic efficiency actually increased depended crucially on the size of any behavioural response to price incentives, and any such efficiency effects should be compared to the economic costs of charging a price (administration expenses plus forgone benefits for those who do not get milk when a price is charged) and to the moral costs of the unequal treatment of small children.

Indeed, any claim that a particular economic policy will improve economic efficiency will always depend crucially on how large any changes in individual behaviour actually are. My biases since grad school have therefore always included a conviction that the empirical evidence is crucial. The theoretical paradigm which dominates most economics departments in North America sees people solely as materialistically selfish atomistic agents who interact only through market transactions. That paradigm often generates useful hypotheses to test against the data. However, in my opinion, it is also an incredibly shrivelled perspective on human nature and a sometimes misleading predictor of human behaviour. And as the carbon-pricing policy debacle illustrates, the prediction errors of economists can be very costly.

Fortunately, economics has in some respects become more interesting in the last twenty-five years. There is a new recognition in "behavioural economics" of the actual decision-making processes of real people[24] and a rapidly expanding literature on the "economics of happiness." Since economists now increasingly ask real people about their present happiness or long-term life satisfaction and try to determine what it is that actually matters for them, they have discovered some of the limits of money income. Although, at any point in time, the relatively rich tend to report more happiness and greater life satisfaction than the poor, this cross-sectional relationship does not imply economic growth necessarily makes a country happier on average. Indeed, average national income, measured as Gross Domestic Product (GDP) per capita, has grown substantially in advanced countries over the last seventy years, but average self-reported happiness has barely budged.[25]

That finding is consistent with the hypothesis that in rich countries relative income — one's own income compared to others' — is what primarily matters for most people, because "keeping up" in material terms determines one's place in the hierarchy of respect. But even comparing the relatively rich and the not-so-rich at any point, annual income is just not that large a predictor of self-reported happiness[26] compared to social relationship variables, like being unemployed, divorced or not having friends. Higher unemployment rates always strongly predict individual unhappiness. Even the employed are more likely to be unhappy when the unemployment rate rises because they worry more about the probability of unemployment.[27]

To my way of thinking, this evidence implies that economics, and economic inequalities in particular, are important in very different ways in rich countries than in poor countries. Before going to graduate school, I worked for two years as an economist ("Mtalamu wa Mipango na Maendeleo" was my official job title) in Tanzania. When you are working with practical problems of economic development in a place where owning a bicycle is a sign of significant household wealth and, as recently as 2014, "stunting or chronic malnutrition was identified in 34.7 per cent of children 0–59 months of age,"[28] it is easy to see that material living standards and economic growth and economic inequality are hugely important. But there are diminishing returns to material growth. The happiness and health and well-being returns to ever more growth in national income per capita decrease as societies become richer and richer — and Canada, in the early twenty-first century, is already one of the richest countries the world has ever known.

One of the most robust principles in economics is the law of diminishing marginal returns — a concept that one can usefully illustrate in large undergraduate classes by asking for a couple of volunteers and feeding them marshmallows (or chocolate chip cookies or whatever else they initially really like). Each volunteer is asked to draw a bar graph on the board to illustrate the pleasure that they got from the last marshmallow eaten, and the professor just keeps feeding the volunteer students marshmallows until they ask him or her to stop — please! Students differ in exactly how many marshmallows they have to eat before the pleasure of eating one more marshmallow goes to zero (which illustrates the general idea of differences in preferences among individuals). However, they always do find that at some point, when they have already eaten a lot of marshmallows, further increases in marshmallow consumption just do not produce any additional pleasure. The issue is not *if* increasing material consumption eventually reaches a point where the gains from further increases in material consumption are very small or non-existent; the issue is *when*.

So I think that in countries as rich as Canada is now, we should start having a discussion about when the total material output of Canadian society will be "enough" — a question which is particularly important if we recognize the environmental costs[29] to ever-increasing material production, and that the growth rate of national income is, in any event, slowing substantially. The truly important economic issue then will be how we share both the wealth we have and the contributions we make to creating that wealth.

In my view, in rich countries' economics now often matters in a negative sense. By creating unnecessary levels of anxiety about the future or high rates of unemployment and poverty or rising resentments about relative rewards, misguided economic policies can make most Canadians worse off in ways that are not at all reflected in a statistic like "per capita national income" or GDP. Since 1998, Andrew Sharpe, of the Center for the Study of Living Standards, and I have collaborated in trying, with our Index of Economic Well-Being (IEWB),[30] to provide a better method of measuring economic well-being. Unlike some other authors, we explicitly restrict the IEWB to economic variables. This is not because we think non-economic issues (e.g., political freedoms and civil liberties such as freedom of expression and association) are unimportant; quite the opposite, in fact. We think non-economic issues such as civil liberties or political democracy are too important to be submerged within an overall index which also contains economic variables.[31]

In my view, although economic growth matters, a fair division of the gains from growth matters even more because increasing unfairness and rising economic insecurity eventually have very worrying implications for political economy and for civil liberties. As the "Make America Great Again" (MAGA) phenomenon in the United States illustrates, economic inequalities which increase year after year can eventually have disastrous social and political consequences — not least because the big collective challenges of climate change and periodic pandemics are not going away. If nothing is actually done about increasing inequality and insecurity, the anxieties and anger and resentments they generate will make it ever more difficult for Canadians to get it together to find solutions to our big collective problems. The scandal of increasing economic inequality is that we have seen that we actually could reverse this trend.

Chapter 1
CANADIAN INCOME INEQUALITY — THE BIG PICTURE

The first thing to remember about Canada's "Big Picture" is that we are a rich country, which has been getting richer year by year for a long time. Economic inequality is about how much we each share, as individuals, in that economic growth and this book is about the changing sizes of peoples' shares of Canada's economic pie. However, Figure 1.1 begins by illustrating the growth of the total size of the economic pie. It presents data on the total output per person of the Canadian economy — i.e., GDP per capita — for the 155-year period from Confederation in 1867 to 2022. Since there has been a lot of price inflation over this long period of time, it adjusts for inflation and presents "real GDP per capita" measured in 2022 dollars.

At the time of Confederation, Canada was not a rich country by modern standards. Measured in 2022 Canadian dollars, GDP per capita in 1867 was $3,377 — roughly comparable to the per capita GDP of India in 2022.[1] There was little change in average living standards during the 1870s, but the Wheat Boom more than doubled Canada's average income between 1880 and 1912 (to $9,010). However, economic growth before WWII was inconsistent, coming in occasional surges followed by severe downturns. Per capita GDP grew by 13 per cent during WWI, crashed by 26 per cent between 1917 and 1921, surged in the late 1920s and then crashed again during the Great Depression of the 1930s. In 1936, GDP per capita was only a tiny bit higher ($9,110) than it had been a quarter century earlier in 1912 — a combination of instability and long-run income stagnancy that led many economists to question the efficiency of the market system.

During World War II, Canada industrialized and urbanized and per capita GDP rose by 60 per cent. Motivated by fears of the economic collapse that had followed WWI, and by worries about the social and political instability that mass unemployment had produced in the 1930s, post-war economic policy was firmly Keynesian. Until the late 1970s, managing aggregate demand to maintain full employment was a policy priority of Canada's federal government.

Figure 1.1

GDP Per Capita in Canada, 1867-2022

(2022 dollars)

Source: FON Macroeconomic Database, Finances of the Nation

Growth slowed after 1980, and slowed even more after 2010, but altogether the eighty years from 1940 to 2020, although interrupted by occasional recessions, have been a remarkably long run of increasing average income. Measured in 2022 dollars, per capita GDP was $16,001 in 1946, almost triple that ($45,527) in 1980 and another 60 per cent higher ($72,131) in 2022. Many citizens and policy-makers in Canada have come to assume that economic growth is the normal state of affairs in a market economy — even if the 1920s and 1930s should remind us that there is nothing inevitable about economic growth. However, the benefits of growth have been shared very differently in different historical epochs.

To see how growth in individual incomes has been shared over the last few decades in Canada, Figure 1.2 uses income tax data to graph trends in annual individual incomes.[2] It plots the real (i.e., inflation-adjusted) after-tax income of people at eight very different points in the range of incomes across all Canadian taxpayers. Three are at the very top end: the midpoint of the top 1 percent of the top 1 per cent (the 99.995th percentile), at the midpoint of the top 10 per cent of the top 1 per cent (the 99.95th percentile), and at the threshold of the top 1 per cent (the 99th percentile). Figure 1.2 also plots two people in the upper-middle class: one in the middle of the top 5 per cent (i.e., the 97.5th percentile) and in the middle of the top 10 per cent (the 95th percentile). Three people are in the middle class, at the 75th per cent ranking, at the 50th percentile (the median) in the middle of the distribution and at the lower end of the middle class (the 25th percentile).

However, a big problem with trying to draw a picture of the income distribution is scale. The vertical axis of Figure 1.2 plots incomes in dollars because a dollar will buy the same amount of bread or clothing or any other commodity, no matter who spends it. But the disadvantage of a straightforward dollar scale is that, as demonstrated in Figure 1.2, one cannot actually see income trends for anybody except those in the top 1 per cent, because the size of top 1 per cent incomes is so much greater than those of everyone else in the remaining ninety-nine percentiles.

Figure 1.2

Real Income of Canadian Taxpayers, 1982–2021

(Total income including capital gains, in 2022 dollars)

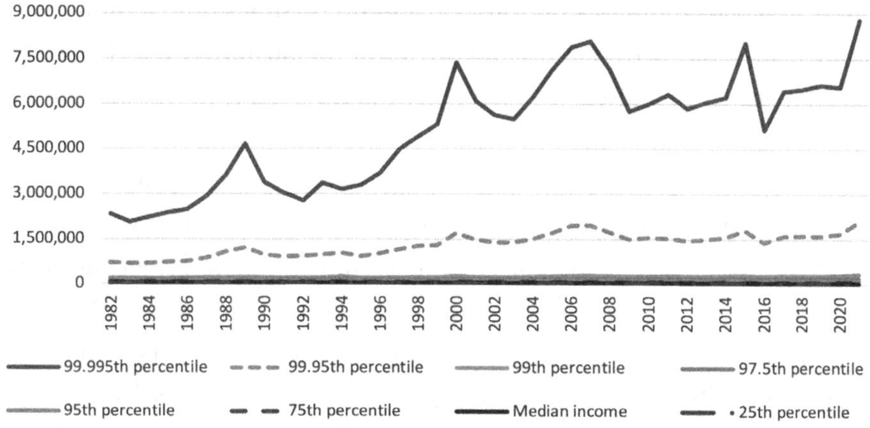

Source: Statistics Canada. Table 18-10-0005-01: 11-10-0055-01

In order to draw an accurate, to-scale picture of the income distribution in Canada and to include the incomes of those at the very top, incomes must be measured in millions of dollars. But when incomes are measured in million-dollar units, income differences in the middle and at the bottom of the distribution are too small to show up. In 2021, the taxpayer at the middle of the distribution (the 50th percentile or median) reported an income of $44,847 (measured in 2022 dollars) and the person at the 25th percentile received $23,812. That $21,035 income difference between them was hugely important to their standard of living, but it is small change to somebody in the top tenth of the top 1 per cent, since it would only be about 1 per cent of the median income for this group. To effectively show the income differences among middle-class people, one has to use a dollar scale of thousands, but using that scale of measurement makes it impossible to fit the very top end onto the same page (or indeed onto the same blackboard) as everyone else because their incomes are so much larger.

Despite these shortcomings, Figure 1.2 is still useful. It illustrates both the upward trend in real incomes at the very top of Canada's income distribution and the occasional volatility of those incomes. Canada's economic recessions stand out clearly: in the early 1990s, in 2000 and in

2008. Top incomes fell during these recessions, partly because capital gains on the stock market turned into losses. Executive compensation is often largely paid in stock options, so top-end incomes tend to move with share prices and with the ups and downs of the business cycle. Figure 1.2 also illustrates how, after a recession, it can take a while for incomes at the very top to recover to their previous levels; for example, the recession of the early 1990s produced a large income drop at the top which lasted until 1995, before an even larger recovery over the next five years. More recently, the effects of the 2008–09 recession were still lingering in the 2014 data, but there was a strong recovery of top incomes in 2015.

In general, Canadian trends in top incomes over the last thirty-five years have followed American top income trends very closely, although sometimes with a lag,[3] and in the US, the data unambiguously indicate that top incomes rebounded strongly from the 2008 recession and continue to increase strongly.[4]

Although the average real income of Canadian tax filers increased by 38.8 per cent between 1982 and 2021, this average income gain statistic can be seen as an example of how misleading averages can be. The average percentage gain across all tax filers hides huge differences. At the top, the average real pre-tax income, including capital gains, of the top tenth of the top 1 per cent of tax filers more than tripled, increasing by $2,439,437. Within the top 1 per cent, the "poorer" nine tenths of the top 1 per cent (i.e., from the 99th to the 99.9th percentile) did not do nearly as well, increasing by $307,142 — but they still doubled their incomes. The upper middle class — those taxpayers who are in the top 10 per cent but not in the top 1 per cent — had better than average real income gains (up by $75,000 for the ninety-fifth to ninety-ninth group and up by $33,000 for those between the ninetieth and the ninety-fifth). The rest of Canada's population lagged far behind. Over the last forty years in Canada, the gains from economic growth have clearly tended to end up at the very top of the income distribution.

But what do these numbers mean in the real lives of people at the top, in the middle and at the bottom of Canada's income distribution?

Figure 1.3

Average Real Total Income in 1982 and 2021

(2022 dollars)

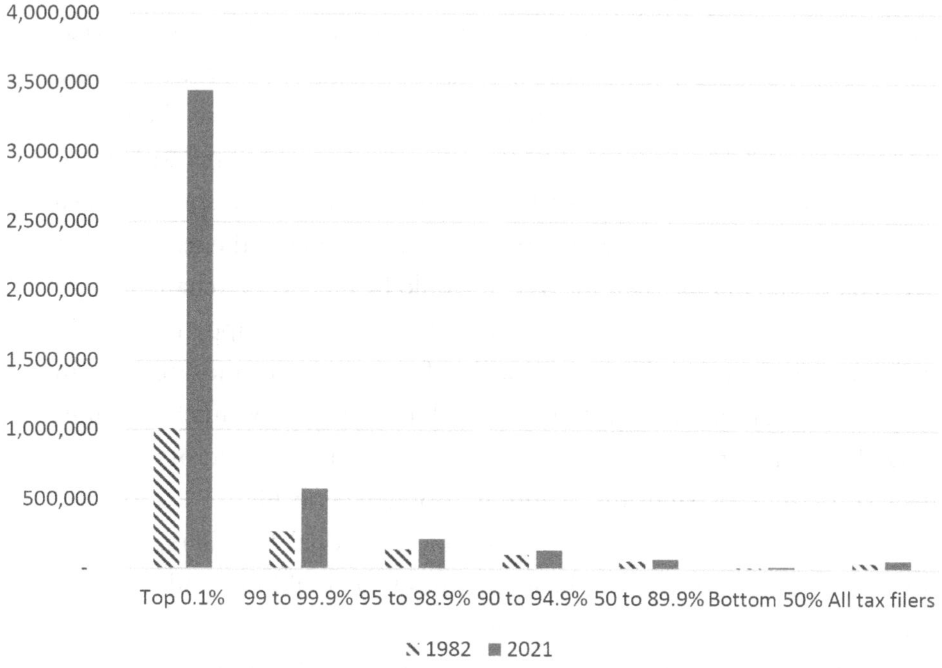

Source: Statistics Canada Table: 11-10-0055-01 (formerly CANSIM 204-0001); Table 18-10-0005-01

The contrasts in the scale of incomes which Figures 1.2 and 1.3 illustrate visually also correspond to an important social reality: an additional dollar of money income matters to a drastically different degree depending on where you sit in the income distribution.

In Halifax, where I live, a disabled person who depended on social assistance would have received $12,687 to live on for the year in 2022.[5] In 2021, the after-tax income of Canada's top 0.1 per cent of taxpayers averaged $3,499,900, so $13,000 would be a bit more than a third of 1 per cent of their annual income (0.37 per cent). For somebody already in the top 1 per cent, another $13,000 would undoubtedly be nice but not all that noticeable. No big change in lifestyle would be implied; another $13,000 might enable a top 1-percenter to tack an additional few days onto their European vacation. By contrast, for a middle-class person making somewhere between $40,000 and $90,000, an additional $13,000 in annual income would be serious money with noticeable effects. It makes a significant difference in quality of life if your family can afford a second car or a move to a larger apartment so the kids do not have to share a bedroom, and another $13,000 can make that possible. However, these changes in lifestyle are still tiny compared to the impact of an additional $13,000 at the bottom of the income distribution. For a disabled person on social assistance who is now struggling to buy groceries and pay the rent, another $13,000 would double their income. It would be literally life-changing.

So although Figure 1.2 lets us see what has been happening at the very top, we have to change the scale of comparisons and measure in thousands, rather than millions, of dollars to see how much incomes have been changing for the vast majority of Canadians across the rest of the income distribution. Another problem with Figure 1.2 and 1.3 is that they record only the income of individual tax filers, thereby omitting people who do not have incomes (e.g., children) and ignoring the family context within which people live.

Focusing on individual income is a reasonable thing to do if we are interested primarily in how income is produced — if, for example, we want to examine the impacts of trade and technology on wages and the returns to capital. However, if we are interested in the inequality of incomes because we care about the inequality of well-being, we should focus on how income is consumed and consider how many people share in consuming each household's income. Looking at individual tax filer income ignores the social reality of consumption sharing within households, which implies that the total after-tax household income of all household members,[6] and the number of people who have to share that total income, both matter for economic well-being.[7]

An annual after-tax income of, for example, $35,000 can buy a very different standard of living for a single person than for a married couple with several children. But although some costs are greater in larger families, it would be misleading to assume, for example, that the cost of living for a four-person household is exactly four times greater than the cost of living of a single person. As students who share apartments during university know from practical experience, living with roommates makes some savings possible. Since the mid-1970s, Statistics Canada has therefore published data on trends in "equivalent" disposable real income which incorporate adjustments of the total disposable (i.e., after-tax) money income of all household members to reflect the lower per-person cost of living of larger households.[8] In those calculations, the after-tax income from all sources (labour earnings plus capital income plus transfer payments from government) of all household members is added up, adjusted for inflation in consumer prices and the savings in cost of living of larger households by dividing by the equivalent number of people in each household who share in household income — the result is called "equivalent personal disposable income," which is then attributed to each person.

Table 1.1

Share of Total Income Received by Each Quintile of Families and Unattached Individuals (%)

	1951	1961	1971	1981	1991	1996	2001	2006	2011	2016	2019	2021
Poorest 20%	4.4	4.2	3.6	4.6	4.5	4.3	4.1	4.1	4	3.9	4.1	4.4
Second 20%	11.2	11.9	10.6	11	10	9.6	9.7	9.7	9.4	9.4	9.5	9.8
Middle 20%	18.3	18.3	17.6	17.7	16.4	16.4	15.6	15.7	15.3	15.4	15.5	15.6
Fourth 20%	23.3	24.5	24.9	25.1	24.7	24.7	23.8	23.8	24	24.1	23.9	23.5
Richest 20%	42.8	41.1	43.3	41.6	44.4	45.2	46.9	46.8	47.1	47.1	47.1	46.6

Sources: Statistics Canada, Income Distribution by Size in Canada, (1998), Catalogue No. 13-207: CANSIM Tables 202-070 and 206-0031; J. R. Podoluk, Incomes of Canadians, Dominion Bureau of Statistics, (1968)

Unfortunately, calculations of the distribution of equivalent personal disposable income are not available before the mid-1970s in Canada, so getting a longer-term perspective on income distribution in earlier years requires reliance on data that is not adjusted for household size. Table 1.1 summarizes[9] such data on income shares in Canada from 1951 to 2021.

It lines up all the households in Canada (both families and unattached individuals) in order of their total household income and divides the population into five equal parts, or quintiles and asks the question: "What is the share of total money income (before tax) received by the poorest fifth of households? How much does the next 20 per cent, the lower middle class, get? What share do the middle 20 per cent get? The 20 per cent who are second from the top? The most affluent 20 per cent?"

One can see from Table 1.1 that Canada has always been an unequal place, but the data show relatively small shifts in top income shares before 1981, compared to considerably larger changes since. For example, although the income share of the top 20 per cent actually declined a bit between 1951 and 1981 (from 42.8 per cent to 41.6 per cent), the size of that change was much smaller than the size of the increase in their share over the next thirty-four years (+5.8 percentage points, to 47.1 per cent in 2019, just before the Covid-19 pandemic). Until 1981, the available data supported the possibly somewhat boring conclusion that in Canada "economic inequality has remained roughly constant since the Second World War."[10]

This all changed in the 1980s and 1990s, as Figure 1.4 shows. It plots changes in the most commonly used single number for summarizing income inequality, the Gini index (also sometimes called the Gini coefficient or the Gini ratio). The Gini index reports the average dollar difference in incomes between all possible pairs of people, expressed as a fraction of average income. Since most people, and hence most possible pairs of people, are in the middle of the income distribution, changes in the Gini index are, in practice, dominated by what is happening to incomes in the middle and are quite insensitive to changes in top 1 per cent income shares.[11] If there were no differences in incomes at all (i.e., a perfectly equal society), the Gini index would have a value of zero. If one person had all the income (i.e., a completely unequal society), the Gini index would have a value of one.

In actual societies, the Gini index is almost always somewhere between 0.2 and 0.5. For equivalent personal disposable income in

2022, it was, for example, 0.268 in Denmark and 0.256 in Belgium, but considerably higher in the United States (0.395) and in Mexico (0.42). Figure 1.5 presents the data on all Organization for Economic Cooperation and Development (OECD) nations.[12]]

Although the Gini index is not very good at picking up changes in the income share of the top 1 per cent, it does a reasonable job of measuring inequality in the middle part of the income distribution. In Canada, after adjusting household income for household size, the Gini index of equivalent market income (i.e., the wages and salaries received by labour and the interest, rents and dividends received by owners of capital, before taxes and transfers) was 0.384 in 1976. By 2015, it had increased to 0.435 and in 2021 it was 0.432.

Although in most countries transfer payments have a considerably bigger impact on income inequality than taxes, both taxes and transfer payments always make a significant difference. Figure 1.4 illustrates their impacts in Canada by plotting the change since 1976 in the Gini index of equivalent household income when: (a) market income, not including capital gains, from labour and capital is all that is considered; (b) transfer payments (e.g., from Canada Pension Plan or Employment Insurance or Workers Compensation or Social Assistance) are added to market income to get total income; and (c) income tax is subtracted from the total income to get disposable personal income. As Figure 1.4 shows, the Gini index of inequality of income after transfers are added to the market income but before income tax is subtracted is always lower than the Gini index of market income. The Gini index is lower still when both income taxes and income transfers are considered — but transfer payments always make the bigger difference.[13] In 2021, for example, the Gini index of market income was 0.432 while the Gini index of total income was 0.332 and the Gini index of disposable personal income was 0.288 — so measured in Gini points, transfer payments made a difference of 0.1 while income taxes changed the Gini index by 0.044, or less than half as much.

In general, statistics like the Gini index are primarily interesting for comparison purposes. When people ask the seemingly simple question of whether inequality in Canada has increased or not, Table 1.1 may not give a clear answer because every year it provides five numbers — one for each 20 per cent group of the population. (If Table 1.1 had presented data on decile shares there would have been ten numbers, one for each 10 per cent group of the population.) Since the data on income shares for particular groups can sometimes move in differing directions, getting a clear answer to the seemingly simple question of whether inequality is greater now than it used to be requires us to boil all differences between all people down to a single number. There is a specialist literature in economics which discusses the biases implicit in different indices, but the Gini index is the most popular index now in use.[14]

Figure 1.4 therefore plots the changes in the Gini index of equivalent market income, of equivalent total income (including transfer payments) and of equivalent disposable income (i.e., after both taxes and transfers) of individuals in Canada since 1976. For market income inequality, total income inequality and disposable income inequality, an individual's equivalent income is calculated by first adding together the total income from all sources of all members of each household, adjusting total household income for the economies of scale that larger households enjoy, and then attributing to each individual the average equivalent income of the household that they live in.[15] The Gini index of inequality of the equivalent incomes of all individuals is then calculated.

Figure 1.4 calculates the change of the Gini index since 1976 by subtracting the initial 1976 level from its current level, to show when and how changes have occurred over the forty-five years, 1976 to 2021. The top line shows the change, compared to 1976, in the Gini index of inequality of market income. As can be seen in Figure 1.4, from 1976 until 1981, the change was negative and was similar for all income concepts. Because market incomes became more equal and the impacts of transfers and taxes did not change, the Gini index of inequality of all income concepts fell. However, there was a sharp increase in market income inequality from 1981 to 1983, mirroring exactly the increase

Figure 1.4
Gini Index of Income Inequality in Canada, 1976-2021

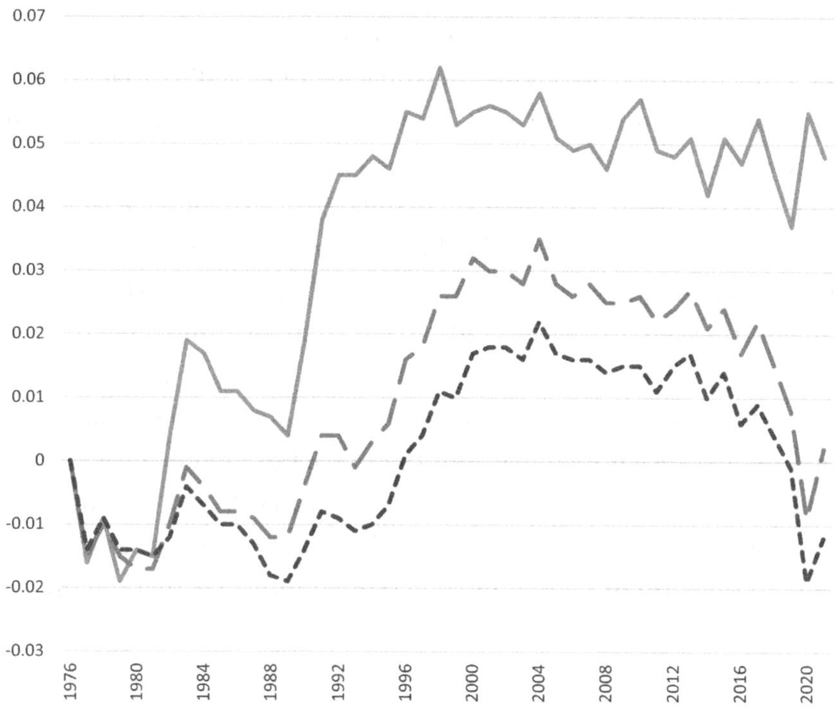

Source: Statistics Canada. Table 11-10-0134-0, Gini coefficients of adjusted market, total and after-tax income, www150.statcan.gc.ca/t1/tbl1/en/tv.action?pid=1110013401

in unemployment during the 1981 recession. The Gini index of market income inequality then trended sharply downward as unemployment declined and the economy recovered from recession between 1983 and 1989. The second big surge upwards in the Gini index of market income in Canada was from 0.388 in 1989 to 0.429 in 1992, followed by a more gradual increase until 1996 — again matching exactly the upward surge in unemployment during the recession of the early 1990s, but this time also reflecting the long period of high unemployment which followed. Since then, the Gini index of market income inequality has been fairly flat (0.439 in 1996 and 0.432 in 2021). In the quarter century 1996 to 2021, there was a slight downward trend, reflecting trends in unemployment, and a series of small ups and downs.

Transfers and taxes have always made a considerable difference to the inequality of annual incomes in Canada. The second line in Figure 1.4 is the Gini index of total income inequality and the third is the Gini index of disposable personal income (DPI), that is, total individual after-tax income. As Chapter 5 will discuss, the majority of income transfers in Canada are most accurately thought of as "social insurance" payments intended to maintain annual income when an individual's market income falls, due to events like unemployment or workplace accidents or retirement. But whatever the reason for transfer payments, they add to a household's after-tax income, allowing for more consumption of goods and services. Arguably, DPI is more relevant than market income or total income for the inequality of annual "living standards" because it includes both the impact of income taxes and all types of transfer payments. Between 1976 and 1980, the Gini index of both total income and DPI inequality declined, mirroring exactly the decline in the Gini of market income (which indicates that the impact of taxes and transfers did not change).

In the recessions of 1981 to 1983 and the early 1990s, the market income Gini shot up while the total income and DPI Gini rose by much less. Increased inequality in market incomes was largely offset by greater transfer payments during these recessions, so there was a much smaller increase in both total income and disposable income inequality[16] than in market income inequality. In Canada in the 1980s and early 1990s, unemployment benefits and social assistance were higher and were received by many more people than is the case today. As unemployment surged upward in the early 1980s recession, increased unemployment insurance and other social assistance transfer payments were able to offset a large part of the increase in market income inequality. During the 1983 to 1989 recovery phase, the Gini of market income inequality and the Gini of total income and DPI inequality declined in parallel, reflecting the fact that there was not much change in the inequality-reducing impacts of taxes and transfer payments.

When unemployment and the Gini index of market income inequality simultaneously surged upward again during the 1989 to 1992 recession, the offsetting impact of Canada's tax and transfer system kicked in, as it had in the recession of the early 1980s. Because transfer payments had a large impact on the Gini index and offset much of the increase in market income inequality, there was a much smaller increase in the Gini index of total income and disposable personal income.

Indeed, although the Gini index of DPI moved upward in the early 1990s, it was not until 1995 that it finally rose above its 1976 level. Throughout those nineteen years, whenever Canadian inequality was mentioned in international conferences on economic inequality, the standard observation was that, unlike other countries, Canadian inequality was not increasing because the Canadian tax and transfer system had successfully offset the increased inequality in market incomes.

Added together, the total impact of the Canadian tax and transfer system on income inequality in Canada has always been quite significant: in 1976, a reduction of 0.084 Gini points, in 2015, a reduction of 0.122 Gini points and in 2021 a reduction of 0.144 Gini points. Two periods of peak impact stand out. During the peak unemployment year of the early 1990s recession, in 1994, the tax and transfer system reduced the Gini index by 0.142 Gini points. During the Covid-19 pandemic, although the pandemic caused a surge in unemployment which increased the inequality of market incomes, the rapid creation of new transfer programs like CERB more than offset that increase in inequality — the impact of income taxes and income transfers on the Gini index was even larger, surging from 0.122 in 2019 to 0.158 in 2020.

As Figure 1.4 shows, from the mid-1990s to 2004, changes in the impact of transfers and taxes on the Gini index accentuated the changes in market income inequality, instead of offsetting those changes. Altogether, 1989 to 2004 was a period of substantial increase in the DPI Gini index.

Nevertheless, observant readers may be asking themselves how a fairly flat Gini index of market income inequality since roughly 2000, as shown in Figure 1.4, could be consistent with the upward trend and large fluctuations in top incomes pictured in Figure 1.2. The answer is partly the way the Gini index is constructed: because there are very few people at the very top end, the Gini index is just not very sensitive to changes in the top 1 per cent income share.[17] As well, over the last thirty years, economists have become very conscious of the fact that when we analyze data on income distribution, we should think about where the data came from. The data underlying Figures 1.2 and 1.3 come from income tax records, while Table 1.1 and Figure 1.4 are based on data from sample surveys of the Canadian population.

It has long been known that surveys do not give us a good picture of the very rich, in part because multi-millionaires and billionaires are so very few in number that they are not often selected in random sample surveys of the population. Additionally, the financial affairs of the very affluent are often quite complex, and if, by chance, a multi-millionaire is randomly selected for an income survey and a Statistics Canada interviewer happens to knock on their door, they often refuse to answer. Hence, the very rich are usually not found in the household surveys measuring income inequality.

Sample surveys can also be quite unreliable at the very bottom of the income distribution. Some of Canada's most deprived citizens live in isolated northern First Nations communities which are not sampled in most Statistics Canada surveys (partly because of the cost of administering surveys in very remote areas). Surveys of the Canadian population also start by "knocking on doors." After enumerating a list of residences, Statistics Canada chooses a sample of addresses from that list and interviews the people at those addresses. Since the homeless have no address, they are not included in a sample of residences and are therefore missing from the data. People who are very mobile, who work odd shifts, or who are socially isolated are also less likely to respond to residence-based surveys and can be very hard to sample accurately. Hence, in sample surveys, the reliability of estimates of the number and the incomes of both the very poor and the very rich is often seriously in doubt.

By contrast, household survey data can provide reliable estimates of what is happening in the middle of the income distribution. Middle-class people are many in number, easy to find and, in Canada, they are usually cooperative in answering questions. As Chapter 2 will discuss in more detail, "the middle class" can be an ambiguous concept — objective definitions vary considerably and subjective self-definitions differ even more. However, if one thinks of the middle class as the middle 60 per cent of the income distribution, in 2022 the middle 60 per cent of families and unattached individuals spanned the total income range from $36,400 to $124,100.[18]

The financial affairs of such Canadians are usually straightforward compared to the very affluent, who may need to ask their accountant to know how much money they made last year. Middle-class Canadians are also likely to get their income from one or a few main jobs, and the household income survey is planned to coincide with tax time, so their pay stubs are handy and their annual salary is easily remembered. Indeed, in recent years, Statistics Canada has been asking respondents for permission to get the income data directly from the tax records. Survey-based statistics, although less accurate at the bottom and very top of the income distribution, are quite reliable for the middle 60 per cent, or probably even the middle 90 per cent, of the population. Discussions of income distribution based on survey data (like that underlying Table 1.1 and Figure 1.4) are therefore most reliable when the middle class is the focus of analysis. For discussion of trends at the very top and very bottom, it is a good idea to supplement survey data with tax or census information.

The next three chapters of this book focus separately on what has been happening to Canadians at the top, in the middle and at the bottom of the income distribution. There are three basic reasons for splitting up the discussion like this. First, as already noted, the best data sources to use differ; income tax data is, for example, what we have to rely on for analysis of trends among the very affluent. Second, the types of income and the implications of unequal incomes differ greatly. While capital gains on their stock options are an important income source for CEOs, it is the housing market that matters most for middle-class wealth. But the poor and the homeless have neither stocks nor houses. Third, and most importantly, economic inequality at the top, in the middle or at the bottom of Canada's income hierarchy matters for different reasons.

Increasing elite concentration of income, the disappearing middle class and the poverty of the disadvantaged are all different aspects of inequality; they could even be called different inequalities. They are very much linked, but they do not always coincide. Because they have different social and economic implications and different policy solutions, this book will look at them separately. Summarizing all inequalities in a single number, like the Gini index,[19] can never reveal what has been happening at different points in the income distribution. Chapters 2, 3 and 4 of this book therefore look separately at what is going on in the middle, at the top and at the bottom of Canada's distribution of income. Chapter 5 discusses why annual money income is often an inadequate indicator of economic well-being. Chapter 6 examines the inequality of wealth.

How does Canadian income inequality compare internationally? As Figure 1.5 indicates, comparing the Gini index of inequality of the equivalent disposable personal income in 2022, Mexico (0.42) and Chile (0.448) stand out as the most unequal, with higher Gini indices than Türkiye (0.403) and the United States (0.395). At 0.292 in 2022, Canada was a bit below the average of 0.318 for all OECD countries and had a substantially larger Gini index than many European countries — e.g., the Slovak Republic (0.217), Slovenia (0.242), Czechia (0.255), Norway (0.285) and Denmark (0.268).

Figure 1.5

Gini Index of Inequality of Equivalent Disposable Income in OECD Nations

(2022 or latest available year)

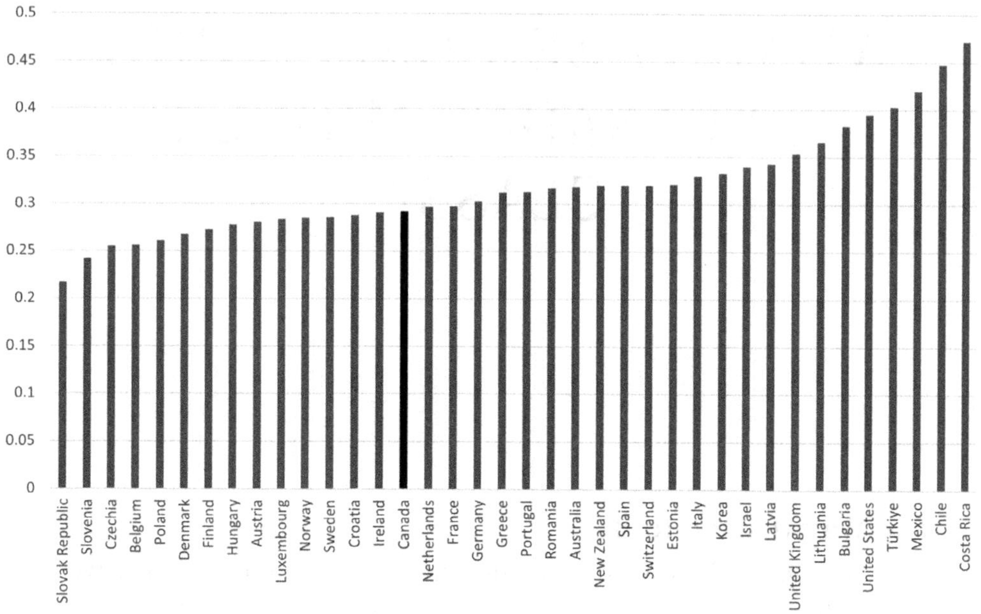

Source: OECD Income Distribution Database (IDD). http://www.oecd.org/social/income-distribution-database.htm

Chapter 2
WHAT'S BEEN HAPPENING TO CANADA'S MIDDLE CLASS?

The Way It Used to Be

For many years, the vast majority of Canadians thought of themselves as "middle class." When I was growing up, my father was vehement in his insistence that he was "ordinary middle class." Although he had a better-than-average job as a chemical engineer, I suspect that his childhood experiences as an immigrant kid in rural Alberta meant that self-identifying as "middle class" was his way of saying that he was just as Canadian as anybody else. And in the 1960s middle-class families like ours shared some broadly common experiences and concerns. Middle-class families shopped at the same stores and sent their children to the same public schools. Their primary asset was the family home, and they knew the main way they could make a difference in their children's economic future was by helping them acquire a good education. Although they worried about retirement and medical bills in the 1950s and 1960s, those anxieties were reduced as the Canada Pension Plan (CPP), Quebec Pension Plan (QPP) and Medicare were introduced in the late 1960s and early 1970s and started to provide a sense of security about what would happen in sickness or old age.

Perhaps most of all, they had experienced increasing prosperity in their own lives, and they expected even more prosperity for their children.

Back then, income inequality was stable and economic growth was strong. Although, as Table 1.1 shows, there was substantial inequality (the before-tax income share of the top 20 per cent of households was roughly ten times the share of the bottom 20 per cent), incomes grew strongly and at roughly the same rate for rich and poor alike. When everybody's income grows at a roughly similar rate, income inequality remains relatively constant. Throughout the 1950s, 1960s and 1970s, almost everybody thought this was the "normal" state of affairs.

In many ways, the lack of change in post-war income inequality in Canada was quite remarkable, because Canada changed profoundly in many other ways over the thirty-five years between 1946 and 1981. The "baby boom" and high immigration doubled Canada's total population, but because national income (GDP) was 4.5 times larger in 1981, per capita GDP more than doubled (to 237 per cent of its 1946 level).[1] Urbanization and industrialization transformed the country: while farmers were 27.1 per cent of the population in 1941, they made up well less than 5 per cent by the 1970s. During the post-war period, horse-drawn wagons and steam engines were replaced, the telecommunications/computerization revolution got underway and married women joined the paid labour force in unprecedented numbers. Medicare was introduced nationwide, post-secondary education expanded dramatically, the 1960s and 1970s hippy phenomenon challenged social mores and the Old Age Security (OAS)/Guaranteed Annual Income (GIS) and Canada/Quebec Pension Plan (CPP/QPP) pension systems were established. Despite all these changes in Canada's economy and society, the distribution of annual income hardly budged, because incomes grew at roughly the same rate from top to bottom. The rich, the middle class and the poor all shared in economic growth.

Keynesian full-employment macroeconomics and welfare-state social policy made balanced growth possible. It was a historic bargain of political economy, an implicit social contract in which capitalists got growing markets, increasing dividends and continued political dominance while workers got jobs, rising wages and a taste of economic security. This post-war recipe of stable income shares and strong, balanced economic growth produced social stability. There is still a deep nostalgia for those days among many Canadians. Although the post-war period of shared prosperity ended around 1981 — more than forty years ago — the rhetoric of Canadian politicians, economists, businesspeople, civil servants and political commentators still routinely express a desire to get back to the good old days of inclusive growth. And although there were spirited debates about the fairness of the income distribution during the thirty-five years from 1946 to 1981, it was at least plausible then to claim that economic inequality was the price Canadian society must pay for vigorous increases in everyone's absolute living standards.

But that was then, and this is now.

The New Normal

Between 1981 and 2008, national income (GDP) in Canada grew by about $800 per person per year (from $45,595 to $66,445, measured in constant 2022 dollars) — a total increase of 46 per cent. Per capita GDP growth slowed considerably after the 2009 financial crisis and ensuing recession, but the 2022 data still showed some increase (to $72,131). One would think that growth of that magnitude, in an already-wealthy country, could have (or perhaps should have) produced a widespread sense of economic well-being and optimism.

However, in a 2022 poll by the Pew Research Center 75 per cent of Canadian respondents said they thought that "when children today grow up, they will be financially worse off than their parents" — a number that has steadily increased[2] since a 2014 EKOS poll asked whether the next generation will be worse or better off than the current generation, and a 60 per cent majority believed their children's generation will be worse off. (64 per cent had similar responses in Pew polls in 2013 and 2015.)

A poll by EKOS Research in 2014 also found that less than a third

(32 per cent) of Canadians aged 25 to 44 thought they were doing better than their parents at the same age,[3] and only 40 per cent among those aged 45 to 64 felt they were better off than their parents. Although 85 per cent of respondents agreed that "a growing and optimistic middle class is an essential component of societal progress," most were in fact deeply pessimistic. Almost three-quarters (74 per cent) agreed with the statement "the middle class is shrinking and falling backward." The fraction of Canadians willing to identify themselves as "middle class" has also fallen sharply, from 67 per cent in 2000 to 47 per cent in 2014 and 42 per cent in 2023. By contrast, the percentage who self-identified as "working class" increased to 33 per cent, of whom half (51 per cent) said they were middle class ten years ago.[4]

Other polls are just as pessimistic. A Pollara poll in 2023 indicated a majority of the middle class feel they are either "just getting by, with no savings" (43 per cent) or "falling behind on monthly expenses" (15 per cent). It provided a slightly different estimate of Canadian self-identification as "middle class" (53 per cent), "working class" (32 per cent) and "poor" (13 per cent)[5] but also found a huge drop in middle class optimism in recent years: only 31 per cent were optimistic about the future of Canada's middle class, down from 53 per cent in 2020. Faced with the question of whether or not respondents think they themselves are better or worse off than their parents, the result is basically a coin toss.[6]

In 2014 Pollara data, a huge majority (85 per cent) believed "income inequality is no longer about the gap between the rich and the poor, but rather the very rich and everyone else," with 38 per cent "strongly agreeing" and 47 per cent "agreeing." A similarly worded EKOS question got 77 per cent agreement. In both the EKOS and the Pollara data, we can see pessimism about Canada's future and personal anxieties about retirement and the employment prospects of children. Self-assessed downward mobility is also an important issue: a large fraction of Canadians (around one-fifth) used to see themselves as "middle class" and now self-identify as "working class."

The Pew, EKOS and Pollara polling data reveal a widespread perception in Canada that the middle class has missed out on economic growth and the government has not assisted. The EKOS poll found[7] that, by a large majority (79 per cent), Canadians agreed "the fuel which drives middle class progress is the fair sharing of the financial rewards of a healthy, productive economy." But when asked how important various factors were "in causing the stagnation or decline of Canada's middle class," a nearly unanimous 95 per cent thought wage and income stagnation was "important" (57 per cent) or "somewhat important" (38 per cent). There was similar unanimity (94 per cent) on the idea that "excessive concentration of wealth at the top" was either "somewhat important" (25 per cent) or "important" (69 per cent). A slightly smaller percentage (85 per cent) of Canadians thought the "diminished role of government in providing universal social programs" was "important" (39 per cent) or "somewhat important" (46 per cent), while 82 per cent thought the "sharp decline in corporate and individual tax rates" to be "important" (34 per cent) or "somewhat important" (48 per cent) in the decline of the middle class.

What happened?

Middle Class Income Trends in Canada Since 1980

Disappointment occurs when actual events fall short of expectations. From the 1940s until about 1980, growth in real wages from one year to the next was something most Canadians had come to expect, so the actual evolution of middle-class living standards in Canada since then has come as a major shock. Since middle-class Canadians depend on wages and salaries for their economic well-being, a useful indicator of trends in their prosperity is how much labour receives, on average, for an hour's work. Around 1980, the reliable growth of average inflation-adjusted (or "real") hourly wages in Canada came to a sudden halt. As Figure 2.1 shows, average real hourly labour compensation rose strongly for most of the twentieth century, but this trend ceased after the late 1970s.[8]

Since the total compensation of all employees includes the pay of the CEO and other top executives, the trend to rapidly rising top executive pay during the 1980s and 1990s both increased the inequality of wages

Figure 2.1
Average Hourly Labour Compensation in Canada, 1914–2000
(2022 dollars)

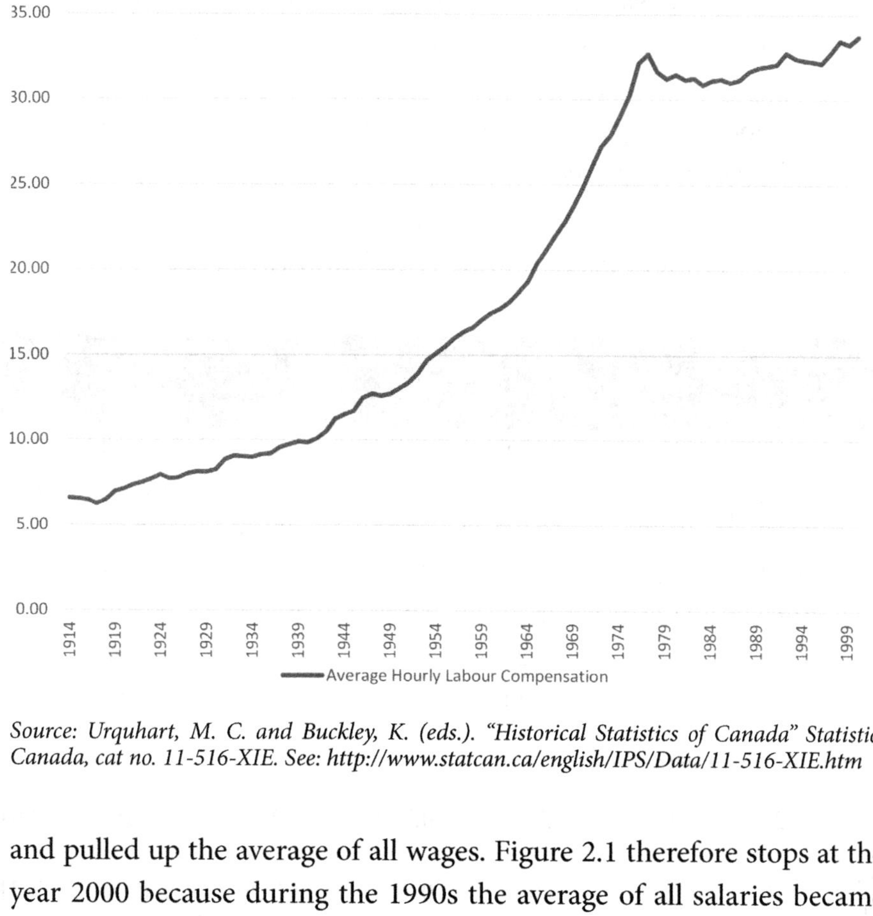

Source: Urquhart, M. C. and Buckley, K. (eds.). "Historical Statistics of Canada" Statistics Canada, cat no. 11-516-XIE. See: http://www.statcan.ca/english/IPS/Data/11-516-XIE.htm

and pulled up the average of all wages. Figure 2.1 therefore stops at the year 2000 because during the 1990s the average of all salaries became increasingly unreliable as a measure of the wages of an "average" worker. To look at what has been happening at each point in the income distribution, Table 2.1 presents data from Duclos and Pellerin (2016: Table 3) to unpack the trends between 1980 and 2010 within the distribution of real hourly wages. It lines up all full-time Canadian workers in order of their hourly wages, adjusts for inflation and examines the real hourly wage at the bottom, midpoint and top end of the hourly wage distribution — specifically, at the 10th, 50th, 90th, 99th and 99.9th percentiles. Since Duclos and Pellerin use data on individuals which come from the long-form Canadian Census, they have millions of observations, which enables them to examine directly the very top end of the hourly wage distribution. The disadvantage is that Census data are only collected at five-year intervals, and the most recent long-form Census data available to them were from 2010. Nonetheless, their findings repeat a very common conclusion about income distribution: "Most of the action has been at the very top."[9]

Table 2.1

Hourly Real Wage: Full-Time Workers

(2022 Dollars)

Year	Average	10th Percentile	50th Percentile Median	90th Percentile	99th Percentile	99.9th Percentile	$ Gap 99.9th–50th
1980	30.73	13.90	27.91	49.56	85.91	180.33	152.41
1985	30.04	12.22	27.43	49.23	85.02	186.55	159.12
1990	30.62	12.13	27.82	50.45	90.40	203.59	175.78
1995	30.11	11.51	27.05	49.79	90.99	227.54	200.49
2000	31.67	11.69	27.43	52.59	109.72	317.13	289.69
2005	33.81	12.31	28.27	55.70	122.58	444.48	416.21
2010	37.02	13.62	31.14	62.18	133.81	406.69	375.55
Compound annual growth rates							
1980–2010	0.62%	-0.07%	0.36%	0.76%	1.48%	2.71%	3.01%
1980–2000	0.15%	-0.87%	-0.09%	0.30%	1.22%	2.82%	3.21%
2000–2010	1.56%	1.52%	1.27%	1.68%	1.98%	2.49%	4.81%

Source: Duclos and Pellerin (2016-Table 3) plus author's calculations

Although Figure 2.1 may give the impression that average real wages recovered toward the end of the 1990s, and although an increase in average wages can also be seen in the first column of Table 2.1, this increase in the average real hourly wage is largely because the average was pulled up by the huge increases at the very top end (99th and 99.9th percentiles).

However, in 2010 the hourly wage of low-paid workers (the 10th percentile), after adjustment for inflation, was still below its 1980 level. Wages at the midpoint (the median real hourly wage) only returned to their 1980 level around 2005. Although the median real wage then surged until 2010, that late surge accounted for almost all of the increase in the inflation-adjusted hourly median wage for the thirty years from 1980 to 2010. For the full thirty-year period from 1980 to 2010, the compound annual growth rate of the median real hourly wages of full-time workers was an anemic 0.36 per cent annually — roughly one-eighth of the growth rate of wages at the very top.

At the very top, in the 99.9th percentile, average real hourly wages more than doubled, from $180 per hour in 1980 to $406 an hour in 2010. The dollar gap between the midpoint and the top end (i.e., between the median and the 99.9th percentile) therefore widened from $152 hourly to $375 hourly — i.e., by $223 per hour. Simultaneously, there was also an increase of about $10 in the gap in hourly wages between the upper-middle class (the 90th percentile) and the median — but the increase in the gap between the median and the 99.9th percentile was more than twenty-two times larger.

The sudden stop of average real hourly wage growth in Canada, and the continued stagnation of middle-class wages throughout the 1980s and 1990s, occurred despite the fact many changes in Canada increased average labour productivity and arguably should also have increased hourly wages — in particular:

1. Canada's workforce became much better educated: the fraction of full-time workers with some college or more increased by 26.6 percentage points over the 1980 to 2010 period.[10]
2. Between 1980 and 2010, Canada's baby boomers entered the most highly paid years of their working lives.
3. Labour productivity benefited from transformative technological change and from investment in new capital equipment as the capital/labour ratio increased.

4. Canadian governments made a host of institutional reforms with the stated objective of increasing market efficiency. Deregulation and the privatization of Crown corporations like CN Rail, Air Canada and Petro-Canada[11] were only part of what some have called the "neo-liberal" agenda that dominated economic policy-making after 1980.
5. Canada signed a host of accords and free trade agreements, including the Canada–US Free Trade Agreement (FTA), the North American Free Trade Agreement (NAFTA) and the World Trade Organization (WTO) accords.
6. Canada committed to a new monetary policy framework which solely targeted low inflation. Full employment was no longer mentioned as a policy goal.
7. Social spending cuts reduced social assistance and unemployment insurance benefits and eligibility (and UI was rebranded as EI — Employment Insurance) — cuts which were justified by the argument that they "increased work incentives."

Canadians have been repeatedly assured this new policy framework and all these institutional reforms would produce increased prosperity, but the real hourly wages of the middle class have stagnated. Labour productivity and GDP per capita did increase, but workers did not benefit. As Duclos and Pellerin conclude, "Wages within educational and potential experience groups have stagnated between 1980 and 2010. Hourly compensation growth among full-time workers is driven largely by rising educational attainments. Once we remove the wage effects of changes in the composition of the labour force, average hourly compensation stagnates or even declines over the period."[12]

The same pattern can be observed in income tax data. Table 2.2 provides some of the numbers underlying Figure 1.2 in Chapter 1. The first two columns show the real income in 1982 and 2021, measured in 2022 dollars, of taxpayers at the top (i.e., within the top 1 per cent) and at the 75th, 50th and 25th percentiles. The remaining columns draw out some of the implications.

Income gains were greater, in both percentage and dollar terms, for those higher up in the income distribution — which widened considerably the gap in incomes between the middle and the top in Canadian society. In the middle, income gains have not been large — the 50th percentile (median) taxpayer saw a gain of 0.5 per cent annually, or roughly $200 per year, as they went from $36,905 in 1982 to $44,487 in 2021. Within the middle class, dollar gaps have also not changed all that much. The 25th percentile taxpayer was $20,380 below the median taxpayer in 1982 and $21,035 below the median in 2021 — remarkably little change. The 75th percentile taxpayer was $27,816 above the median in 1982 and nearly 40 years later in 2021 the gap had widened to $31,928, which amounts to a widening of about $105 every year. Within the broad middle of the Canadian income distribution, there was not a lot of change in dollar income gaps.

However, income gaps between top income groups and the middle class have changed much more dramatically. As the first two columns of Table 2.2 show, over the thirty-nine years from 1982 to 2021, annual income at the very, very top (the midpoint of top 1 per cent of the top 1 per cent) grew by nearly $6.5 million from $2.3 million to $8.8 million — an average annual gain of $165,665 and a compound annual percentage increase of 3.41 per cent. Comparing the top tenth of the top 1 per cent to the median, a gap of $686,000 became a gulf of $2.05 million, widening by an average of $35,000 every year. And although at the margin of the top 1 per cent (the 99th percentile) the dollar gap with median income "only" doubled from $159,000 to $305,000 — that increase is still well more than enough to enable significant widening of the differences in lifestyle to be observed at the top and in the middle of Canada's income distribution.

When changes of this magnitude in the income gaps of Canadian society have been observed in the recent past, it is natural to wonder what Canadians might expect in the future. If we suppose that the rate of income growth actually observed over the period between 1982 and 2021, as presented in column 6, continues on for twenty years into the future, we get the italicized columns of Table 2.2 in 2041.[13] The arithmetic of growth dictates that when

Table 2.2

Real Total Income of Canadian Taxpayers, 1982–2021

(Including capital gains, in 2022 dollars)

Income group		1982	2021	*Projected 2041*	Gain 1982–2021	Annual gain	Growth rate
Top 1% of 1%	**Midpoint: 99.995**	2,329,692	8,790,636	*17,173,202*	6,460,944	165,665	3.41%
Top 10% of 1%	**Midpoint: 99.95th percentile**	722,675	2,100,569	*3,603,979*	1,377,894	35,331	2.74%
Top 1%	**Midpoint: 99.5th**	257,784	522,046	*747,239*	264,262	6,776	1.81%
Top 1%	**Threshold: 99th percentile**	195,816	349,917	*470,221*	154,101	3,951	1.49%
Top 5%	**Midpoint: 97.5th percentile**	142,111	218,898	*272,851*	76,787	1,969	1.11%
	Threshold: 95th percentile	115,398	159,422	*188,031*	44,025	1,129	0.83%
	75th percentile	64,721	76,775	*83,786*	12,053	309	0.44%
	Median	36,905	44,847	*49,550*	7,943	204	0.50%
	25th percentile	16,525	23,812	*28,693*	7,287	187	0.94%

faster annual growth compounds on a much larger initial base, the dollar gulfs between elite and middle-class lifestyles widen drastically.

Both Census data and tax data lead to the same conclusion: in Canada, there has been very strong income growth at the very top of the income distribution but not much change for the middle class. Indeed, for the 1982 to 2021 period as a whole, the median taxpayer's real income only grew by 0.5 per cent annually. Long-term growth at the 75th percentile (0.44 per cent) was quite similar but 90th percentile incomes grew at 0.83 per cent yearly.[14]

Within the top 1 per cent, the further up one goes, the greater the acceleration of income growth. The very top income percentiles grew

Income group		Dollar gap with median 1982	Dollar gap with median 2021	Dollar gap with median *2041*	Ratio 2021/1982	Annual widening of gap with median 2021–1982
Top 1% of 1%	**Midpoint: 99.995**	2,292,787	8,745,789	*17,123,652*	3.77	165,462
Top 10% of 1%	**Midpoint: 99.95th percentile**	685,770	2,055,722	*3,554,429*	2.91	35,127
Top 1%	**Midpoint: 99.5th**	220,879	477,199	*697,689*	2.03	6,572
Top 1%	**Threshold: 99th percentile**	158,911	305,070	*420,671*	1.79	3,748
Top 5%	**Midpoint: 97.5th percentile**	105,206	174,051	*223,301*	1.54	1,765
	Threshold: 95th percentile	78,492	114,575	*138,481*	1.38	925
	75th percentile	27,816	31,928	*34,236*	1.19	105
	Median	0	0	*0*	1.22	0
	25th percentile	-20,380	-21,035	*-20,857*	1.44	-17

Source: Statistics Canada, Table S 18-10-0005-01 & 11-10-0055-01

at a compound annual rate of 3.4 per cent for the full thirty-nine year period, with extremely rapid market income growth from 1982 to 2000 (roughly 6 per cent annually) and market income declines during the Great Recession and its immediate aftermath (as Figure 1.1 illustrated).

But for middle-class Canadians, the big question is why? Why did middle-class hourly wages and labour earnings stagnate for twenty years between 1980 and 2000? Why was there some recovery after 2000 (but not enough to catch up)? Why was income growth so much stronger at the top than in the middle? What can Canada's middle class expect for the future?

Killing Inflation: 1981 to 2000

Since middle-class families in Canada get most of their incomes from their jobs, they depend primarily on growth in wages and salaries for increases in their economic well-being. But a widespread increase in earnings only happens if there are enough jobs for the people looking for employment, enough hours of work for the people with jobs and enough competition by firms for workers to generate upward pressure on hourly wages. If there is not enough demand for labour, one cannot expect earnings to increase.

In continental Europe, wage-setting is often quite institutionalized. It is common there for unions to negotiate nationwide wage settlements, and for the wages set by collective bargaining to be extended automatically to all workers in a particular industry. Canada has never been like that. Roughly 90 per cent of Canadian workers are covered by provincial labour legislation[15] and all Canadian jurisdictions follow the Wagner Act model of the United States, in which labour boards certify a single bargaining agent at the company or establishment level to negotiate a wage contract. Although the overall rate of unionization in Canada decreased from 37.6 per cent in 1981 to 30.9 per cent in 2021, the stability of public sector unionization rates contrasts with larger declines in the private sector: by 2021, the private sector unionization rate in Canada was down to 15.3 per cent.[16]

Since the influence of unions on wages in the private sector in Canada is limited to a small fraction of employees, demand and supply in the labour market sets the general level of unemployment and real wages. When there is not enough aggregate demand for labour — when unemployment is high — one cannot expect to see a general increase in real wages. And the 1980s constituted a regime shift for Canadian unemployment. As Figure 2.2 shows, between 1946 and 1974, Canada's annual unemployment rate averaged 4.6 per cent and was never above 6.4 per cent.[17] However, unemployment was consistently greater than 8 per cent throughout the 1980s and 1990s, averaging 9.5 per cent over those two decades. When there is high unemployment, stagnant wages are a predictable implication. But if real wages did not rise because Canadian unemployment suddenly shifted up, the next obvious question is why this sudden shift to a high unemployment/low labour demand situation happened.

Figure 2.2

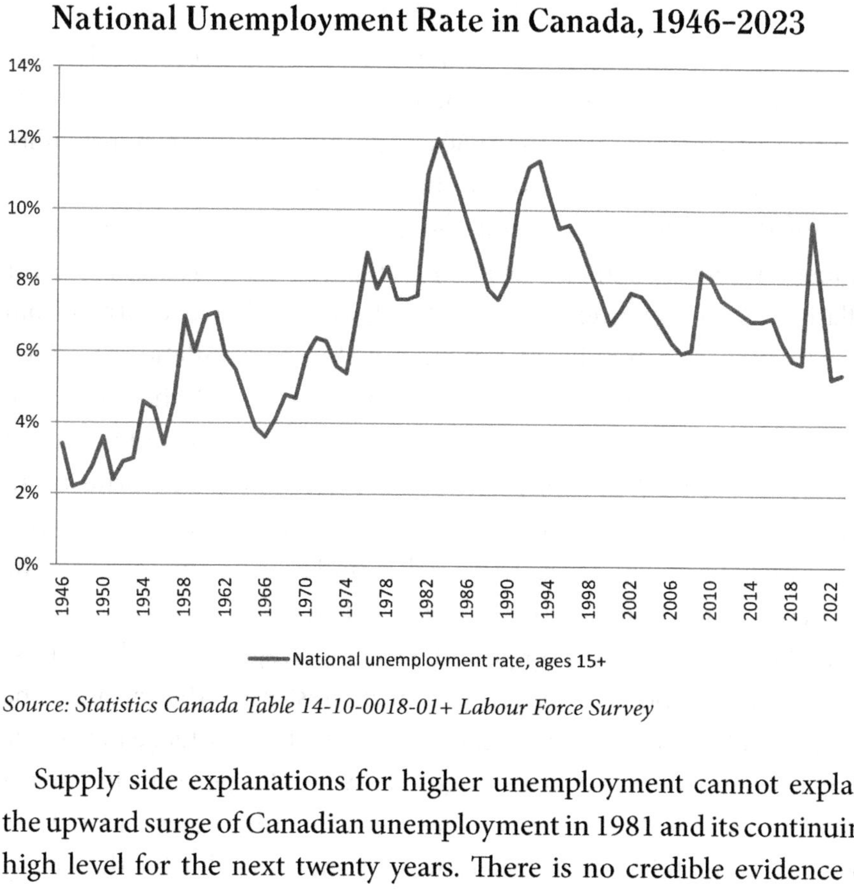

Source: Statistics Canada Table 14-10-0018-01+ Labour Force Survey

Supply side explanations for higher unemployment cannot explain the upward surge of Canadian unemployment in 1981 and its continuing high level for the next twenty years. There is no credible evidence of any sudden shift in Canadians' preferences for unemployment time. Any "incentives" to prefer unemployment to waged labour embedded in Canada's social assistance systems were reduced, not increased, throughout the 1980s and 1990s.

The alternative hypothesis is the demand side explanation: two decades of high unemployment were collateral damage in Canada's successful war against inflation. During the 1970s, price inflation rose steadily in Canada, as it did in the United States and other countries, partly because energy and other commodity prices rose dramatically following the oil price shock of 1973–74. Canadian economists had long known that governments can always kill off price inflation if the central bank is willing to engineer a severe enough recession. Businesses will not raise prices when they cannot sell what they are currently producing. But during the post-war period in Canada, until about 1980, there was still a lingering memory of the mass unemployment of the Great Depression in the 1930s, the social and political instability that it created and its legacy of war in the 1940s.

Until the 1980s, both Liberal and Conservative governments were reluctant to increase unemployment and looked for other solutions for inflation. Canada even experimented with wage and price controls from 1975 to 1978 (which reduced, but did not eliminate, inflation[18]). When the world price of oil spiked upward again in late 1979, threatening to set off a new upward spiral of prices, getting inflation under control became the federal government's macroeconomic policy priority. In both Ottawa and Washington, the decision was made to raise interest rates by whatever was necessary to reduce inflation — and to accept the increase in unemployment which that implied.

Anybody who owned a home and had a mortgage in Canada in those days can remember vividly the rise in interest rates that ensued: the average lending rate for a five-year term residential mortgage in Canada jumped from 11.8 per cent in August 1979 to 21.3 per cent in August 1981.[19] If your mortgage came up for renewal anytime between 1979 and 1981 (as mine did in 1980), there was an enormous hit for the family budget. When I had to renew the 10.5 per cent mortgage on our house at an interest rate of 16.5 per cent, all other household expenditures had to be cut to the bone. When a large number of people cut their spending on goods and services, businesses cannot sell what they are producing. When sales disappear, firms lay off workers. The unemployment rate in Canada shot up, reaching a high of 12 per cent in 1983, and only declining slowly throughout the next few years.

The 1980–81 recession demonstrated clearly something that Canadian governments had long known — that inflation can be reduced if the central bank is willing to raise interest rates (and unemployment rates) high enough for a long enough length of time. Consumer price inflation fell precipitously from its 12 per cent peak in 1981 to an average of 3.81 per cent from 1984 to 1988. But by 1988, the federal Department of Finance was worried about a possible resurgence of inflation. In Ontario, the Liberals had just ended over forty years of Conservative rule, and they were spending heavily. The Conservative federal government was proposing to replace the old Manufacturers Sales Tax with the new Goods and Services Tax, but was concerned that introduction of the new tax, especially in an "over-heated" Ontario economy, might change inflationary expectations and set off an upward wage/price spiral. I well remember the senior macroeconomic forecaster from the Department of Finance explaining to me, over lunch in the Dalhousie Faculty Club, that a small recession would be necessary to "cool off" the economy.

As part of this new anti-inflation push, in January 1988, John Crow, then the governor of the Bank of Canada, committed the Bank of Canada to "a path that leads towards underlying price stability."[20] Shortly thereafter, the Bank of Canada began raising interest rates again. Between March 1988 and March 1990, the Bank of Canada raised the rate at which banks borrow funds (the "bank rate") from 8.7 to 14.05 per cent, (an increase of 5.27 percentage points), and other short-term interest rates followed in rough parallel.

Very few homeowners in the 2020s[21] can really imagine what it was like to buy a house in the early 1990s, when the real interest rate on home mortgages was consistently over 8 per cent, hitting a high of 10.6 per cent in 1994.

Raising interest rates that much had quite predictable impacts: investment and consumer spending collapsed and unemployment increased. Unlike the early 1980s, this was a "Made in Canada" recession; American interest rates did not follow the same path. But because higher interest rates in Canada produced a historically large interest rate differential with the United States, financial capital flowed north and the inflow of foreign exchange bid up the value of the Canadian dollar (from 0.72 to 0.89 USD), which priced Canada's exports out of foreign markets and decimated employment in manufacturing industries.[22]

Canada's macroeconomic decision-makers had forecast, and indeed had intended, some of this. But they had not expected Iraq to invade Kuwait in August 1990. When that happened, and the Gulf War started, investor and consumer confidence in the United States evaporated, and the US also went into recession from 1990 to 1992. With the American recession now overlaying the domestic recession already underway, Canadian exports took another hit and unemployment surged upward again, averaging 10.3 per cent nationally in 1991, 11.2 per cent in 1992 and 11.4 per cent in 1993. The recessions of the early 1980s and early 1990s, and the "Twin Peaks" of unemployment in Canada they caused (see Figure 2.2), correspond exactly to the two big upward surges in middle-class inequality of market incomes in Canada discussed in Chapter 1.

In recessions, it is typically the youth cohort who have not yet acquired seniority in a permanent job, along with marginalized groups (such as recent immigrants or Indigenous or racialized Canadians), who lose the most in earnings. Older, established workers with higher pay rates are often somewhat protected from layoffs by their greater seniority. Since the earnings of those most likely to be laid off are lower to begin with, the inequality of market incomes increases during recessions.

In Canada in the 1980s, unemployment benefits were received by a far higher percentage of the unemployed than is now the case; the ratio of UI/EI beneficiaries to the number of unemployed has been cut from roughly 80 per cent to under 40 per cent.[23] Provincial social assistance payments were also considerably higher, in inflation-adjusted terms, in the 1980s than they were after 1996.[24]

As already discussed in Chapter 1, when unemployment surged upward during the recession of the early 1980s, increased transfer payments were able to offset a large part of the 1981 to 1983 increase in market income inequality. But while transfers and taxes played an increasing role in offsetting rising market income inequality until the mid-1990s, they played a decreasing role after 1995. From the mid-1990s to the early 2000s, changes in the impact of transfers and taxes accentuated the changes in market income inequality, instead of offsetting them. Why did Canadian governments shift from offsetting to accentuating rising market income inequality?

The short answer is that Canada's "debt crisis" of the mid-1990s produced major cuts to social programs. But that just forces the question: where did the debt crisis come from?

Interest Rate Policy, the Public Debt and Social Programs in Canada

As already noted, the Canadian recessions of the early 1980s and 1990s were the result of conscious interest rate policy decisions (even if the depth of Canada's 1990s recession was accentuated by the unanticipated shock of a US recession). The increase in unemployment in these recessions was the expected result of raising interest rates to reduce total (or "aggregate") demand for goods and services and thereby reduce inflation. But this short-run cost of recessions was not the only impact — recessions also leave a legacy of increased government debt. Higher interest rates both slow the growth of national income (which reduces tax revenue and increases spending on unemployment insurance and welfare) and simultaneously speed up the compounding impact of interest rates on the accumulated stock of debt. Higher interest rates thus can have disastrous effects on government finances.[25] The larger the debt is to start with, the higher the increased cost of interest on it. That interest cost on past debt adds to the debt, increasing the debt even further, which in turn means even higher interest costs the next year. When interest rates are raised substantially (as in the early 1980s and early 1990s), they can add so much to the debt that a debt crisis occurs.

For both countries and households, the affordability of debt depends on how large it is relative to income and what interest rate is being paid.

In financial markets, the most closely watched statistic for measuring the affordability of government (public) debt is the ratio of public debt to national income (i.e., the debt/GDP ratio). The compounding impacts of interest rates mean the numerator of that ratio (the debt) tends to grow at the rate of interest.[26] Meanwhile, the denominator grows at the rate of growth of national income (i.e., the GDP growth rate). When the growth rate of the economy is greater than the interest rate, GDP increases in size faster than the debt, so governments do not have to worry as much about the debt/GDP ratio.[27] Like a skier racing an avalanche, the key issue is which is going faster. But higher interest rates both slow down the skier (GDP) and simultaneously speed up the avalanche (accumulating debt), resulting in a double-whammy for the sustainability of the national debt.

In Canada, the federal debt/GDP ratio peaked during the Second World War, but thereafter declined until 1975, largely because of strong economic growth.[28] After that, there were three distinct phases. In the first phase, from 1975 to 1980, the federal government ran a series of deficits, as the result of a succession of tax policy changes which decreased the tax share of total GDP.[29] The second period, 1981 to 1989, saw a rapid rise in Canada's debt/GDP ratio. Higher interest rates increased the speed at which the debt compounded, and slower GDP growth cut the size of the national income that could be used to pay down the debt. However, by the latter part of the 1980s, Canadian governments had raised taxes and cut spending considerably. By 1989, the provincial and federal governments were running sufficiently large excesses of taxes over expenditures to begin to reduce the debt/GDP ratio.

When, in 1988, the Bank of Canada embarked on its new policy of "price stability," higher interest rates[30] and slower growth destroyed the debt stabilization plans of the federal and provincial governments. The debt/GDP ratio soared to new heights, and by 1995, all Canadian governments perceived no alternative but to engage in major expenditure cuts.[31] In 1996, federal Minister of Finance Paul Martin declared he was going to eliminate the federal government's budget deficit, "come hell or high water," by cutting spending. Massive cuts to unemployment insurance benefits, and a name change to "employment insurance," were combined with cuts to federal transfers to provincial governments, who then cut their social assistance payments.

During the federal budget cuts of the mid-1990s, unemployment insurance benefit recipients fell, as a percentage of the unemployed, by roughly 40 percentage points (i.e., by half) — and have never recovered. Federal cost-sharing of social assistance was abolished, and provinces cut welfare benefits substantially (e.g., a 24 per cent cut in Ontario) — and never reversed those cuts. Although the late 1990s saw a recovery in public finances, transfer payments were never restored. The decision of the federal Liberal government of 2000 was to cut personal and corporate tax rates and thereby lock in the decline in public spending as a fraction of GDP.[32]

During the 1970s and before, the Bank of Canada, like the US Federal Reserve, had a dual mandate,[33] which recognized that since there might be costs in higher unemployment to achieving better inflation performance, the Bank should find a balance between these objectives. Unlike the US Federal Reserve, macroeconomic policy-makers at the Bank of Canada have focused exclusively on low inflation since 1980, as explicitly formalized in inflation targets after 1991 (the target inflation rate is 2 per cent, with a band of plus or minus 1 per cent). The Bank of Canada was an "early adopter" of the policy of targeting only the inflation rate, and this target has been consistently achieved.

Minimizing the probability of inflation is not really all that difficult. Economists have long known that wages and prices will not increase if unemployment is kept high enough for long enough and that can always be achieved with higher interest rates. The difficult part of monetary policy is also maintaining economic growth, but policy formation is simpler when trade-offs are not acknowledged. Once the objective of the Bank of Canada was limited to inflation control, its policy mandate was to raise interest rates (and unemployment) whenever it grew anxious about higher inflation,[34] which it often has been and continues to be.

Figure 2.2 plotted the unemployment rate and Figure 2.1 plotted the resultant trend in average real hourly wages. Since the recessions of the early 1980s and 1990s were extremely costly and were both induced by a monetary policy aimed at reducing inflation, the Bank of Canada has had a lot of institutional credibility invested in continuing to achieve inflation targets. Promotion from within[35] has meant that incoming governors of the Bank of Canada have reproduced the same policies they had earlier helped to develop as junior central bankers.

Success in killing inflation has therefore had both direct and indirect impacts on Canada's middle class. From 1980 to 1995, Canada was a case study in how the direct impacts of interest rate policy choices and the priority given to "price stability" can choke off growth of the market income of the middle class by restricting labour demand, raising unemployment and thereby smothering growth in real wages. Increasing inequality of market incomes is one result, but as Figure 1.4 shows, until 1995 much of that increase in market income inequality was offset by increased transfer payments from unemployment insurance and social assistance. However, the second-round impact of anti-inflation interest rate policies has arguably been more important for long-run inequality in Canada, because high interest rates destabilized the public debt, producing lasting cuts to the income transfer programs that before 1995 had partly protected Canadian workers from the income losses produced by unemployment. After 1996, these cuts to transfer payments meant Canadian governments shifted from offsetting to accentuating increases in market income inequality — an impact which remained, even when unemployment declined during Canada's later resource boom. For middle-class inequality in Canada from 1980 to 2000, interest rate policy has mattered, in major ways.

The Income Gains of Canada's Oil Boom

Unlike most of the other rich nations of the OECD, Canada is a significant exporter of oil, natural gas and other resource commodities, and its terms of trade have been quite sensitive to their international prices.[36] Between 2001 and 2014, Canada's labour market was heavily influenced by a steady surge in real oil prices from $22 USD[37] per barrel in late 2001 to $142 USD per barrel in June 2008. That surge spawned a confident expectation that oil prices could only continue to go up, which motivated a surge of investment in the oil sector. (Although the upward march of oil prices was interrupted by a collapse to $42 per barrel in December 2008 as the Great Recession hit, price recovery was swift, rebounding to $119 per barrel in March 2012.)

As Prime Minister of Canada from 2006 to 2015, Stephen Harper was clear about his belief in "Canada's emergence as a global energy powerhouse — the emerging 'energy superpower' our government intends to build."[38] High oil prices were widely believed to be a near certainty, in Canada and elsewhere. Indeed, a technically excellent study in 2012 from the International Monetary Fund[39] analyzed geological data on world oil reserves, technological capabilities in the petroleum industry and economic projections of world oil demand and supply and forecast 2016 price of $130 per barrel, rising to $180 per barrel in 2020.[40] The expectation of continued increases in oil prices and Canada's status as a secure supplier to the nearby American market produced a surge of investment. Between 1999 and 2013, approximately $201 billion CDN was invested in the Alberta oil sands industry,[41] and when that much investment goes into a highly paid sector[42] that fast, there are impacts across the economy. During the oil boom, as charter flights were flying crew changes into Fort McMurray construction sites from Atlantic Canada and rural B.C. and everywhere in between, labour market impacts were apparent to Canadians from coast to coast.

Although Canada's oil and gas sector directly employs only a small percentage of Canadian workers, the rapid expansion of oil sands investment established new reference points for wage-setting nationwide. With an interlude of a governor appointed from outside, the Bank of Canada allowed national unemployment to trend down. Low unemployment and high wages in Alberta attracted substantial interprovincial migration, which combined with the explosive growth of interprovincial commuting to bid up real wages throughout the country.

Canada's resource boom also meant the impact of the Great Recession of 2008–09 was considerably less severe in Canada than in the United States or Europe. As Figure 2.2 indicated, the increase in Canadian unemployment in 2009 was relatively small and of short duration. The rapid recovery of oil prices following the 2008–09 recession seemed to validate the general expectation of continued energy price increases and continued profitability of investment in oil sands production facilities. For most Canadians, the growth of real after-tax income during the 2001 to 2014 period was a welcome contrast to the flat-lining experienced from 1980 to 2000 (see Figure 1.2 in Chapter 1).

A top priority of the Harper government between 2006 and 2015 also was cutting taxes — for example, the 2015 cut of 2 per cent in the GST tax rate. However, although tax cuts can produce a one-time increase in the purchasing power of voting households, tax cuts cannot happen every year forever since, eventually, government will run out of revenue entirely. Unless tax cuts cause an increase in the growth rate of household income[43] (which so far has not happened), they only have a short-term impact on private consumption.

Additionally, the flip side of taxes is the quantity and quality of public services that government can provide. Households benefiting from education, healthcare, police services, fire protection and other government services must expect that when governments have less tax revenue, they will provide fewer and/or lower-quality public services. Counting an increase in after-tax money income as the benefits of a tax cut overstates the well-being gain of households because the costs of decreased public services are not recorded. Canadians are not necessarily better off if, for example, a tax cut increases their after-tax money income but less tax revenue for government means less public spending on road maintenance and pothole filling, so their private spending on shock absorbers and mufflers goes up along with their after-tax household money income.

Nevertheless, whether one uses survey, income tax or Census data, there are some common findings on after-tax money income inequality. Within the middle 80 per cent of the income distribution, whatever the data used, in Canada there was a common experience of real income stagnancy from 1981 to 2000 when annual real income growth averaged 0.3 to 0.4 per cent at most throughout the middle class. During the oil boom period which followed, until 2014, there was faster income growth for some demographic segments. Some increase in the income gaps within the middle 80 per cent is also a common finding. For example, from 1980 to 2010, census data on real hourly wages at the 10th percentile fell at 0.07 per cent yearly but rose by 0.76 per cent yearly at the 90th percentile.[44] Some authors[45] have interpreted this fanning out of incomes as the divergence of fortunes of the highly educated professional and technical occupations in Canada's upper-middle class and the poorly educated factory workers of the lower-middle class. Others[46] call it the "hollowing out" of the middle class, the result of long-term job polarization combined with upskilling of segments of the workforce.

However, income gaps within the middle class grew by far less than income gaps between the middle and the top. Differentials in income growth within Canada's middle class have been much, much smaller than the differences in income growth between the middle and the top percentiles. Most of this increase in income gaps within the "middle 80 per cent" of Canadians also happened before 2000 — after that, there was less fanning out in after-tax middle-class family incomes.[47] In fact, the similarity in total growth across equivalent disposable income percentiles from the 10th to the 90th is really quite striking: one often has to look to the third decimal place to find differences in income growth rates across deciles in any given year.[48] Basically, Canada's "middle 80 per cent" of households experienced rising real incomes and pretty much unchanging income inequality among themselves from 2001 to 2021.

But how then can we explain the polling data on public attitudes presented earlier in this chapter? Some of those polls were collected before the decline in commodity prices pricked the balloon of Canada's resource boom and after a long period in which relative real household incomes within the middle part of the income distribution changed very little. So why were so many Canadians even then pessimistic about the middle class? Why did the Pollara data report 85 per cent agreement with the statement "income inequality is no longer about the gap between the rich and the poor, but rather the very rich and everyone else," and why did a similarly worded EKOS question garner 77 per cent agreement?

Life After the Commodity Boom?

In the United States and Europe, the decline in lower middle-class wages and employment opportunities, particularly for males with relatively poor education, has had a major impact on inequality within the middle class. The reasons have been much debated. Some authors have emphasized the importance of institutional changes, particularly declining unionization and cuts in the real value of the minimum wage. Other authors have stressed the role played by automation and technical change and the disappearance of many manufacturing jobs. Still others emphasize the importance of globalization and trade competition from newly emerging low-wage competitors. Whatever the cause, the impact has been uneven, and poorly educated older males have often encountered particularly sharp declines in their labour market options.

Until 2014, Canada was a bit of a bystander in this debate on the future prospects for the traditional working class, because Canada's construction boom after 2000 provided many well-paying jobs for exactly this demographic. In the oil patch, construction jobs are particularly well-paid, and their numbers rise and fall with oil prices. However, Canada's oil boom has gone and is unlikely to return. Although sudden price surges (e.g., due to the outbreak of the war in Ukraine in 2022) can add unpredictability to the short-term evolution of oil prices, the long lead times involved in major investments mean that oil companies have to try to predict oil prices decades into the future. Their current worry is that the increasing global policy emphasis on decarbonization and the declining costs of competing energy technologies such as solar and wind mean the "low for long" scenario for oil prices will imply that past oil sands investments will become stranded assets. Oil boom days are gone.

Summary

The crucial issue for long-term inequality trends is differences in income growth rates. After World War II, increasing real wages fueled rising living standards for Canada's middle class for thirty-five years. Since 1981, the middle class has seen two decades of wage stagnation, followed by a period of tepid growth. The issue for the future is whether middle-class market income growth can speed up to match top-end income growth — especially since two big trends that have supported middle-class family income growth are unlikely to continue. Over the last forty years, women's earnings have increased substantially as a percentage of household income because both their wages and their probability of employment have increased, but female labour force participation cannot keep going up forever.[49] The Canadian workforce is also better educated than ever, but educational attainment also cannot continually increase. In Canada, the middle class thus faces significant challenges, in addition to the problems (common to all affluent nations) of coping with the accelerating impacts of artificial intelligence and the continuing globalization of production.

Chapter 3
INEQUALITY AT THE TOP

Economic inequality is not exactly a new phenomenon. In feudal times, there was enormous inequality between the nobility and the peasantry and during the Industrial Revolution of the nineteenth century the gulf between the great fortunes of the new factory magnates and their workers was gargantuan. Concern about the extremes of economic inequality has always been central to discussions of inequality. But before the twentieth century, attempts to measure these inequalities were rare. Since surveys of household income distribution were largely unknown before the 1950s, early studies of income inequality had to depend primarily on income tax return data, which was only available in a few countries before the early 1900s. Because only the very affluent then paid income tax, when Vilfredo Pareto (1896) published his path-breaking analysis of income inequality, he could only examine the income of the uppermost percentiles of the income distribution. That did not stop him from declaring that he had discovered a universal law of income distribution[1] but because Pareto did not have a reliable way to calculate total income, he could not calculate shares of total income. It was not until the 1930s and 1940s that economists developed the concepts needed to measure GDP. The national income accounting systems which made GDP measurement possible enabled Kuznets (1953) to combine income tax data with national accounts data and obtain pioneering estimates of the percentage share of top income-earners in total income.

Measuring just how much inequality exists in a country is thus a fairly recent innovation. Chapter 2 relies heavily on the data from representative sample surveys of households which Canada now uses to track inequality trends, but these surveys date from the 1970s. Hence, Chapter 2 primarily discusses trends over the last fifty years, because that is when the survey data started to become available — but survey data is not available to examine longer-run trends. As well, survey data often leave the very poor and the very affluent out of the picture,[2] and thus make it difficult to say anything reliable about the most extremely unequal parts of the income distribution.

Many people would argue the growth of the middle class during the mid-twentieth century was a new, enormously positive trend because it reduced the polarization between extremes of wealth and poverty. Since the very wealthy still control so much income, accurate measurement of their share is crucial to the measurement of inequality trends, but they are very few in number and often unwilling to answer surveys. As a result, we cannot depend on sample surveys in Canada to measure top-end trends accurately.[3]

Income tax data have both important advantages and some severe disadvantages for the study of top-end inequality. One of the advantages is that income tax records include the complete population of the affluent, since filing an income tax return is compulsory. When combined with reliable estimates of total income, tax data enable the estimation of trends in the top 1 per cent income share. In Canada, income tax data have also become increasingly representative of the entire adult population. Income tax coverage has expanded because social transfers like the GST/HST tax credit are now administered through the income tax system. Also, the long span of tax data, combined with historical estimates of total income, enables discussion of very long-run trends in top-end inequality.[4]

However, tax return data are greatly limited in possibilities for analysis. Since the administration of income tax only retains data relevant to income tax collection, many variables which may be important for the analysis of income determination (e.g. education or ethnicity) are not recorded in the data, so many of the causes and correlates of individual income cannot be examined.

Estimates of inequality are also influenced by the fact that taxation creates incentives to avoid or evade payment — especially at the top. Avoidance is distinguishable from evasion in that tax avoidance alters the legal reporting of economic income in ways that will lessen or entirely avoid taxation while evasion is illegally escaping taxation entirely by not reporting income. Well-paid tax lawyers and tax accountants are available to help the very affluent devise sophisticated tax planning strategies to keep clients on the legal side of what can be a very fine line.[5] But whether it is avoidance or evasion, the net result of "tax planning" for the measurement of income inequality is that income disappears from any inequality statistics based on income tax records. If tax avoidance and evasion could be assumed to be constant over time, trends in taxable income would at least mirror trends in economic income, but it is clear that income reporting in tax data is sensitive to both anticipated enforcement and changes in tax rates and tax law.

Although most analysis of inequality builds up estimates from the bottom (i.e., from the income tax returns of individuals or the responses of individuals to surveys or the census), some recent papers have started from the top, attributing to individuals the income that is missed by tax returns or surveys. The under-reporting of income is especially important for capital income because in Canada "only 66.6% of net national income is observed in tax data each year — in other words, one third of national income is not allocated to anyone in traditional inequality statistics . . . Including this missing income in inequality statistics tends to increase estimates of inequality because while most of labour income is observed (76% on average), only 29% of capital income is observed annually, and capital income is more unequally distributed than labour income."[6]

Nevertheless, international research using income tax data has conclusively documented a long and historic swing in top-end income shares and an increasing realization that in income distribution, "most of the action has been at the very top."[7]

Figure 3.1

Top 1 Per Cent Share of Pre-Tax National Income in the USA, 1910–2022

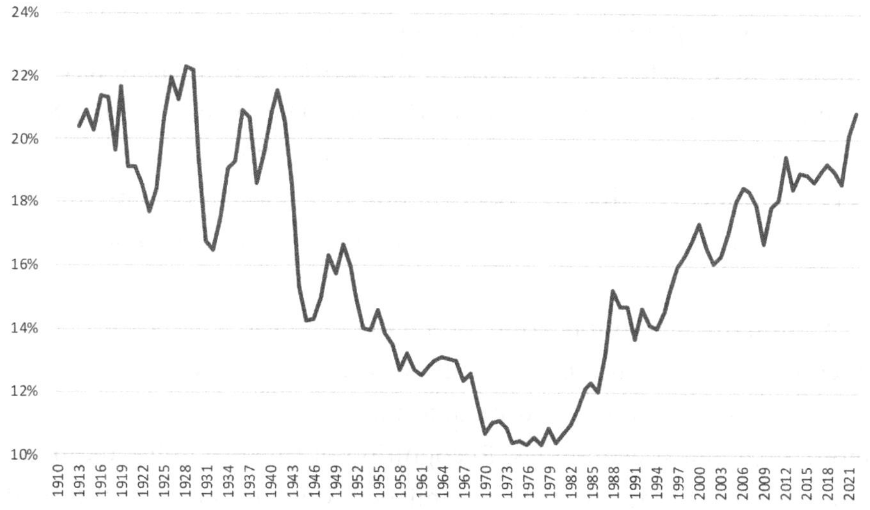

Source: WID – World Inequality Database

As Figure 3.1 shows, the income share of the top 1 per cent in the United States was very high in the 1920s, fell abruptly during the 1940s and then edged down marginally during the 1950s, 1960s and 1970s. Since the 1980s, however, there has been a clear long-run trend upward in the income share of the top 1 per cent (with ups and downs around this trend during booms and recessions).[8]

The further up the income pyramid one goes, the faster the rate of increase in income. As already documented, the income growth rate for the top 0.01 per cent is greater than the growth rate for the top 0.1 per cent, and the growth rate of the top 0.1 per cent is significantly greater than the income growth rate for the top 1 per cent. This realization has changed the focus of much of the debate about economic inequality. Since incomes at the top are already large, a large percentage change each year means the absolute size of increases in the income share of the top 1 per cent dwarfs the magnitude of shifts historically observed and those occurring elsewhere in the income distribution. In the thirty-six-year post-war period before 1981, for example, the income share of the middle 20 per cent of Canada's income distribution fluctuated by only 0.6 percentage points.[9] Since 1981, the gain in income share of Canada's top 1 per cent has been more than ten times larger than this. In the United States, the increase in the top 1 per cent share has been even larger — from 10.8 per cent in 1982 to 20.9 per cent in 2022. Since the 20 per cent of US households making $22,300 or less received 3.2 per cent of income, that 10.1 per cent point <u>increase</u> in income share by the top 1 per cent was more than three times the <u>total</u> income share of the bottom 20 per cent.[10]

A fundamental implication of Figure 3.1 also is that, by clearly documenting the long-term ups and downs in the income share of the top 1 per cent, it shows that income inequality has not been stable in modern capitalist economies. Recognition of this instability requires a huge shift in perspective for economists. If one looks only at the 1970s in Figure 3.1, one will see an income share of the top 1 per cent which did not change much. That decade of stability, and the small size of shifts in the income quintile shares reported in Table 1.1, had a big impact on the way economists thought about economic inequality and economic growth in the 1970s. If the level of inequality does not change much within a country, thinking of income distribution as the result of a stable process of balanced growth makes sense.[11]

Furthermore, if income inequality is roughly constant for each country, but differs across countries, the natural question to ask is whether countries with higher levels of income inequality are better off or worse off in other ways. For example, if income inequality is stable, one can ask if more unequal countries are also less healthy, less democratic and less happy, or if they have more crime, more social conflict and less equality of economic opportunity than countries with lower levels of inequality. Richard Wilkinson and Kate Pickett's 2010 book, *The Spirit Level: Why Equality Is Better for Everyone*, is a particularly famous example. In it, the authors compare inequality of income with a host of social indicators — average levels of health status, trust, social mobility, infant mortality, educational performance, violence, obesity, mental illness, teenage births, homicides and imprisonment — both across OECD countries and across states within the United States. They conclude that, along all these dimensions, there are more social problems in places where there is more income inequality.[12]

If one can expect inequality within each country to remain roughly the same over time, comparing the level of inequality across countries can therefore help answer a hypothetical question like: "What type of society would I like to live in?" Since this is an important question, and since there was a significant period during which within-country levels of income inequality changed only slightly, much of the literature on income inequality has emphasized these cross-sectional comparisons of the level of inequality. But times have changed. The level of inequality can only remain constant over time when income growth is balanced, that is, when the rate of income growth is roughly equal at all points in the income distribution. When some people's incomes grow much faster than others, income shares and the level of inequality necessarily change over time. Table 2.2 documents how much faster income growth at the top in Canada has been since 1982. The increase in the top 1 per cent income share since the early 1980s in the US illustrated by Figure 3.1 is just the logical implication of unbalanced growth.

In Canada, the United States and elsewhere since the 1980s, higher rates of income growth at the top end of the distribution have been compounding on ever-higher base incomes, so one now must ask if and when increasing top-end inequality will ever stabilize, and what the implications are if it does not. If unbalanced growth can be expected to continue, fundamentally new issues are raised. It is one thing to say that Canada is more unequal now than it was in 1980, and quite another to say Canada is more unequal now than it was in 1980 and that Canadians can expect it to get ever more unequal each year into the indefinite future.

Table 2.2 shows how income stagnation for most Canadians contrasted strongly with very robust income growth at the top, with an accelerating rate of increase in real (inflation-adjusted) incomes the further up one goes within the top 1 per cent. Table 2.2 and Figure 1.1 both also show how temporary declines within the business cycle have accompanied this long-run trend. The econometric evidence[13] indicates that American and Canadian top 1 per cent trends have become closely linked. Since the passage of the FTA and then NAFTA and the greater ease of mobility for Canadian executives into the United States, the share of the top 1 per cent in the US has been an excellent predictor of the income share of Canada's top 1 per cent.

When top-end incomes grow faster than the incomes of everyone else, income gaps necessarily continue to widen. Income inequality will only stop increasing if/when growth rates equalize — either as a result of middle-class incomes growing much faster or top-end incomes growing much slower (or some combination of both). As long as income growth rates differ, income shares will change over time.

Although Figure 3.1 shows a decrease in the income share of the top 1 per cent from the late 1930s to the mid-1970s in the US, this was never due to any actual decline in the real incomes of the top 1 per cent. Rather, the *share* of the top 1 per cent fell because the real incomes of the other 99 per cent of the income distribution grew more rapidly than top incomes did. This equalizing process has turned around since the early 1980s, as the incomes of the top 1 per cent have grown dramatically faster than everyone else's. And, as Table 2.2 shows, income growth rates have been even larger the further up the income distribution one cares to look.

What can explain these historic shifts in income growth? In particular, why did the income of the bottom 90 per cent grow so rapidly in North America after 1940?

Full employment matters. As Chapter 2 has already noted, people need jobs if they are to earn labour income, so strong demand for labour — i.e., full employment — was a large part of the reason middle-class incomes grew strongly throughout the 1950s and 1960s. Keeping unemployment low was then, unlike now, a clearly stated priority of Canada's federal government. But aggregate demand for labour can only ever be part of the story. The potential supply side of the Canadian economy also grew strongly, partly for reasons that are unlikely to be repeated. The rapid growth from 1940 through the 1970s of the real incomes of the bottom 90 per cent in Canada started from a situation in which:

- the mass unemployment of the 1930s was rapidly absorbed into wartime production during the early 1940s;
- price and wage controls during the Second World War were able to compress wage differentials and reduce profit margins;
- a large percentage of the population still lived on the farm in 1940 and rural outmigration significantly boosted average wages and productivity;
- initially low secondary and post-secondary enrollment meant the level of education had substantial room for increase;
- after WWII, post-war investment embodying up-to-date technologies could make up for years of under-investment during the Great Depression and Second World War and produce substantial increases in labour productivity;
- rising unionization rates produced a labour movement with significant influence in both workplace bargaining and social policy determination;
- the initially low share of women in the paid labour force meant that increased female employment had a big impact on disposable household money income; and

- communism was a credible hard-left political option, which had a "threat effect" on political elites, who agreed to progressive taxation and expansion of social programs like unemployment insurance, social assistance and public pensions, thereby recycling top-end incomes and reducing political discontent.

Wartime mobilization and price and wage controls were "one-time" events which ended by 1946. Structural changes of economic development also happen only once, but urbanization, rising female labour force participation and widespread increases in secondary and post-secondary education were spread over a long period and showed up as an increase in the growth rate of average income in the post-war era, right up until the 1970s.

Overall, however, balanced growth is not the norm in Canada or elsewhere. Canada's post-war period of fairly equal growth rates at the top and the bottom appears to have been a happy accident of history. Balanced growth then made it plausible for academics to ignore changes in income distribution. (In many university departments of economics, gullible undergraduates have been taught since the late 1970s about the steady-state properties of imaginary worlds in which, by assumption, poverty and inequality cannot exist at all because these theoretical worlds are entirely inhabited by identical "representative agents.") But balanced growth was a historical anomaly. Since the early 1980s, unbalanced income growth at the top has been our "new normal."

Will Market Processes Spontaneously Restore Balanced Growth?

"Increasing income inequality over time" and "more rapid income growth at the top" are actually just two different ways of describing the same reality. A stable income distribution can only happen when income growth rates are the same for everyone. Achieving that now requires either a substantial acceleration of the income growth rate of the bottom 99 per cent or a decline in the income growth rate of the top 1 per cent (or some combination of the two). But two fundamental aspects of the modern market economy make it unlikely that spontaneous "equilibrating" market forces will produce enough of either: (1) the very different processes driving pay in top-end labour markets,[14] and (2) the increasing importance of capital income and inheritance.

Segmented Labour Markets: Growing Globals and Lagging Locals

In 2022, J. Patrick Doyle, Executive Chairman of Restaurant Brands International, Inc., headed the pay parade of Canadian CEOs with $151,812,911 in total compensation, well ahead of the $98,864,268 that Matthew Proud of Dye and Durham made or the $36,398,662 of Seetarama Kotagiri of Magna International. The bottom guy (the one hundred top CEOs were almost all male) on Canada's list of one hundred highest paid CEOs was Randy Smallwood of Wheaton Precious Metals, at $6,698,241. To put these pay packages in context, one might remember that $6.7 million is about one hundred and fifty times what Canada's median taxpayer made that year. The rest of the top one hundred CEOs made even more.[15] These sorts of salaries represent dramatic increases in top-end incomes. What can explain them?

Pay at the top of Canada's corporate heap has always depended on firm size, and for many firms, size depends on the scale of the market. Since 1980, and particularly since the FTA of 1988, many firms in Canada that previously operated on a national scale have expanded into continental and global markets or been bought out by global multinationals. As trade barriers and transportation costs have fallen, innovations in telecommunications and information systems have made effective centralization of management of large, dispersed organizations more feasible. When the scale of these firms' global operations and global profits grows, their top management team takes a share. These payments (which economists often call "positional rents") increase with their rank in the hierarchy and with market size (which is growing at the global growth rate).

As well, internet start-ups and innovation in the high-tech sector have an underlying technology characterized by high fixed development costs and very low variable costs. Developing the initial concept, business model and source code can be expensive but reproducing it around the world is relatively cheap. Although the initial development costs of Facebook, Shopify, Airbnb or online poker may have been large, once the business is up and running, marketing the same service in Argentina, India, Germany or Australia costs very little. The owners of the first entrant in a market niche can therefore reap outsized returns from the global marketplace — especially if they can squeeze out upstarts who try to enter the market.

Historically, collective bargaining by unions was a constraint on the pay of senior management. When the CEO is getting multimillion-dollar bonuses, it is hard to persuade the union that workers' wages cannot go up, so the Board of Directors may limit executive pay increases. However, as the percentage of workers covered by collective agreements has shrunk, top executives have become less constrained.[16] The growth of CEO salaries has therefore been inversely correlated with union density — fastest in the United States, but slower in some other countries (e.g., France). In bygone days when slower communications, tariffs and transportation barriers produced more localized markets, it can also be argued that Canadian pay scales in CEO compensation were somewhat socially insulated from US trends. However, the FTA with the US in the 1980s and then NAFTA in the 1990s erased the barriers to executive mobility, producing a close matching of American and Canadian trends at the top.

Both the top managers and the owners of big businesses sit at the very top of the Canadian income distribution, but it is much easier to know about managers than about owners. In 2022, Bradley Shaw was CEO of Shaw Communications and was paid $13.1 million dollars.[17] Tony Staffieri had a very good year in 2022 as CEO of Rogers Communications, receiving $31.52 million. We know these numbers because the stocks of both companies were publicly listed on the

Toronto Stock Exchange and a requirement of public listing is that top executive salaries be disclosed. However, there is no requirement for public disclosure of the income of the Rogers and Shaw families, who controlled these companies.[18]

Even prior to the merger of the Rogers and Shaw telecommunications companies in 2023, the stockholdings of the Rogers Family Trust in those companies were worth approximately $9 billion and those of the Shaw Family Trust were worth about $2 billion.[19] The income from those holdings is not publicly available data but the rate of return on wealth of that size can be estimated by comparison with the rate of return observed on large pension plan funds — the ten-year average rate of return earned by the Canada Pension Plan has been 10 per cent.[20] If one assumes that the Rogers and Shaw families are able to manage their own assets as well as the employed money managers of the Canada Pension Plan, they would also get a 10 per cent rate of return — which implies an annual income for the Rogers family of at least $900 million and at least $200 million for the Shaw family.

The publicly available data on the compensation of executives in publicly traded companies enables us to know the $31.52 million income of the Staffieri family, which places them well up in the top 1 per cent of the family income distribution of Canada. However, fundamentally Tony Staffieri was the "hired help." Large as it was, his labour compensation as CEO of Rogers Telecommunications in 2022 was only about one-thirtieth of the ownership returns to the Rogers family. For Bradley Shaw, as for other CEOs who are running the family firm, reported labour compensation (as CEO) and unreported capital income (as owner) can be blurred together.

There is a lot of inequality even within the top 1 per cent. Among the top 1 per cent, as among all Canadians, one gets very different answers to the questions: "Where is the money?" and "Where are the people?" Since twenty-nine million people filed income tax returns in Canada in 2021, there were 290,000 taxpayers in the top 1 per cent — but most of those people did not make millions every year. The lowest income, measured in $2022, within the top 1 per cent was $350,000, but the top 1 per cent of the top 1 per cent (i.e., 2,900 people) started at an annual income of $5.9 million[21] — well below the Staffieri and Rogers families. The occupational composition of the top 1 per cent is dominated by people whose incomes are measured in the hundreds of thousands, not in the millions — but the big money is made by the owners and operators of big businesses who dominate the very top, and they are very few in number.

Owning the store is the main event at the very top. Although Galen Weston, who paid himself $11.8 million to be CEO of George Weston Limited in 2022, was clearly in the top 1 per cent of the top 1 per cent based on his executive pay alone, his labour earnings as CEO were small change for him compared to his capital income. A 10 per cent rate of return on the Weston family wealth of $13.4 billion implies[22] an annual income of $1.34 billion, which is about 114 times greater than his CEO compensation. Although it is true "the majority of top income earners are executives, managers, supervisors, and financial professionals.[23]" Canada's top 1 per cent do not get most of their income from wages and salaries.[24] Executive compensation practices and the billings of top professionals may determine the pay of most of the people in the top 1 per cent, but most of the income of Canada's top 1 per cent depends on the rate of return to capital.

Within the top 1 per cent, hedge fund managers, derivatives traders and private equity specialists can get especially outsized incomes. In 2016, the world's top twenty-five hedge fund managers made a combined $11 billion, an average of $440 million each that year.[25] In 2022, the top twenty-five made $21.5 billion, which works out to an average of about $860 million each.[26] Since incomes like these rely on the scale of financial transactions, there are only a few places within the global hierarchy of financial markets where such massive money can be made. In the global financial system, New York and London offer a range of corporate and financial services and a scale of transactions that second-tier financial centres like Toronto cannot match.

Within Canada, as in other countries, top-end income growth is quite concentrated geographically.[27] Cities like Winnipeg, Regina or Halifax are regionally important and may have a few head offices of local firms that went big, but they are not in the same league as Toronto, which is not in the same league as New York or London. Toronto's dominant role in Canada's financial and legal services and in banking, finance and corporate head offices implies its continued accumulation of Canadian top-end-income share, even if even bigger megabucks are to be made in New York or London. Canada's smaller cities have fewer of the top jobs in banking, finance and associated services and rural areas have virtually none at all.

As a result, there are far fewer Lamborghinis and Ferraris to be seen on local streets in Yarmouth, Nanaimo or Peace River than in Toronto. The social implication is that inequality is more often "in your face" in the lived reality of big cities than in small towns and rural Canada. Because top incomes have risen far more in larger centres, the conspicuous consumption with which the very affluent advertise their wealth is not as much observed in rural areas, even if people there may suspect that the wealth they help create is paying for the supercars on Toronto streets.

In Canada, capital gains have been taxed at half the rate of ordinary income,[28] so top executives have had a huge incentive to arrange their affairs such that much of their compensation is paid in the form of stock options. For the wealthy, capital gains and losses in the ups and downs of the stock market also imply that, in any given year, top-end income can fluctuate quite a lot, as Figure 1.1 shows. During the oil boom period (2000 to 2014), top pay packages in Calgary kept up with the top 1 per cent of Toronto and were significantly more than those of the top 1 per cent of other smaller regional centres. However, the collapse of oil prices after 2014 produced a cyclical slump in the top 1 per cent income share that especially affected Calgary and was still apparent a decade later.

Fundamentally, however, year-to-year fluctuations in top-end incomes are much less important than the average long-run rate of income growth. In Chapter 2, Table 2.1 presents the long-run trend in hourly wages, and Table 2.2 shows the long-run trend in total taxpayer market income. Both tables document the same reality: over the last forty years or so, top incomes have grown at a compound annual rate that outpaces income growth rates at the middle of the income distribution by 2 to 3 percentage points. A difference of 2 or 3 percentage points does not sound like much. Indeed, if it only lasts for a year or two, it does not amount to much. However, over a forty-year period, the difference in growth rates compounds to an ever-larger income gap. As Table 2.1 shows, between 1980 and 2010 the gap in hourly real wages between the 99.9th percentile and the 50th percentile more than doubled, increasing from $152 per hour to $376 per hour.

Individual markets and firms always differ somewhat, but on average, top executives tend to have pay packages that grow with firm size and firm profits. Profits grow with sales and sales tend to grow with market size. The average rate of income growth for "global" players therefore tends to be driven by global market growth rates, which have been significantly faster than domestic growth in Canada or the United States. Continued growth in China, India and elsewhere (including sub-Saharan Africa) implies the growth rate of global markets will continue to be considerably greater than that of domestic markets, and as the firms servicing those markets expand in size and profitability, top corporate pay packages grow in parallel.[29]

There is no plausible evidence that the CEOs of 2024 are any smarter or wiser or work longer hours than the CEOs of 1964 or 1974, but it is very clear they run larger organizations and are paid much more. Administrative hierarchies have always been a type of team production. When the profitability of the firm depends on hundreds, if not thousands, of people doing their jobs well, the exact measurement of each individual's true contribution is often problematic, so pay comparisons are inevitably important. At the top, executive pay scales are determined by compensation committees. What an executive makes depends on hierarchical rank, the span of control at each level of the hierarchy, firm profits and wage norms — what "everyone else" in the industry is currently paying. Before the FTA of the late 1980s, the pay of executives in Canada was usually compared within Canada, and executive compensation lagged behind pay rates in the United States. Since the free trade agreement, compensation committees have looked continentally.

In 2023, Canadian Pacific Railway (CPR) acquired Kansas City Southern and the merged transnational rail network was rebranded as CPKC — the latest chapter in the saga of Canada's iconic big company, dating from the "last spike" which linked Canada from sea to sea. The CPR subsidiary still has massive holdings of land, hotels, oil, gas and other natural resources which date from the initial incentives it received from the federal government to build the transcontinental railway. Even before the merger, its prospectus was clear that executive salaries are determined by comparisons with American railways: "In determining compensation for the executive officers reporting to the CEO, the Committee considers a comparator group of the following Class I Railroads: BNSF Railway, Canadian National Railway Company, CSX Corporation, Kansas City Southern Railroad, Norfolk Southern Corporation and Union Pacific Corporation." [30]

The bottom line finding from a panel dataset spanning thousands of executives working at hundreds of major US firms is that "recent globalization trends have increased US inequality by disproportionately raising top incomes of business executives."[31] Those increases are observed not just among firms which exported more but also among firms that happened to be in industries that increased exports. The growth rate of compensation for those at the top of global corporations thus sets the benchmark for the jobs at the top of the national private sector. Pay escalation for executives in the private sector then determines what their peers at the top of public sector hierarchies — such as university presidents, hospital administrators and senior civil servants — come to expect as the "fair" level of remuneration that is "normal" for somebody with their level of responsibility. Compensation committees charged with determining a "competitive" pay scale then look at what is being paid in "comparator groups" and top salaries ratchet up.

Norms are always central to the propagation of wage trends within labour markets,[32] even for middle-class occupations. However, they are particularly important at the top end of corporate and public-sector hierarchies in rich countries because labour markets are so thin at the top. The "going market rate of pay" for secretaries in Vancouver depends, for example, on the labour demand of hundreds of firms and the labour supply of thousands of people who compete for work, so competition and local demand and supply can explain the average wage of secretaries. However, there is only one president of the University of British Columbia, so local demand and supply cannot determine their rate of pay in the same way. The key issue for university president pay packages is what the compensation committee thinks is "normal."

Comparative or relative pay is the key issue in "satisfaction with pay" for somebody in the top 1 per cent because, at this level, actual needs for creature comforts have long since been satisfied. At this pay level, money income may be a marker that indicates who is "winning" or "losing" in the race for success, but "winning" — or, at the very least, "keeping up" — is the main event. For "the globals and their peers," who sit at or near the top of Canada's organizational and professional hierarchies, the continued growth of globalized markets is key to the rate of growth in corporate scale and top pay.

However, globalization works very differently for the other 99 per cent — the "locals" who are not in top-end internal labour markets and whose pay growth and employment prospects depend on the supply and demand for labour within their own local labour markets.

Since global firms usually can site their production in many possible places around the world, international competition for new investment sets the growth of local labour productivity as an approximate upper boundary to the rate of average income growth of local labour. Of course, when unemployment is high and there is lots of competition for every available job, as in Canada between 1980 and 2000, firms do not have to raise wages to find workers, so pay increases do not have to keep up with labour productivity growth. Slack local labour markets then mean real wages can stagnate even as labour productivity continues to increase, as has been the case in Canada.

The resource sector can sometimes be an exception. As ore bodies and oil sands deposits cannot be moved, workers in some specialized occupations and locations — like Fort McMurray during the construction phase of the oil boom — can sometimes extract part of the resource's potential profits in the form of higher wages. The extent to which this is possible depends on the speed of resource development, the level of unionization of workers and whether local labour can exclude potential competition from foreign workers.

Whenever real wage growth falls short of labour productivity growth, a surplus is created within firms, which is available to be shared between senior management and stockholders. If Canadian unions had been able to mobilize collective action effectively, they might have been able to bargain for a share of these increasing global corporate profits, which could have restrained the escalation of corporate norms of top pay.[33] In those European countries where collective bargaining still plays a key role in wage setting for most workers (e.g., Germany and Sweden), this process has limited the increase in top 1 per cent income share. However, as already noted, in Canada only 15.3 per cent of private sector workers were union members in 2021, and the decline of private-sector unionization in Canada and the United States has made avarice much easier for senior executives in both countries.

Even if the Canadian economy returned to something closer to full employment, in a globalized world the core constraint on the long-run growth rate of market income of "locals" is the local rate of labour productivity growth, which has been slowing in Canada (and elsewhere). But at the top of the economic hierarchy, income growth for "the globals and their peers" depends on the rate of growth of global markets, which continues to be significantly higher. The long-run tendency remains for the growth rate of labour incomes to be higher at the top than in the rest of the income distribution.

Labour's Declining Share

National income (GDP) is always divided between payments to capital and payments to labour, so capital's share of national income has always been crucial to income inequality. In recent years, labour's share of national income has been declining at the same time as labour earnings have been becoming more unequal. Although the capital/labour division of national income was fairly stable until the 1980s, "the average adjusted labour share in [Group of Twenty] G20 countries went down by about 0.3 percentage points per year between 1980 and the late 2000s . . . When GDP is measured at market prices, the average labour share for the 9 countries with data from the 1960s declines from a peak of more than 65 per cent to about 56 per cent."[34] By 2023 in Canada, compensation of employees was only about half (50.8 per cent) of GDP.[35] As Chapter 6 will discuss, the ownership of capital is very unequally distributed, so the fall in labour's share, and consequent rise in capital's share, reinforce the trend to greater market income inequality — especially at the very top.

The trend to lower shares for labour in national income is, from one perspective, understated in the National Income Accounts, because the National Accounts count the compensation of CEOs as part of labour's share. If an accounting of "capital's share" of national income included the income derived from control over capital, as well as the income derived from formal ownership of capital, most of the compensation of senior executives would be counted as part of capital's share, not as part of "labour income." In Canada, the trend to a greater capital share almost doubles in speed if the labour income of the top 1 per cent is excluded.[36]

In assessing trends in the labour share and capital share of national income, one should also recognize that some CEOs have inherited their jobs along with their shares in the family company. When the younger generations of the Rogers, Shaw, Thomson, Weston, Irving or Desmarais families decide to run the family business themselves, their salaries are counted as part of labour income, even though how they got their jobs is very different from the job search of people who needed to work for a living.[37] (Their salaries should also, in principle, be adjusted to take account of the efficiency losses of family-run firms, but that is not done.[38])

The shift in national income from labour to capital has mirrored the shift in bargaining power that occurred as firms have become larger and more often multinational and unions have become rarer and weaker. The rise of superstar megafirms, which increasingly dominate their industries and save on labour costs by outsourcing work to contracting firms, temporary help agencies, independent contractors and freelancers, has also shifted the gains from growth to the owners of firms.

In Canada (as in other market economies) the inequality of wealth ownership has always been considerably greater than the inequality of income. Since the increase in top executive compensation has been going on since the 1980s, the accumulated savings from those earnings are in the 2020s also producing significant wealth.[39] And as Thomas Piketty has emphasized, when the interest rate on wealth exceeds the growth rate of national income, wealth grows faster than GDP does, which produces a long-run tendency for capital's share of national income to increase.

Because the very rich can afford to buy the best investment advice and can negotiate with financial institutions for favourable fees and commissions, the real rate of return on wealth is higher for large portfolios than for small savers. As a result, large wealth holdings tend to grow faster than small ones do, which accentuates the tendency for an increasing long-run concentration of wealth ownership. Increasing inequalities then compound on each other. With labour's share of national income shrinking, more and more of GDP is received by the owners of capital and since large fortunes get a higher rate of return than small portfolios, the ownership of wealth becomes more and more concentrated; more of capital's (increasing) share is received by the owners of large fortunes.

Eventually, of course, the owners of wealth die. A major implication of increasingly concentrated wealth holdings is that the inheritance of wealth becomes increasingly important as a determinant of life chances for the next generation. Income growth at the very top then includes both the growing labour income of "globals" and the growing capital income received from inheritances.

Why Should Anyone Care that the Income Share of the Top 1 Per Cent is Increasing?

As a long-serving university professor, I make good money, but I'm not in Canada's top 1 per cent, and I do not hang around with anyone who is. I do occasionally chat after church with a local businessman who certainly is a member of the top 1 per cent. He is a very pleasant guy, but he does not invite me to his house and I do not invite him to mine, and that is fine with both of us. Repeated social interaction, "hanging out" together, would require some parity of lifestyles. Things eventually get a bit awkward if your friends always want to go out to eat at restaurants which you cannot afford. My pattern of (i.e., my lack of) social interaction with the top 1 per cent is, I think, typical; the reality is that most Canadians associate socially with other people who have a roughly similar income and socio-economic status.

This process of social separation is helped along by the fact that, to a very considerable extent, the top 1 per cent in Canada already live in a separate world. As income inequality increases, the infrastructure of inequality also grows. Gated resorts, exclusive neighbourhoods, high-end shops, luxury car dealerships, top-end hotels and fine dining restaurants are places where the 99 per cent hardly ever go. At airports, ordinary folk queue up to board but elite travellers wait in their airport lounge for their flights and are ushered to the front of a different queue when the flight is called. The super-rich travel by private plane and are never even seen by ordinary mass travellers.

So why don't the 99 per cent just ignore the 1 per cent and let them live their separate lives? Why should the 99 per cent care if unbalanced growth increases the absolute size of income differences and Canada's economic elite becomes ever more disconnected from the lived reality of everyone else? What are the actual negative effects to the 99 per cent if the more rapid growth of top 1 per cent income and consumption continues?

Escalating Consumption Norms

Medieval Europe and Mogul India are just two of the many examples from the history of regimes with very high economic inequality which lasted for centuries.[40] When a high level of inequality persists for many generations, its stability can enable the elite to develop strong norms of gracious living. If income differentials remain roughly constant for a long time, the seeming permanence of these lifestyle gaps can also habituate the masses over time. Habit and inertia can then help to ensure the acquiescence of the lower classes to their own place in life (a process that historically was reinforced strongly by organized religion). Films and television dramas like Downton Abbey or Upstairs Downstairs, which celebrate both the ostentatious consumption of the nobility and the faithful deference of their loyal retainers, have portrayed the sociological reality that highly unequal ways of life can become part of definitions of self-identity, for both the servants and the served. Viewed culturally, extravagant consumption by the nobility can become a fantasy world of materialist dreams. Seen from a macroeconomic perspective, the exaggerated consumption of the nobility recycles income into aggregate demand and creates jobs. If such consumption is done in much the same way, year after year for many years, a given level of great inequality can become viewed socially as the "natural order of things."[41]

However, the British servile tradition was built up over centuries, and our current reality is quite unlike such earlier periods of high, but stable, inequality. Unbalanced growth and rapidly increasing real top-end incomes now create the "problem" (at the top) of finding, every year, new ways to consume — that is, the elite must be increasingly extravagant over time if they are to spend all, or even much, of their increasing income. (The escalating size and extravagance of superyachts is an example: "On average, a 100-meter superyacht with a top speed of

25 knots and 50 crew members should cost around $275 million."[42]) Continued rapid income growth at the top means that ever-growing ostentation has to be expected. Sometimes, as Veblen noted over a century ago, conspicuous consumption is a large part of why great wealth is desired in the first place. However, increasingly, an "if you've got it, flaunt it" lifestyle can also be resented by some of the 99 per cent. The socio-political question then becomes whether the ever-increasing consumption gaps of society are consistent with long-run social stability.

When inequality is not changing much, consumption aspirations (a.k.a. "keeping up with the Joneses") don't change much. However, one of the implications of increasing inequality is an escalating expenditure cascade of consumption norms as the middle class shift their consumption aspirations upward and attempt to keep up with the more affluent, whose incomes are growing faster than theirs.[43]

Consumption aspirations in a rich country like Canada are often influenced more by social comparisons than by actual function. When, for example, an old high school friend of mine renovated their kitchen and showed me their new granite countertop, part of my brain knew perfectly well that although his kitchen countertop was a lot more expensive than my kitchen countertop it did not actually do anything any better. Nevertheless, our aspirations for our own home renovations the next year changed all the same, and we now also have a granite countertop.

Housing and automobiles are two of the more socially visible markers of relative consumption and relative status so when the top 1 per cent build larger houses or buy more expensive cars, they shift the frame of reference that defines what others slightly below them on the income scale consider an acceptable or desirable house or car, which in turn shifts the frame of reference for those just below them and so on all the way down the income distribution ladder.

When income growth is balanced and everyone's income is growing at roughly the same rate, consumption and consumption aspirations are increasing, but the income available to satisfy those aspirations is also increasing at roughly the same rate, so the gaps of unsatisfied aspirations are not growing. However, unbalanced income growth means that consumption norms are shifting upward at the top faster than the income growth of those lower down the income ladder. As the lifestyles of the top end pull ever further out of reach, the middle class whose incomes are growing more slowly fall ever further short of their aspirations. Goods that only recently were "good enough" now begin to look inadequate, but since middle-class incomes are not growing fast enough to keep up with the escalation of consumption norms, they have to pile on the debt if they are to "keep up" in consumption. Debts and discontent rise together.

Manufacturing Discontent: The Advertising of Luxury Goods

In modern times, escalating material discontent also has some very powerful accelerants. Medieval Europe and Mogul India and many other ancient societies had extreme inequality that lasted for centuries, but they did not have an advertising industry. In the twenty-first century, one can expect advertising to increase market envy and stoke discontent. Rapid income growth at the top means increasing market opportunities for firms which service top-end consumers. Yacht builders, supercar makers, haute couture fashion designers and five-star hotels and restaurants have a growing market. In general, as top-end inequality increases, luxury goods grow as a fraction of total consumer spending — and the large and increasing relative size of the top-end market is a powerful incentive for an ever-increasing volume of aspirational advertising.

Because the necessities of life must be purchased even if they are not advertised at all, advertising of groceries and housewares focuses heavily on conveying price information. But the flyers that advertise bargains on hamburger at the supermarket are appealing to different motivations, and a different clientele, than the glossy elite publications that advertise Patek Phillipe or Omega watches.

Luxury goods are necessarily advertising-intensive items because they are discretionary expenditures which people really do not have to make. Persuasion — i.e., advertising — is key to sales. In rich countries like Canada, the top 1 per cent of the income distribution have long since satisfied their normal creature comfort needs. If they are to be persuaded to spend even more when their income increases, the top 1 per cent have to be convinced somehow to purchase goods they do not "need." So advertising is essential. Because creature comforts are already satisfied, luxury goods makers have to appeal to ideas of exclusivity and status to motivate sales. As Francois Henri Pinault, CEO of PPR Group (whose luxury brands include Gucci, Bottega Veneta, Yves Saint Laurent, Balenciaga, Stella McCartney and Alexander McQueen) has put it, "You don't buy luxury to enter a community but to set yourself apart from others."[44] And to achieve this an advertiser cannot restrict their messaging just to those who could actually afford to buy.

Patek Phillipe and Omega watches do not tell time any more reliably than a cell phone. A BMW, Mercedes or a Porsche does not get through traffic jams any faster than any other car, and the highway speed limit is the same for all vehicle brands. But functionality is not the issue for luxury goods. The main reason people spend thousands of dollars more to buy luxury goods is because they think their purchase will confer enhanced status. But status goods can command a premium price only if they are widely known to be status goods — there is no point in paying thousands of dollars extra for a fancy watch or an expensive car if no one else recognizes it as "special." Hence, advertisers have to market luxury goods like expensive watches and cars in a way that targets both those who can afford to buy them and those who cannot, because the people who do buy have to know that everyone else knows that these are very expensive, very exclusive items.

Although some high-status goods can acquire their cachet via tradition and word of mouth, the expanding pool of disposable income among the affluent creates ever-greater incentives to create new status goods using advertising. In such marketing campaigns, desire is created by repeating the message that "everybody wants this, but only special people have it" — that is, by inspiring envy among those who do not possess the good, so that those who do buy it can obtain status and deference. Because the market value of luxury brands will depreciate without continued advertising to reinforce their message of exclusivity, privilege and wealth, mass media become increasingly saturated with their messaging.

Continually increasing income gaps between those at the top and everyone else therefore imply a continuing shift in production toward advertising-intensive luxury goods; and increasing incentives to produce more advertising messaging telling the 99 per cent about what only the top 1 per cent and top 0.1 per cent can afford. The aim of aspirational advertising is to create product awareness in the broader audience in order to motivate purchases of the advertised commodity by the much smaller target clientele. But as income differentials grow, the benchmarks of luxury move ever further away from the consumption possibilities of middle-class households, thereby ensuring the less affluent are increasingly often told about the pleasures of goods they cannot remotely afford.

Unbalanced growth and increasing income inequality in a market economy therefore produce greater incentives for advertising expenditures that create envy about material goods. Furthermore, since advertisers necessarily have a product to sell, their messages always emphasize the importance of buying.[45] And status from relative material consumption is a positional good, in which more status for me necessarily means less status for you. For the 99 per cent, one of the costs of rising top 1 per cent incomes therefore is the ever-increasing volume and the messaging associated with this pervasive bombardment of aspirational advertising. As such advertising increases, and is increasingly tilted toward emphasizing the importance and the desirability of luxury goods that most people cannot remotely afford, greater discontent and less human happiness among the 99 per cent is the result.

Elite Political Influence and the Erosion of Democracy

Even if the bottom 99 per cent might want to ignore the top 1 per cent, the top 1 per cent do not want to be ignored. Increasing income inequality gives the top 1 per cent more resources to intervene in the political process and to ensure that their opinions matter. There is clear evidence[46] that the political and social preferences of the very affluent are quite different from those of the general population. The top 1 per cent are much more active politically than the 99 per cent and legislative action is heavily influenced by their policy priorities.

In Canada, campaign spending legislation constrains somewhat the power of money during the election period. However, between elections, donations to "think tanks" and policy institutes and the ownership of media outlets give the wealthy the ability to push their point of view and influence the climate of opinion in a way ordinary people cannot match.

As well, great wealth is accompanied by the economic power to withhold or to grant investment and needed jobs, and the political influence that goes with that economic power. Canadian politicians return the phone calls of billionaires, but only sometimes get back to ordinary citizens. If billionaires and multi-millionaires had similar perceptions and preferences as "ordinary folk" this would not be as costly for the 99 per cent. However, the increasingly separate world of the top 1 per cent means their perceptions and their preferences are increasingly disconnected from those of ordinary people. Their informal power to shape events and their growing influence over the political process diminishes the relative influence of the rest of society, to a degree that will increase over time as top-end inequality continues to increase.

On some issues, the differences in perceptions that come with wealth are what create a gulf — it can be hard to explain economic insecurity and anxieties about job loss and the importance of a social safety net to somebody whose family has always had millions in the bank. However, on many important issues, elite objectives are just inherently in direct conflict with the interests of middle-class people. For the wealthy, it is not a problem that lower taxes will imply fewer and poorer quality public services — they have the money to buy high-quality private substitutes whenever they need them. Families which are already at the top also have no self-interest in supporting greater equality of opportunity. The affluent can only lose from greater intergenerational income mobility, because if your family is already at the top their only possible future social mobility is downward. The political agenda of the top 1 per cent therefore tends to tilt very differently than that of the 99 per cent — so increases in their political influence matter.

Summary

Although the real wages of the Canadian middle class have not grown much over the last forty years, incomes have certainly not been stagnant for Canada's economic elite. The incomes of the top 1 per cent, and especially the top 0.1 per cent have had their ups and downs, but on average those incomes have grown significantly since the early 1980s — much faster than middle-class incomes. As a consequence, the income share of the top 1 per cent and top 0.1 per cent has increased substantially — as was also seen in the late 1920s.

Income tax data has enabled a long-term perspective with an important lesson: that the distribution of income is not stable. The period from 1952 to 1980 in Canada (when income growth was balanced and the level of inequality was therefore roughly stable) was historically unique. That period of balanced growth enabled rising household incomes to keep up with rising consumption aspirations, at essentially the same rate throughout the income distribution. In those days, when inequality was not changing much, the social implications of inequality did not change much. When income growth was balanced, political spending by the elite and advertising of luxury goods for the elite also did not change much over time. And people do "get used to stuff"; habituation conditioned the expectations of many Canadians and dulled any tendency toward discontent with a fairly constant level of inequality.

But that was then and this is now. Since the 1980s, unbalanced growth has implied increasingly large absolute income differences between income classes, particularly between those at the very top and everyone else. Some of the consequences have been increasingly ostentatious lifestyles at the very top, increasingly large expenditures by the elite to influence the political process, greater attempts to secure the advantages of their own children and ever-increasing advertising reminding everyone of the desirability and exclusivity of the luxury goods most people cannot remotely afford.

Chapter 2 reports on the public opinion polls which found broad agreement among Canadians[47] with the statement: "Income inequality is no longer about the gap between the rich and the poor, but rather the very rich and everyone else." That polling data become easier to understand when one looks at growth in the absolute size of the income gap between the top 1 per cent and the median or between the top 0.1 per cent and the median.

To my mind, this all adds up to ever-increasing political stresses, particularly if it is not actually feasible to accelerate the rate of growth of middle-class incomes and stabilize income shares with faster middle-class income growth. Those political stresses will make it ever harder to solve big collective problems — like climate change and periodic pandemics — which affect everyone.

Change in this pattern of growth will face the barrier that the top 1 per cent have no reason to be unhappy. Canada's current economic system has been very good to them. However, I think many among the 99 per cent are becoming impatient. Telling them that inequality of opportunity is the real issue and they should wait for another thirty or forty years to see how things will turn out for their children is not likely to be seen as an adequate response. An unhappy majority, for whom the current system has produced stagnant wages and increasing insecurity, is (I think) unlikely to acquiesce in the proposition that rapid top 1 per cent income increases should continue indefinitely while their incomes lag behind. The social question is which direction their resentments take, and how much that anger gets in the way of solving our big common problems, like climate change.

Chapter 4
POVERTY AND INEQUALITY

Wednesday mornings are garbage collection time in my neighbourhood, so every Tuesday evening everybody puts their empty wine and beer bottles out with their recycling. It seems to me a commentary on our society that the bottles are invariably gone within a half-hour, picked up, for the five or ten-cent refund on the deposit,[1] by one or another of the many people who cruise the neighbourhood, in all seasons and all weather, sometimes pushing supermarket grocery carts and sometimes in very old cars. They have to work hard for their money, especially during winter snowstorms. It takes five hundred small bottles to make $25 a day. But I think, for many Canadians, most of the time they are invisible.

Expensive cars and large houses may advertise the lives of Canada's billionaires, but Canada's poor are largely unseen. Part of this is due to residential segregation, but that does not really explain why we look away from the people who pick up empty bottles every week. Could it be that thinking about street people as real people can be uncomfortable? Is that because it would raise the possibility, however remote, that if real people can be homeless in our society, it could also happen to me or you?

Counting the Poor

Statistically, because they have no fixed address, the homeless are just not included in the sample for residence-based surveys, so they do not appear in the data on income distribution and poverty based on those household surveys. Also missing from the household surveys which give us annual estimates of income distribution are the inhabitants of isolated Indigenous communities in Northern Canada. The income distribution surveys are done as add-ons to Statistics Canada's labour force survey (LFS), whose main purpose is to estimate monthly unemployment numbers. Since remote northern communities are far too small to have any appreciable impact on the national or provincial unemployment rate, but are very expensive to survey, they are left out of the sample. As a consequence, the hardships facing many of Canada's Indigenous communities do not get counted in standard surveys.

Even if the homeless were interviewed in a survey, putting a dollar value on their "income" would also be very problematic, because some depend heavily on donations and in-kind services such as a meal or a night's lodging in a shelter. At any given time, the visible homeless people in tent encampments across Canada's cities are also only the tip of the iceberg of the precariously housed — the many people imposing on relatives or couch-surfing at friends' or living out of their car are also usually missing from standard residence-based surveys. Hence estimates of the number of homeless people and the depth of their poverty vary widely.[2]

Trends in Low Income

These data problems reinforce the general point that household surveys do a much better job of estimating what is happening to the "middle 80 or 90 per cent" of Canadians than they do in counting those at the extremes of affluence and deprivation. Nevertheless, survey numbers are still very useful for the assessment of trends in low income. Although surveys may be underestimates in any given year, if they give us much the same underestimate every year, these numbers can still provide a reasonable estimate of long-run trends.

Figure 4.1

Equivalent Disposable Income of Lower Income Canadians, 1976–2021

(2022 dollars)

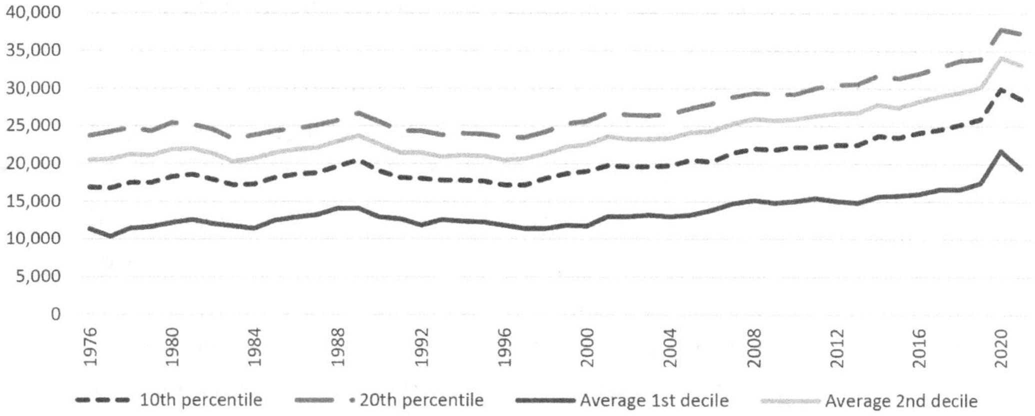

Source: Statistics Canada. Table 11-10-0193-01

Figure 4.1 therefore presents household survey data estimates of what has been happening to the real after-tax equivalent disposable income (i.e., after subtracting income tax from market income and including transfer payments and adjusting for inflation and household size) of the lowest income 20 per cent of Canadians. The two dashed lines plot the incomes of the people at exactly the 10th percentile and 20th percentile rank in the income distribution, so they tell us that in 2021, 20 per cent of Canadians received equivalent incomes of $37,400 or less, and 10 per cent of Canadians received less than $28,600. The two solid lines plot the average equivalent income of people in the bottom 10 per cent ($19,400 in 2021) and the average of those in the second decile ($33,200).

Over the twenty-year period from 1980 to 2000, measured in constant 2022 dollars, the average equivalent income of those in the bottom 10 per cent actually fell, declining from $12,600 in 1981 to $11,750 in 2000 (a negative compound growth rate of -0.18 per cent), while the average income of the second decile barely budged (increasing from $22,000 to $22,530 — which is +0.14 per cent per year). After missing out on those twenty years of income growth, the bottom two deciles then saw a resurgence of income growth — the average income of the bottom decile increased at a compound annual rate of 2.1 per cent between 2000 and 2019 and the second decile's average income increased at 1.6 per cent annually.

Figure 4.1 thus paints a picture that can be described as two long periods (1980 to 1999 and 2000 to 2019) sandwiched between two short periods (1976 to 1979 and 2020 to 2022). As Figure 2.1 shows, average real wages were still going up in the late 1970s — wage stagnation started with the 1980 increase in unemployment. The two decades afterwards saw an unemployment rate which averaged 9.5 per cent throughout the 1980s and 1990s and a general stagnation of incomes at the bottom of Canada's income distribution. After 2000, the unemployment rate came down during the oil boom, and as jobs became available (and as Table 2.1 reported earlier) the real hourly wages of the 10th percentile started going back up — lower-income households saw some growth in market incomes. After 2015, families with children also benefitted from the introduction of the Canada Child Benefit.

When Covid-19 came to Canada in March 2020, unemployment spiked upward dramatically as the global economy tanked. Because the Covid-19 pandemic lockdowns had their biggest impacts on jobs in restaurants, hotels, retail sales and personal service industries, low-wage workers were particularly exposed and the inadequacy of Employment Insurance as a social safety net was immediately apparent. It was a remarkable administrative achievement to get the CERB program up and running within weeks — payments arrived in bank accounts in May 2020. Because CERB payments were lump sums ($500 per week) CERB provided a significant boost for low-income households — as the income spike in Figure 4.1 shows. The impact of winding down Covid-19 transfers in 2021 also shows up clearly in Figure 4.1. As this was being written in early 2024, the income numbers for 2022 and 2023 were not yet available, but it was already clear that a surge in inflation in 2022 to 2023, which particularly affected food prices and apartment rents, combined with the winding up of CERB and a softening of employment growth to stretch the budgets of many low-income Canadians.

However, just where at the bottom of the income distribution should one draw the poverty line? Indeed, what does poverty mean in Canada, one of the richest countries the world has ever seen?

What is Poverty in Canada? How Should the "Poverty Line" Be Drawn?

The dictionary definition of "poverty" is "want of the necessities of life,"[3] but for many years Statistics Canada only published data on the "low-income measure"[4] or LIM and on two other "low income" criteria — the "low income cut off" in "before tax" (LICO-BT) and "after tax" (LICO-AT) versions. Statistics Canada long resisted calling any of them "poverty lines." Writing in 1997, the Chief Statistician argued: "Before anyone can calculate the minimum income needed to purchase the 'necessities' of life, they must decide what constitutes a 'necessity' in food, clothing, shelter and a multitude of other purchases, from transportation to reading material. The underlying difficulty is due to the fact that poverty is intrinsically a question of social consensus, at a given point in time and in the context of a given country."[5] Believing there was an "absence of politically sanctioned social consensus on who should be regarded as 'poor'" Statistics Canada preferred for many years to say it was measuring "low income" (meanwhile in practice recognizing the widespread use of their "low income" statistics as indicators of poverty). That Canadian reluctance to officially recognize and define "poverty" was a distinct contrast to many other countries — e.g., the United States, where official estimates of poverty have been published since 1969.

The designation in 2019, following a widespread national consultation process, of the "Market Basket Method" (MBM) criterion as Canada's "official poverty line"[6] was therefore a major initiative, for Statistics Canada and for the federal government as a whole. The MBM sets the local poverty line in each province and major city across Canada by calculating the cost, at local prices, of "a specific basket of goods and services representing a modest, basic standard of living." That basket is defined, and occasionally updated over time, in a consultative process "with Canadians, experts, and federal, provincial and territorial stakeholders" using surveys, focus groups, online forums, personal interviews and expert panels and working jointly with Employment and Social Development Canada (ESDC).[7]

In the literature on poverty, there are two main perspectives on how to draw the poverty line. The "absolute income" perspective on poverty would say that the necessities of life are the minimum amounts of food, clothing and shelter necessary for the physical survival of humans — which implies the poverty line is always the same. From an absolute income perspective, a poverty-line income is what it would cost to buy the goods and services (e.g., food and housing) that are the physical necessities of life, so updating the poverty line from one year to the next only involves adjustments for price inflation. The origin of this budget standards definition of the poverty line has often been ascribed to Rowntree's pioneering work in late-nineteenth-century England.

However, even Rowntree's poverty budget, constructed on the rule: "Nothing must be bought but that which is absolutely necessary for the maintenance of physical health, and what is bought must be of the plainest and most economical description," still contained an allowance for tea — an item of no nutritional value.[8] The "relative income" perspective on the measurement of poverty therefore argues that Rowntree's recognition that poor people in England in the 1800s should be able to have a cup of tea illustrates the fact that humans are fundamentally social animals and implicitly acknowledges the importance of social necessities. If necessities are partly social, the necessities of life will change as societies change, which implies that the poverty line should always be drawn relative to "normal" living standards in a particular society at a particular time.

More than 240 years ago, at a time when the per capita national income of England and Scotland was significantly less than that of India today,[9] Adam Smith left no doubt as to his opinion. He thought the definition of "necessities" should be "not only those things which nature, but those things which the established rules of decency have rendered necessary to the lowest rank of people." As someone who had travelled widely in Europe, Smith was well aware of the large differences then existing in the standard of living of European countries. He noted that in the late 1700s, leather shoes were normal — considered a necessity of life — in some countries (like England) but not in others (like France), because at that time the general standard of living was significantly higher in England. Smith argued strongly that the "established rules of decency" of a society change as a society changes. As he put it, "a linen shirt, for example, is, strictly speaking, not a necessary of life. The Greeks and Romans lived, I suppose, very comfortably though they had no linen. But in the present times, through the greater part of Europe, a creditable day-labourer would be ashamed to appear in public without a linen shirt, the want of which would be supposed to denote that disgraceful degree of poverty which, it is presumed, nobody can well fall into without extreme bad conduct."[10]

Adam Smith's "established rules of decency" would today probably be called "social norms," and when Jenny Podoluk did the first major statistical monograph on Canadian poverty in 1968, she gave some practical examples. She noted that with respect to such things as indoor toilets or installed baths or showers, "Amenities which in the mid-1960s are considered to be necessities as recently as twenty-five years ago were not available to nearly half of Canadian households."[11] She therefore argued that "poverty is a condition of possible deprivation relative to prevailing levels of living."

The idea that the poverty line should be defined relative to prevailing income levels has often been justified by Adam Smith's criterion of whether or not people are "ashamed to appear in public" because they cannot manage to afford a "decent" life for themselves and their families, where "decent" depends on what most other people have and take for granted. But that is only part of the picture. Equally important is the fact that the cost of living for poor people rises when a country's average income increases. Rising living standards for the majority mean some cheap necessities of life become unavailable — and sometimes also means that some expensive items become necessary.

The food distribution system is, for example, necessarily set up to meet the needs of the average consumer. When the house which I now live in was built in Halifax around 1908, the typical Canadian household did not have either a refrigerator or a car. Indeed, as late as 1941 only 21 per cent of Canadian houses had a refrigerator.[12] To meet the needs of the average consumer, there were corner stores on nearly every block in our neighbourhood because urban families shopped daily by walking to the corner store on foot. In rural areas, people then could often buy from the grocery man who came by with his wagon or truck every few days. But corner stores and travelling grocery wagons cannot offer much variety, and when middle-class people started to get cars, they began to drive to supermarkets for their weekly shopping (which they stored in their new refrigerators). Supermarkets were able to offer more variety and lower prices, so local neighbourhood stores and grocery wagons mostly went out of business.

As Canada's food distribution system has adapted to meet the changing requirements of the average consumer, the option of walking to the corner store to buy food has disappeared in most of the country. To buy food in Canada today — which is surely an essential "capability" — most Canadians have to be able to get to a supermarket, which is often kilometres away, and they need a refrigerator to store their food once their weekly purchases have been carted home. Today, calculations of the cost of food should include the cost of transportation and storage of food as well as the direct cost of groceries. And when bus or taxi service does not exist, as in Canada's rural areas and most small towns, having a car becomes a necessity — not an option and certainly not a luxury.

But it is not just the operations of the market mechanism that increase the cost of living of poor people. When societies get richer, their legislation also changes to suit the majority, which often makes life more expensive for everyone, including poor people. If you travel, for example, in sub-Saharan Africa today, you will see everywhere how the ingenuity and energy of poor people can enable them to make their own shelters, from whatever little bit of building material they can find available, on whatever small plot of land they can get access to. There may be building code legislation in these countries, but it really does not matter for most people. The political will to enforce housing standards and the bureaucracy of building inspectors necessary to ensure compliance simply do not exist — and quite rightly. In a poor country, it would make absolutely no sense to tell people they cannot have a roof over their heads unless it has fully inspected wiring and indoor plumbing and uses certified building materials.

In Canada, our National Building Code says a house cannot be built unless it satisfies a long list of such characteristics. For generations, houses in rural Canada were built from rough-hewn lumber, which people often harvested themselves from their own backyard woodlots. Although many of those houses are still standing, such lumber does not meet the current building code. People in Canada today do not have the same option of building for themselves as they would have had a century ago, or that people in poor countries now have. In the tent encampments of Canadian cities in the 2020s, homeless people are not allowed to build a small shed to better protect themselves from winter blizzards, because the shed would not be "up to code." Canadian society enforces, by law, strict social norms of housing adequacy and safety — and poor people have to live with the consequences.

In poorer countries like India, it is also normal to see whole families piled onto a single motor scooter (five is not uncommon: Dad at the controls, the youngest child between his knees, the second youngest sandwiched between him and Mom on the back and the oldest child holding on for dear life at the very back end). Everyone in these families absolutely knows that it is safer and more comfortable to ride in a car — which they cannot afford. In India, they get to go on a family outing using cheap transportation, but we prohibit that in Canada in the name of safety. The bottom line is that when rich countries prohibit by law the cheaper goods that are available in poor countries, the cost of living of poor people necessarily increases.

Some cheap things may become unavailable as society changes and some expensive things can become necessary. Cellphones were, for example, clearly not a necessity of life in Canada in the 1970s, when they did not exist, or in the 1990s, when cellphone ownership was rare. Since cellphone ownership by other people was non-existent or rare in those days, it was possible to participate in normal social and economic interactions, from arranging a social life to finding out about shift reassignments on one's job, without a cellphone.[13] However, as "everyone else" has acquired cellphones, and as their capabilities have expanded, remaining on the outside without one has become ever more difficult.

What people themselves believe they need can sometimes be inferred from their purchases. The World Bank has noted: "More households in developing countries own a mobile phone than have access to electricity or clean water, and nearly 70 percent of the bottom fifth of the population in developing countries own a mobile phone."[14] The fact that very low-income people, in very poor countries, buy cellphones, although they can only do so by sacrificing other obviously important purchases, is strong evidence for the social necessity of cellphone access, from the point of view of individuals themselves.

The cost of meeting Adam Smith's "established rules of decency" thus changes as society changes. But just how and where should we draw the poverty line? If we want to measure income poverty, we have to specify a particular "poverty line" income, in order both to identify who is "poor" (because their income is below the poverty line) and how big their "poverty gap" is (how much their income is below the poverty line).

Any particular dollar value of the poverty line is an estimate of the point at which income has become so low that a "normal" household would be deprived of necessities. The qualifier "normal" is important because we all differ in our capabilities and needs. Some people are allergic to some types of food, so a minimally adequate diet for them may cost more. Other people differ in their ability to cope with low incomes (e.g., some people are excellent cooks and careful budget planners while some are not).[15] A poverty line is an *on-average* estimate of the income at which a Canadian household will be materially deprived, and there are several alternative ways to draw it.

Starting in 2000, versions of the MBM poverty line have been available in Canada and since 2019 it has been Canada's official poverty line. The MBM starts by using expert panels to specify a minimally adequate basket of goods that a family of four needs in the Canadian context, and then pricing out what those goods would cost in different cities and rural areas across Canada. That estimate is then updated for price inflation from one year to the next, as an absolute poverty line[16] would be updated.

However, in order to remain relevant, the minimally adequate "basket of goods and services representing a modest, basic standard of living" has to be revised over time. When the MBM was adopted as Canada's official poverty line,[17] the defined list of necessities was based on 2008 data (which had been updated from the 2000 list). In 2019 the MBM was updated again. The 2019 revision included the cost of cellphone services since they "have become a necessity since the 2008-base MBM was developed."[18]

The MBM explicitly considers local variations in the cost of living by using local prices (e.g., for food and rent) to cost out the fixed bundle of commodities.[19] In calculating the MBM poverty line, there is also explicit recognition of several important drivers of the cost of living of poor people which the other poverty-line methodologies ignore — e.g., childcare costs. Transportation is also now recognized as necessary for access to many public services as well as for access to food — i.e., both a physical and a social necessity. The MBM includes an allowance for bus passes in localities served by public transit and where public transit is unavailable, as in most of rural Canada, the MBM calculations include the costs of running a small used car. The MBM also recognizes income sources like child support payments — which are important for many poor families, both in paying and in receiving. A 2019 innovation in its calculation of income which is particularly important for elderly and rural households is the fact it takes into account the cost savings of owner-occupied housing. For these and other reasons, the MBM methodology was chosen when Canada designated an official poverty line in 2019.

Because the MBM prices out the cost of necessities and the list of necessities changes in a changing society, the MBM has to be revised periodically — Figure 4.2 below presents the poverty rate in Canada according to the three available versions of the MBM, which use the three different specifications of the necessary bundle of goods considered appropriate in 2000, 2008 and 2018. As is apparent in the overlapping years when multiple versions of the MBM are calculated, the poverty rate calculation is sensitive to the choice of base year. Also, since each version is only published for a dozen or so years and the MBM has only been available, in any version, since 2000, long-term comparisons and analysis of trends in poverty are just not possible.

Changes in the methodology of poverty line construction can shift somewhat perceptions of what type of person is most likely to be poor — which may affect policy choices. In the years before the MBM was designated Canada's official poverty line, the unofficial poverty line most often referred to in public debates was Statistics Canada's "low-income cut-off" (LICO). The LICO has the longest publication history in Canada, going back to Podoluk's 1968 monograph, and even if Statistics Canada employees were always careful to refer only to "low income," for many years most everybody else thought the LICO measured "poverty."

The LICO is based on the idea that a family is poor when most of their income is spent on food, clothing and housing, with very little left over for discretionary spending. It can be seen as partly a "relative" poverty line (since the percentage spent on necessities criterion was initially defined relative to the average household) and partly as an "absolute" poverty line (since the LICO is only updated for changes in consumer prices). A disadvantage of the LICO always has been its Canadian uniqueness.

Since no other country uses the LICO methodology, it has never been possible to use the LICO in international comparisons of poverty.

However, because the LICO was often used in Canadian debates about poverty, shifting to the MBM criterion of poverty implied a shift in perceptions of the type of person most likely to be poor. The LICO methodology assumes that the urban cost of living is always higher than the rural cost of living because of the higher cost of rent in big cities, so the LICO varies by the size of the city — but the LICO ignores the cost of transportation. Since the MBM recognizes transportation is a costly necessity, the MBM poverty line can sometimes be higher in rural areas than in cities. For example, in 2022 (for a family of four), the MBM was $48,476 in rural Nova Scotia but $46,027 in Montreal. As well, the MBM recognizes the cost of childcare, while the LICO does not. As a result, more rural people and more families with children will be counted as poor by the MBM than by the LICO. Conversely, the LICO emphasizes more heavily the deprivation of the elderly and urbanites.

However, neither the LICO nor the MBM can provide the answers to the important and often-asked set of questions which revolve around international comparisons. What kinds of policies actually succeed in reducing poverty? Is poverty greater in the US or in Canada, Germany, France or Sweden? Answering those questions satisfactorily depends on measuring poverty using the same poverty line methodology in different countries. A poverty line which, like the MBM, relies on costing out a bundle of commodities cannot provide a common basis for comparisons since different countries choose different bundles to cost[20] — and the appropriate bundle within each country changes over time. The LICO methodology also cannot provide an answer, since other countries have never adopted it. To compare poverty in Canada with poverty in other countries one has to use Statistics Canada's Low Income Measure (LIM) which defines the poverty line as "one-half the median equivalent disposable income."[21] Median income (i.e., the 50th percentile) is used as the basis for comparison rather than average income because changes in large incomes at the top may have a big impact on the average, while still leaving most people's living standard unaffected,[22] so the median is a more reliable indicator of prevailing living standards for most people than the average. The poverty line is drawn at 50 per cent of the median after-tax disposable equivalent income, where an equivalence scale is used to adjust household income for the economies of scale in consumption by the household. However, although the LIM can be used to make international comparisons, a major disadvantage is that it does not recognize local cost of living differences within Canada (in 2021 the LIM was $58,400 for a four-person family, after tax, in all parts of the country).[23] That neglect of cost of living differences will tend to mean counting a higher percentage of the people living in rural areas as poor than would be the case if the MBM was used.

In Canada, we therefore have data using four different poverty lines to measure poverty, each of which tells an important part of the story[24] and each of which has shortcomings. The LIM, because it is explicitly drawn relative to median income, can be easily compared internationally[25] and over time, but it takes no account of variations in the local cost of living.[26] The LICO reflects the idea of very little discretionary income. It has been published for a long time but is not updated automatically if prevailing living standards change, and ignores important costs, such as childcare and transportation. The MBM includes these costs, and is now Canada's official poverty line, but is only available since 2000, changes with each revision and therefore cannot provide a longer-term perspective.

How Many Canadians are Poor? How Big is the Poverty Problem?

The poverty rate (i.e., the percentage of all Canadians whose incomes are below the poverty line) is the most widely quoted statistic on poverty, but these different poverty-line criteria generate somewhat different estimates of its level, composition and trend. As Figure 4.2 shows, in 2021 the official MBM (2018) poverty line implies the poverty rate was 14.5 per cent per cent in 2015, declining to 7.4 per cent in 2021. Using

Figure 4.2
Poverty Rates in Canada, 1976–2021

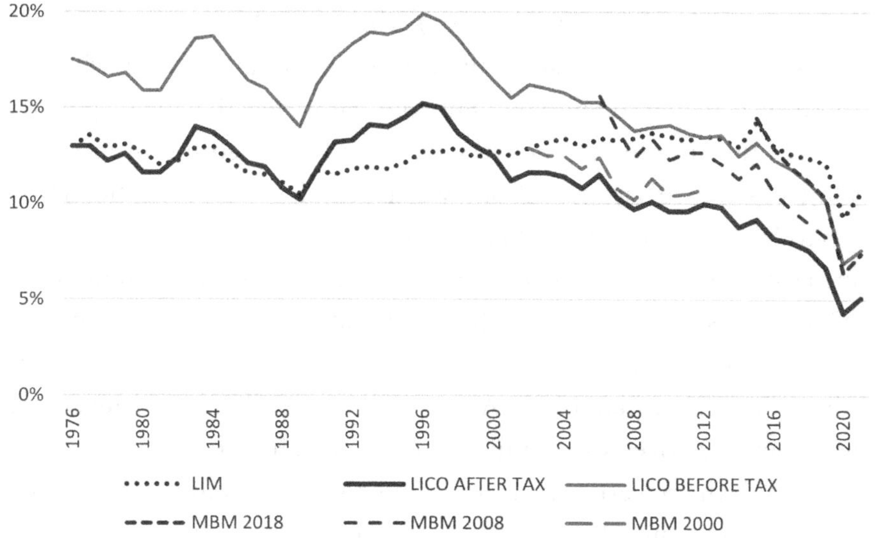

Source: Statistics Canada, Table: 11-10-0135-01 (formerly CANSIM 206-0041)

the LIM poverty line, one would say the poverty rate was 14.3 per cent in 2015, declining to 10.6 per cent in 2021. The LICO-AT says it was 9.2 per cent in 2015 and 5.1 per cent in 2021.[15] Canada's different poverty-line methodologies thus disagree somewhat in their estimates of the size and the composition of the poverty population, but they do agree on the direction of trends in 2015 to 2021. All these poverty measures indicate that it is possible to reduce poverty significantly, within a fairly short period of time, such as the 2015 to 2020 period. What was not clear, at the time of writing in 2024, was whether that downward trend in poverty would continue — all the poverty line methodologies agree both in detecting a downward trend 2015 to 2020 <u>and</u> in measuring an increase in the poverty rate from 2020 to 2021, as Covid-19 transfer payments were wound down and unemployment started to increase.

Furthermore, hiding in Figure 4.2 is a case study in how one can play tricks with statistics in talking about trends. If one wants to conclude that "poverty has been declining for the last thirty years," then all one needs to do is ignore the LIM and MBM poverty lines, focus only on the LICO and start the clock in 1996 at the peak poverty rate of the early 1990s recession (ignoring all previous years). The LICO-AT and the LICO-BT poverty rates have both fallen since 1996, in rough parallel with the decline in Canada's unemployment rate. However, the LICO poverty rate went up substantially between 1989 and 1996, so the twenty-year decline basically disappears if one winds the clock back another seven years to 1989, when both LICO poverty rate measures were virtually the same as in 2013 — a longer-term perspective is sometimes essential.

Nevertheless, the MBM (2018 base) estimated that in 2021 2.76 million Canadians were poor. This was a lower estimate than the LIM (3.96 million) but higher than LICO-AT estimate (1.9 million). Whatever way one defines the poverty line, millions of Canadians live below it.

Although the poverty rate is undoubtedly the "headline statistic" on poverty, it just counts the percentage of people whose incomes are below the poverty line and pays no attention to the depth of their poverty — i.e., how much incomes are falling short for poor people. If the only statistic on poverty we pay attention to is the poverty rate, politicians who want to claim to be "reducing poverty" can be tempted to focus on "helping the most people get out of poverty." Policies that give money to those just below the poverty line would reduce the rate of poverty (by pushing the marginally poor up just enough to get them out of poverty). However, if the political imperative is to not spend any more money and if these transfers are at the expense of people whose incomes are well below the poverty line, that would deepen the deprivation of the very poor. If the poverty rate is all that is counted, it would look like poverty is decreasing because the poverty rate only counts the number of poor people as a percentage of the population.[27]

A poverty policy that "most supports the people who need it the most" would do the opposite, by directing the most resources to the least well-off, the poorest of the poor. The less a person has, the more important each dollar of income is,[28] so for people who have very little income, adding a few dollars has a big impact on their well-being, even if it is not enough to push them over the poverty line. Secular philosophers like John Rawls and Papal pronouncements have long agreed that priority should be given to the well-being of the least well-off.[29]

In general, it does not take much money to make a big difference in the lives of people who have very little. One way of seeing this is to ask how much additional money it would take to totally eliminate poverty in Canada. The poverty gap for poor people — i.e., the amount it would, on average, take to raise a poor person's income to the MBM poverty line — was 31.6 per cent of the poverty line in 2021. In dollar terms, choosing the market basket method poverty line in 2021 as an example, the average per person poverty gap in Toronto was about $4,332, and about $3,400 in rural Quebec. On average across Canada, the MBM poverty gap per poor person was $3,851.[30] Filling that gap would make a big difference to the quality of life of poor people, but spread over the non-poor population as a whole, it is not a large amount of money. In 2021, 7.5 per cent of all Canadians were poor according to the official MBM criterion, which implies 92.5 per cent of Canadians were not poor — i.e., there were roughly 12.3 non-poor people for each poor person. If each of those dozen people had chipped in to fill the poverty gap for each poor person, it would cost each non-poor person $313 per year (i.e., less than a dollar a day) to eliminate poverty. Compared to the incomes of the non-poor 92.5 per cent of Canadians, the dollar amount of the total poverty gap is not large. Eliminating poverty is not something that would be unimaginably expensive to do in Canada. Indeed, the elimination of poverty is quite within the realm of fiscally feasible policies, if there were the political will to do so — i.e., if some or all non-poor Canadians were willing to pay for it.[31]

Social Assistance in Canada

In Canada, however, this has not been the trend. In all provinces, the incomes of people on social assistance are well below the poverty line, even after adding together all applicable federal and provincial transfers. Table 4.1 provides the 2022 data.[32]

Table 4.1

Highest and Lowest in 2022: Adequacy of Example Household Total Welfare Incomes Among the Provinces

		Jurisdiction	Welfare Income	Official Poverty Line	% of Poverty Line
Unattached single considered employable	Lowest	New Brunswick (Moncton)	$8,031	$24,395	33%
	Highest	Quebec (Montreal)	$20,905	$23,014	91%
Unattached single with a disability	Lowest	Alberta (Calgary): BFE	$11,268	$27,886	40%
	Highest	Newfoundland and Labrador (St. John's)	$20,400	$25,466	80%
Single parent, one child	Lowest	Nova Scotia (Halifax)	$21,724	$37,074	59%
	Highest	Prince Edward Island (Charlottetown)	$30,162	$36,081	84%
Couple, two children	Lowest	New Brunswick (Moncton)	$28,664	$48,790	59%
	Highest	Quebec (Montreal)	$58,338	$46,027	127%

Source: Data & measuring — Maytree, https://maytree.com/changing-systems/data-measuring/

As Figure 4.3 shows, Canada has not shared the benefits of growth with its poorest citizens over the past thirty years. Except in Newfoundland, people on social assistance have never fully recovered from the big cuts of the mid-1990s. (And cuts since then have often occurred quietly when benefits have been frozen or increased by less than inflation.) Figure 4.3 adds together all applicable federal and provincial transfers and presents the real value of total income (in 2022 dollars) from 1989 to 2022 for a single, disabled, social assistance recipient in Ontario and Nova Scotia and compares that to Canada's real per capita GDP for the same years.

Figure 4.3

Annual Welfare Incomes in Ontario and Nova Scotia and GDP per Capita in Canada, 1989–2022

(2022 dollars)

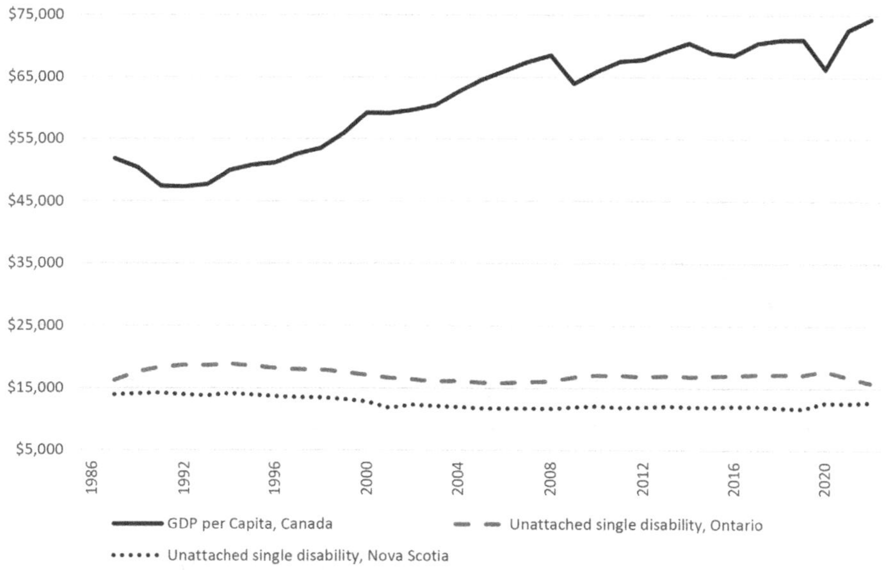

Source: Data & measuring — Maytree, https://maytree.com/changing-systems/data-measuring/

Similar illustrations of the long-term trends in social assistance rates are available for other provinces and for other categories of claimants.[33] Compared to other developed countries, Canada is very stingy in anti-poverty policy. When the OECD compared the adequacy of minimum income benefits of 39 nations in 2023 by measuring the income, as a percentage of the median disposable income in the country, of jobless families relying on guaranteed minimum income benefits, Canada was not the absolute lowest (that was Romania) but it was very close to the bottom, as Figure 4.4 shows.[34]

It is not as if Canada as a country has gotten poorer over the last thirty years. In 2022 dollars, real GDP per capita was $49,944 in 1994 and $72,577 in 2022 — an increase of 48.9 per cent.[35] But the most disadvantaged of Canadian society did not share in this growth. Instead, Canadian governments have cut their real incomes. Measured

Figure 4.4

OECD Comparison of Income Adequacy

(Net income of minimum income benefit recipients, as percentage of the median disposable income)

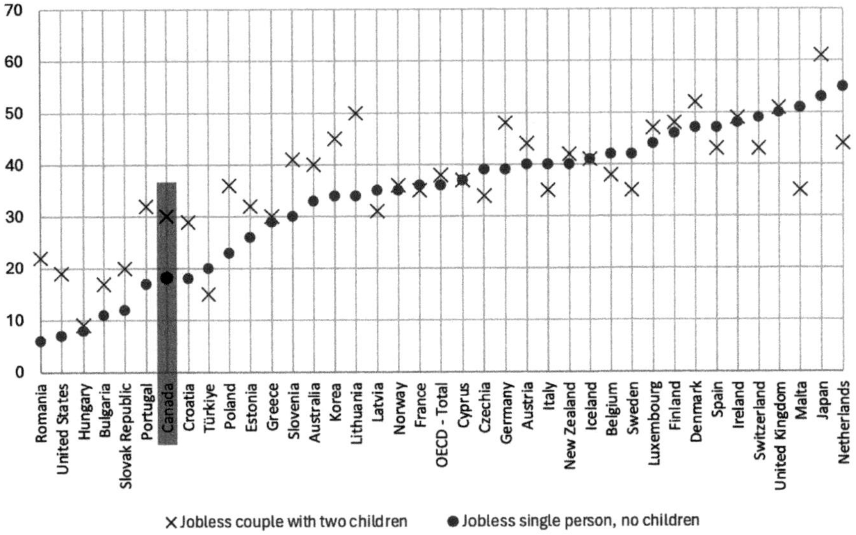

Source: https://data.oecd.org/benwage/adequacy-of-minimum-income-benefits.htm#indicator-chart

in 2022 dollars, a single disabled social assistance recipient in Ontario got $18,882 in 1994 and $15,871 in 2022 — a cut of 16 per cent. In Nova Scotia, a disabled single adult got $14,104 in 1994 and $12,687 in 2022 for a cut of 10 percent. The benefits of economic growth have just not trickled down in Canada.

Only some of the poor receive social assistance in any given year and over the last twenty-five years, the social assistance caseload in Canada has both declined and shifted in composition. In Ontario, for example, social assistance beneficiaries fell from 9.4 per cent to 5.6 per cent of the population from 1997 to 2022. Increasingly, they are disability beneficiaries, who were 25 per cent of the caseload in 1997 but 60 per cent in 2022.[36]

In Canada, most poor people work for their poverty. Even a full-time, year-round job (i.e., fifty weeks at forty hours weekly, or two-thousand hours per year) at the minimum wage is not nearly enough to produce a poverty-line income for a family. In 2024 in Ontario, for example, the general minimum wage was $16.55 an hour — two thousand hours at that pay rate implies $33,100 annually (before any deductions) which is a long way below the $54,419 MBM poverty line for a four-person family in Toronto or the $53,428 threshold in Ottawa.

Of course, calculating the annual income for 2,000 hours of work at minimum wage makes the assumption that full-time, year-round work will always be available, and this is often laughable. Getting enough working hours is a huge problem for many low-income people. Furthermore, intermittent unemployment and underemployment affect much more than just earned income. Statistics on low annual income do not capture the instability and precariousness of working hours for the marginally employed, but these facts of life create real costs. On-call working arrangements and work schedules that are only available at the last minute can make planning for the rest of life difficult to impossible, with serious implications for, for example, childcare, community participation and social life.

Although today's "gig economy" labour market also stresses out many high-wage workers, the stresses are greater for poor people because having money means you can buy time and flexibility. Higher incomes, for example, enable most Canadian parents to drive their kids to daycare and then go on to work, which is much more flexible and takes much less time than if they had to take the bus to do the same things. Since poverty means, among other things, not having the money to buy time and flexibility, poor people's lives are more stressful — and the health and educational implications of that greater stress are borne directly by both parents and children,[37] as well as indirectly by the broader society (e.g., in greater healthcare costs).

But "the poor" are definitely not the same people every year, year after year. In social assistance and the low-wage labour market, there is constant turnover. For quite a few people, social assistance is a very temporary stage: they go through bad spells in their lives and touch the social assistance system for a short time under the "temporary financial need" category, having exhausted their other options, and are able to exit fairly quickly. But others are there for the longer term, often because of disabilities.

Economists have written hundreds, if not thousands, of academic papers on social assistance and poverty. Very often their focus of analysis has been on whether economic incentives such as tax rates or other financial costs and benefits cause people to "choose" their current situation of low earnings. This is not the sort of book to attempt to survey all that literature, much of which is highly technical statistical analysis. Very often, however, real stories about real people can make a point more powerfully than tables and tables of statistics — and who is more real than your own relatives? And is the history of my own extended family all that different from the histories of many other families? Perhaps the very rich or the very young may not personally know anybody who has gone through a bad patch in their lives, but I would wager most of the rest of us do.

"Betty"

Years ago, Betty (not her real name) was a beautiful, vivacious, radiant young bride at her dream wedding. She had just graduated as a nurse, he was an engineer and like many other young people at the time they headed out west where the big-money jobs were. But it turned out that Prince Charming was actually an alcoholic — violent and abusive when drunk and endlessly belittling when briefly sober. Years of abuse, social isolation and alcohol can do a number on anybody's self-confidence. By the time Betty worked up the determination to take her child and leave, she had deep psychological scars.

Of course, her family took her in at home, but living together again after years apart can be stressful. Recriminations, old grievances and the assignation of blame are probably the ingredients of many people's family dynamics, not just the occasional diet of my own extended family. As the weeks became months and months and she did not "just get over it and get a job," tensions grew. The bottom line was that after one fight too many, she was sleeping in her car — and a week later applied for social assistance. After a couple of months, she had a small apartment and was getting back on her feet when (this is the happy ending), she bumped into a guy she had kind of liked way back in Grade Eight, whom she is still happily with today. Her case is what I think of when I read the statistics about how many Canadians have been in "temporary financial need" and required the support of social assistance during a down phase of their lives.

"Jimmy"

Bad luck comes in both short-term and long-term varieties. Part of my family's oral history is the story of the very youngest brother of one of my grandmothers, who was developmentally delayed from birth. In the late 1800s, he could stay on the family farm all his life. In those days there were many simple tasks he could help out with. By all accounts, he had a useful, socially integrated and reasonably happy life.

These options are not available today. Very few families now live on farms and those that do depend on very expensive machinery that is complex and often difficult to operate accurately. In agriculture and everywhere else, job demands in today's labour market are far more demanding and far more stressful than they used to be. Entry-level job requirements have escalated. In all the OECD countries[38] there is now an increasing percentage of the population who are unable to get paid work because of physical or psychological disabilities. Older males with back problems after decades of unhealthy manual work are part of the increasing disability caseload, but there is also an increasing frequency of young males with psychological disabilities.

"Jimmy" (also not his real name) is now in his early thirties, but he still cannot really figure out whether he should get change back from a $10 bill when he buys a hamburger and a soft drink at McDonald's. He therefore avoids going on his own, since he is socially aware enough to be hyper-anxious about the transaction, as he is about many other "normal" events of daily life. Born to high-achieving parents, with a super high-achiever older sibling, he had "bad luck" at birth. A century ago on the family farm, there would have been a place for him — but there is no obvious way he can participate without a lot of help in the ordinary work world of the twenty-first century.

As firms today replace repetitive, low-skill jobs with robots, computerized delivery systems and "total quality" management, they demand a faster pace of work and increasingly high levels of cognitive and social skills in the jobs that remain. So Jimmy has no marketable skills to offer. With an anxiety disorder and limited cognitive abilities, he is uniquely vulnerable to bullying or "teasing" by customers, co-workers or bosses, so even sheltered work placements can be a challenge. With no job-relevant skills and no job experience, he spends many of his days at home alone, watching cartoons on TV and drawing social assistance. His mother worries herself sick about how he will cope when she is no longer there and keeps looking for some combination of counselling and supportive work that will enable him to feel productive about his life. It is no consolation at all for her to know that creating and finding this kind of employment is an increasingly important social issue in all OECD countries.

Finding a job is about much more than money. Many years ago, I ran across a summary of research on the psychological impacts of unemployment which concluded:

> There are latent consequences of employment as a social institution which match human needs of an enduring kind. First among them is the fact that employment imposes a time structure on the waking day. Secondly, employment implies regularly shared experiences and contacts with people outside the family. Thirdly, employment links an individual to goals and purposes which transcend his own. Fourthly, employment defines aspects of status and identity. Finally, employment enforces activity. It is these objective consequences of work in complex industrialized societies which help us to understand the motivation to work beyond earning a living; to understand why work is psychologically supportive, even when conditions are bad, and, by the same token, to understand why unemployment is psychologically destructive.[39]

Jimmy is losing out on much more than money when he cannot get a job. I know that some people might say something like, "He's a big healthy guy — all he needs is a kick in the butt." Some economists repackage such sentiments as the importance of improving "incentives" to get people off social assistance. However, I do not think cutting off Jimmy's benefits would produce anything but deepened misery. Financial calculations are just not driving his reality.

My opinion is the number of people who have a real choice and actually prefer life on social assistance is not zero, but it is very small. Particularly when jobs are available and can be seen to probably lead to something better, having employment is much preferred to the stigma, social isolation and boredom of social assistance. But when there are few jobs available getting a job is hard for everyone — and particularly for the disadvantaged. In a high unemployment labour market, employers have queues of candidates with unblemished credentials available for every opening (between 2011 and 2019 in Canada there were an average of 5.3 unemployed people for every vacancy),[40] so they do not have to take any chances on people with poor work histories or "undesirable" personal characteristics. Getting a job always requires both a job offer from a firm and a job acceptance by a worker. The individual's choice to look for a job is never enough.

Whether or not a person's current situation is due to "choice" can also become a problematic issue for people with mental or emotional problems — and long-duration joblessness can have its own psychological consequences. Being rejected for job after job is hard on one's self-confidence. Particularly when unemployment is high, the probability of getting a job offer diminishes the longer a person has been out of work (partly because potential employers start to wonder why this person has been rejected for other jobs). Faced with this reality, and especially if many others in the neighbourhood or peer group are in a similar situation, bravado and self-excuses can become a psychological refuge from the anxiety that trying would otherwise produce (as in "I didn't want that job anyway" or "They never hire people like me there, so why bother to apply?"). Either way, the long-term jobless can easily get into a psychological space which is hard to get out of without counselling or social support. So I'm not surprised that most research studies find very small impacts on labour supply of changes in work incentives.[41]

Summary

The homeless and the inhabitants of isolated Indigenous communities are largely missing from household survey data, so the poverty of some of Canada's most deprived citizens is poorly measured. Nevertheless, the data that is available indicates that the incomes of the bottom 10 per cent and the bottom 20 per cent of Canadians barely changed when the unemployment rate was high between 1980 and 2000, before moving up in the 2000s as unemployment went down.

Because social norms about what constitutes a "decent" standard of living change when the average income changes, and because the cost of living of poor people goes up when the average income increases, the "poverty line" also goes up when economic growth occurs. Where exactly to draw the "poverty line" has been much debated in Canada, so estimates of the size of Canada's poverty population vary. Nevertheless, it does not take much money to make a big difference in the lives of people who have very little, so all poverty line methodologies agree that it would take a relatively small percentage of total household income to eliminate poverty in Canada. However, in Canada, social assistance payments were cut substantially in the mid-1990s and have never fully recovered.

Nonetheless, recent Canadian data clearly show that poverty can be reduced. Poverty rates fell significantly from 2015 to 2019 and fell further during the Covid-19 pandemic. An implicit lesson of that experience is that governments can move quickly and can create transfer programs that make a significant difference to the poverty rate — if the political will is there. However, in 2024 it was not yet clear whether post-Covid Canada would revert to the "old normal" for Canada's poorest citizens.

Chapter 5
THE MOVING PICTURE OF INCOMES

The world of economic inequality which we experience every day is about many, many daily differences — about Mercedes and BMWs driving past people waiting for the bus, about homeless people sleeping on the pavement outside luxury condominiums, about economy-class passengers watching elite travellers push to the head of the queue at the airport, and on and on. How should we summarize all the different dimensions of the many inequalities between people in their daily command over economic resources?

The statistics on annual money income which this book has so far presented rely on the idea that having enough income every year could equalize many, if not most, of these daily experiences (e.g., by having enough to buy a car, if not a BMW). Since money income can be put to many purposes and since different people often prefer to spend their money on different things, it would be misleading to look at each dimension of individual material differences in isolation. (Some of the people at the bus stop may have chosen to spend their income renting a really nice apartment rather than buying a car.) Because income enables the consumption of many different goods, in different proportions, each person's command over economic resources in general (i.e., total income) provides a better basis for inequality comparisons than looking at inequalities in the consumption of each particular commodity in isolation.

But very often in economics, "the devil is in the details." How exactly should we measure "income"? The common-sense understanding of "income" is the total cash payments which we receive from wages and salaries and dividends or interest returns on capital plus any transfer payments from the government. But cash income is often only part of a person's command over resources. People often also benefit from goods or services they may receive without explicit payment (like living rent-free in a house you own). Capital gains in the stock market or in housing also enable more consumption. A major issue in calculating the inequality of total command over resources therefore is how best to put a dollar value on the benefits people receive without explicit cash payment (e.g., in owner-occupied housing).

Another huge issue in inequality measurement is how best to account for time. Lifestyles and possessions and expectations and anxieties about the future do not just depend on our incomes right now; they also depend on how much those incomes have fluctuated in the past and what we expect for the future. In many ways, comparing statistics on annual income to the real world is like comparing a snapshot photograph to a movie: although a good photograph may capture the outline of an event at a moment in time, the real world is always changing. The faster the shutter speed of the camera, the sharper the image will be — but when movement is frozen at a point in time one can only imagine what happens before or after. Measuring income over a specific period of time freezes a moving process, and is in many respects misleading as a measure of economic well-being. Both the period of time we use for defining income — weekly, monthly, yearly or lifetime — and the concept of income we adopt will alter our perceptions of poverty and inequality in important ways. Hence, this chapter considers why and how a discussion of economic inequalities should go beyond annual money income.

A Year Can Be So Long . . .

Even a snapshot of a year's income is too long a period of time for some purposes. Somebody who is unemployed in January and February may find a job in April, May, June or July (or they may not). If they do, and if they make good money from then to December, their total income for the year may be above the official poverty line (which is measured in terms of annual income). In annual data, it may even look as if this family was prosperous all year. But people need to pay their utility bills every month and their grocery bills every week. Some basic consumption spending cannot be deferred; families that cannot pay their heating bills in Canada in February can get very cold in just a few days. The dependability of income and the availability of savings or access to credit is therefore crucial for well-being.

In polling data, a clear majority of Canadians have for years reported they are either "just getting by, with no savings" or "falling behind on monthly expenses."[1] As Chapter 6 will discuss in more detail, the distribution of wealth is highly unequal. Roughly a quarter of the population does not have enough assets to tide themselves over even a few weeks of missed income. The lower and more uncertain a person's income has been in the past, the less likely they are to have savings available to pay bills in the present. And in personal finance, one bad thing can easily lead to another. When savings or easy credit are not available to smooth consumption over time, an unexpected income shock can be the beginning of a downward cycle of missed payments, poorer credit ratings and less access to credit, higher interest costs and ever-mounting debt.

Rainy weather means roofers and house painters have to sit at home without pay. A slow day at the restaurant may mean staff are sent home early. But people with steady jobs and dependable monthly paychecks are not exposed nearly as often to interruptions in earnings. Salaried employees do not usually have to deal with week-to-week variations in income. However, hourly paid, low-income workers tend to face both greater short-term variability in earnings and higher costs of that variability, because income interruptions of even a few weeks can be a serious matter for people with little savings and poor access to credit. Given the urgency of needs like food and rent, it is not surprising that Canadians who run out of cash will sometimes be willing to pay whatever it takes for a short-term payday loan advance — even if the $66 cost of a $300 advance for fourteen days translates to an annualized interest rate of 573.57 per cent.[2]

Simultaneously in Canada, home equity lines of credit provide instant credit at low rates to people with good collateral and credit history. And if their car needs a sudden engine repair, professional people can get a few weeks' credit for free by putting the bill on their credit card and paying it off at the end of the month. For many Canadian families, income or expenditure shocks are just not a big deal. But for somebody without such access to credit who has to get to work and has no other option, a sudden need for car repair and a payday loan can produce a spiral of dependency. The interest on the loan mounts so quickly that borrowers can sometimes never get out from under it. An income or expenditure shock that would be a minor event for a secure member of the middle class can thus be a catastrophe for the economically insecure. But the uncertainty of weekly income flows and their potential implications are dimensions of inequality that are just not captured when income is added up at year-end to an annual total and then reported in the annual income statistics.

Seen from a business school angle, the occasional cash shortfalls of the less affluent, and their willingness to pay very high interest rates, create an opportunity for profit. In Canadian cities today, payday loan outlets can be seen throughout poorer urban neighbourhoods. Their frequency is a concrete, visual indicator of how often low-income Canadians run out of cash, how remote the major chartered banks are from their needs and how much money a segment of Canada's financial sector is now making from them. Seen from a statistical angle, the fact that short-term credit has a much higher cost for the less affluent means they get less effective consumption from their annual incomes. To compute the effective income that corresponds to a given money income, we really should subtract the differential in borrowing costs of poor people from their annual income to make their income comparable with the annual income of people with better access to credit.

When statistics on income inequality and poverty use an annual accounting framework, the implicit assumption is that it does not matter whether money actually arrives every week or every month or just once a year in January, July or December because credit is always available to finance daily consumption. However, the studies in the United States and Canada that have been able to examine income on a month-by-month basis find short-term poverty is much more common (often roughly three times more common) than annual income poverty.[3]

Although long poverty spells are clearly worse than short poverty spells, short-term poverty sometimes has longer-term consequences; "fighting about money" is, for example, one of the most common reasons cited for divorce. Furthermore, in considering short-term poverty, we should never forget that although a six-month poverty spell is a small fraction of the life experiences of a forty-year-old, it is a large fraction of the life experiences of a two-year-old — at a crucial stage of child development. Even "short" poverty spells during childhood can have important effects in later life.[4]

A Year Is So Short . . .

From other angles, a person's annual income can be much too short a period to examine. Only some of the people who were in the bottom 10 per cent in, for example, 1995 were still there in 1996 (and the same is true for all the income deciles). People in a long-term job often work their way up to higher incomes.[5] Sometimes career mobility happens because workers are moving up a salary scale (e.g., teachers or civil servants). Sometimes seniority pays off in higher earnings because long-term employees get first call on overtime hours and a lower likelihood of layoff or short-time hours of work. Either way, older workers often end up making more than younger workers, so a key social issue is whether, and how much, this career progression actually happens.

Inequalities in annual income associated with age may often be accepted much more easily than inequalities due to other causes. We all do hope and expect to get older (the only available alternative to getting older is just not attractive). Inequalities associated with age mean the young can believe they just have to wait their turn for the higher incomes they will get when they are older. And many people will accept that. University students often, for example, do not mind having a low-paying job while they are in school. They also may not mind it much if, while in their early twenties, they get a part-time job in a coffee shop — especially if most of their peer group has a similarly low-income job and if they can still expect their incomes will grow when they get a "real job" with career advancement. But when that "real job" does not appear, they do mind.

The crucial issue is whether, in the end, wages actually do go up with age and work experience. I well remember the look of pity at my astounding naivety that I got, years ago, while interviewing a tired forty-something salesclerk at the Glace Bay Kmart, when I got to the section of the questionnaire which asked about career progression and promotion possibilities. "There's no 'up' here," she said, with a tone of flat finality — and looking around the store, I had to think she was probably right. There always have been "dead-end jobs" which lead to nowhere other than more of the same.

And there always has been downward income mobility as well as upward mobility. In recent years, factory closures have often meant that long-term employees, who may have worked their way up the job ladder and developed very particular job skills at a specific plant, suddenly become unemployed. Long-term workers, who put their confidence in their employers and established roots in their communities, suddenly have to look for new jobs — something which is particularly difficult for middle-aged people who often have not had to look for a job in decades and who may be tied to a particular location by their mortgages, their spouse's job and their children's schooling. Canada's forestry industry offers a prime example, with pulp and paper mills closing across the country.[6] Mill jobs were well-paid, so their former workers often have to accept much lower wages, if substitute employment can be found locally at all.

Historically in Canada, education has been the route to both higher initial earnings and access to careers with upward income mobility over time. Throughout the 1980s and 1990s, although their initial real wages averaged a bit lower than the entry wages of earlier birth cohorts, each birth cohort entering the Canadian labour market had real wages that, on average, increased with greater work experience.[7] Until 2000, it also appeared that although the supply of workers with post-secondary education was increasing, demand was increasing even faster than supply, pushing up the relative wages of university graduates.[8] After 2000, it was not so clear that the demand for university graduates continued to increase as fast as it had in the past. One influential hypothesis is that Canada's transition to a more knowledge-based economy required a surge of hiring of highly educated labour, but once information systems were in place, updating them required far less hiring, so demand growth for highly educated workers slowed after about 2000.[9]

But whether or not that is true, what today's youth want to know is what will happen in the future, not what did happen in the past. And the big issue now is the remarkable speed of developments in artificial intelligence (AI) and what that will mean for jobs. For generations, new technologies in manufacturing have enabled greater substitution of capital for labour in the production of goods. The increase in productivity that labour-saving technologies produced has enabled both massive decreases in manufacturing employment and massive increases in economic output. Because new jobs have always, up to now, appeared in new sectors, technological optimists have argued that AI is just the latest in a long series of innovations that have improved humanity's standard of living.

However, AI is a different type of innovation. As the OECD has noted: "The occupations that have been most exposed to advances in, and automation by, AI have tended to be high-skilled, white-collar ones, including business professionals; managers; science and engineering professionals; and legal, social and cultural professionals. This contrasts with the impact of previous automating technologies, that have tended to take over primarily routine tasks performed by lower-skilled workers."[10]

Technological pessimists are therefore not so sure that the impacts of AI will be benign. Because AI enables the replacement of many white-collar and service sector functions it is bringing labour-saving technological change to big employment sectors that used to offer secure and well-paid jobs. As the International Monetary Fund (IMF) noted in 2024, "Artificial intelligence has the potential to reshape the global economy, especially in the realm of labour markets. Advanced economies will experience the benefits and pitfalls sooner . . . In advanced economies, about 60 percent of jobs are exposed to AI, due to a prevalence of cognitive-task-oriented jobs." Because "about half may be negatively affected by AI, while the rest could benefit . . . higher-wage earners can expect a more-than-proportional increase in their labour income, leading to an increase in labour income inequality."[11]

Today, the "millennial" and "post-millennial" generations therefore have good reason to wonder whether the experience of past generations — that earnings and security will increase with age — will be a good predictor of their own futures. Certainly, the American evidence has shown dramatic differences between the income growth experiences of different generations. A massive study using linked income tax records found that the fraction of children whose annual income[12] at age thirty was more than that of their parents at the same age has fallen dramatically in the United States. Although 90 per cent of people born in 1940 had a real income at age thirty that was greater than their parents, only 50 per cent of the cohort born in 1980 had higher annual incomes than their parents. The authors' estimate that most (70 per cent) of this decline is due to the increased inequality of income growth rates.[13]

Similar Canadian data are only available for people born between 1970 and 1984, with the conclusion that "overall rates of absolute income mobility for the 1970 cohort were somewhat lower in Canada than in the United States. However, the US estimates show a substantial decline in rates among later cohorts, whereas Canadian rates remained stable. As a result, mobility rates for the 1984 cohort were similar in Canada and the United States."[14] This finding of a roughly fifty-fifty likelihood (i.e., the same odds as a coin flip) that thirty-year-olds in 2014 would have a higher (or lower) real annual income than their parents at the same age is entirely consistent with the data on stagnancy of middle-class real incomes discussed in Chapter 2. On average, real incomes have stagnated for most families over recent generations, but there are random events for individuals. Half the time these random events push the child's income at thirty above their parents' income at the same age, and half the time they push it below.

Isn't Lifetime Income Inequality the Important Issue?

From one year to the next over a person's lifetime, their income may go up and down, so many economists have argued that analysis of economic inequality should focus on inequalities of lifetime income. An important problem in doing this is, of course, that each of us only knows for sure at the end our lives what that total lifetime income will be. This is a bit late, for many purposes. However, a major American study[15] has used income tax data to compare the fortunes of Americans who entered the workforce at age twenty-five between 1957 and 1983. Adding up their incomes (after adjustment for inflation) from age twenty-five until age fifty-five enabled researchers to compare long-term trends in real lifetime income. There was a trend toward gender parity: the median lifetime income of women rose substantially, albeit from a small base, while the median lifetime income of men fell. However, among both men and women, lifetime income inequality increased, and the increase in lifetime income inequality can be traced to the changes which younger cohorts have experienced before age twenty-five.

These findings increase the importance of understanding the experiences of newer cohorts as they enter the labour market. As just discussed, Canadians now under thirty-five have some reason to worry that the lifetime income experiences of past generations may not forecast very well what will happen to their own future lifetime incomes. Although economists have made simulations of the hypothetical lifetime income that people now alive can expect to make,[16] calculating hypothetical estimates always requires that researchers make a set of assumptions about what will determine each person's future earnings. A different set of assumptions will generate a different prediction of future incomes and a different estimate of the inequality of lifetime incomes.[17]

As a result, specific numerical estimates of the future inequality of lifetime incomes are very much open to debate, but the overall perspective of looking at lifetime income has enormous value. Annual income is a very myopic conceptual framework, with strong and misleading implications. When we calculate the inequality of annual income in any given year, it is, for example, all too easy to discuss income differences by age or by generation. If we compare the annual incomes this year of people aged thirty, fifty and seventy, we can easily see differences in sources of income, as well as differences in amounts of income. Canadians over seventy often depend on transfer payments from the government through Old Age Security (OAS), the Guaranteed Income Supplement (GIS) and Canada Pension Plan (CPP). They are usually not paying income tax on wage income, because most seventy-year-old people are retired. Canadians who are aged thirty or fifty are usually working and paying income tax on their earnings, but they cannot claim OAS, GIS or CPP.

Hence, if we look just at annual income in a given year, it is true to say that younger people are paying the taxes which are supporting the older generations, and perhaps some complaints may be heard about that. However, twenty years from now the thirty-year-olds of today will be fifty, and forty years from now they will be seventy (they hope). The same people who are now paying income taxes on their earnings will, a few years from now, be retired and getting OAS, GIS and CPP. Indeed, we can all look back in time a bit and think about the income transfers and the services we received when we were ten years old or one year old. Children in Canada receive child benefits and free-of-charge health care services and education services. Canadians get these benefits, as children, for roughly twenty years before they are old enough to start earning income and paying taxes. Later on, when they are retired, they will also receive transfers and services from the public sector.

While they are retired and while they are children, Canadians typically do not pay income tax on any labour earnings. During the in-between years of their life cycle, Canadians pay both income tax on their earnings and sales taxes on their consumption. One way of thinking about income distribution is to say that while they are in their working years, Canadians pay taxes to finance both the services and the transfers that they are currently consuming in their middle age and the services and transfers that their "younger selves" and their "older selves" have consumed and will consume. A full calculation of redistribution of income by the government should therefore look at the lifetime incidence of taxes and transfers — not just the impact in a particular year.

And What About Chance?

Years ago, on a hot day in early June just before his graduation in engineering from Queen's University, my best buddy John went to a party at a friend's cottage. Other people were diving into the lake from the dock, and he did too — and broke his neck just below the fourth vertebrae. He has been in a wheelchair ever since. John was and is a great person: hard-working, super-smart, a wicked sense of humour and a really nice guy. There is no doubt at all in my mind that he was headed for the top of corporate Canada, but his life changed in an instant. Among many other things, his lifetime income suddenly dropped dramatically.

John's story illustrates the important reality that even if lifetime income is the important issue, our individual lives are unavoidably risky. Hence, when we think about economic inequalities, and the role government may be playing in affecting those inequalities, we should distinguish between redistribution of lifetime income and social insurance of annual income. Redistribution of lifetime income occurs when government taxes and transfers increase the expected lifetime income of some types of people while decreasing that of others. Social insurance programs (like workers' compensation or employment insurance) mostly transfer, in any given year, income between individual people who have approximately the same expected lifetime income.

The nature of insurance is that people pay premiums because they want to cover themselves against a future risk — i.e., to be compensated, at least partially, for possible future losses — in order not to have to worry about that risk. As a result, all insurance programs look different financially before and after the fact. All the people who buy insurance pay premiums before any of them know what will happen, but in any given year only some of them get any money back, depending on what actually happens.

I have, for example, been paying fire insurance premiums on my house every year for many years but I can only receive compensation payments from the insurance company in the years in which I make a claim for fire damage (which I have never actually done). Hence, in all these years of no fire damage, I have paid money in but received nothing back financially. Meanwhile, the people whose houses burned down got compensation payments. Fire insurance transfers income from the lucky (whose houses did not burn) to the unlucky (whose houses did burn). Insurance companies know a certain percentage of Canadian houses will have fires in any given year, but because nobody knows which houses will burn, insurance companies pool the risk by collecting premiums from all the policyholders and only paying compensation to the unlucky few. When people are, in general, averse to losses, pooling the risk of an adverse event through insurance can make everyone better off. I intend to keep paying my fire insurance premiums because I like having the non-financial benefit called "peace of mind" (and I actually hope I never have to make a claim).

In economics, there is a substantial body of literature[18] that examines why and how private insurance markets can effectively pool risks for some hazards (like house fires)[19] and why one cannot expect private insurance markets to work well for some other hazards of life (like unemployment or poverty in old age). Because private insurance markets cannot, for some hazards, effectively provide the peace of mind that citizens want, one observes in many countries that most of the transfer payments of the "welfare state" (like employment insurance, workers' compensation or old age pensions) are social insurance programs[20] that only pay out money under specific conditions, such as being unemployed or having a workplace accident. Using an annual income accounting framework implies that in any given year, it will look like the government is redistributing from higher income to lower income people. However, from a lifetime income perspective, government is "insuring" and transferring income from the lucky to the unlucky.

Market incomes in any given year often depend somewhat on luck, but over a longer period, luck may average out. If, for example, "Bernie" and "Andy" both work for firms that bid on contracts every year and in some years Bernie's firm gets contracts and Andy's firm does not, Bernie then makes money and pays EI premiums while Andy is unemployed and may draw EI benefits. In the years when Andy's firm gets the contracts and Bernie is unemployed, Andy is affluent and paying premiums while Bernie is drawing benefits. If we were to just look at a single year's statistics on annual income, it would always look as if the EI system is redistributing income from the more affluent employed to the poorer unemployed. Statistics on annual income distribution just record the facts of income distribution after the events of the year have actually occurred, so surveys recording annual income will count the lucky as high income and the unlucky as low income. But in this example, in some years the more affluent person is Bernie and in some years it is Andy. Over the longer haul, the premiums paid by Bernie and Andy while employed have to cover the benefits they will claim while unemployed. However, that does not mean unemployment insurance provides no net benefit to them; both Bernie and Andy benefit from the peace of mind that insurance buys.[21]

In any given year, risk is also pooled by the government's commitment to supply particular services when needed. I am, for example, now at an age when several of my friends have recently had heart attacks and expensive operations, which in Canada were provided by our publicly funded healthcare system. Those operations, as well as my buddy John's many healthcare bills, were paid for from the pool of income and sales tax revenues which is raised from the people who (like me) have been lucky enough to avoid heart attacks and diving accidents. In a healthcare system without insurance, these bills have to be paid out of household incomes (healthcare costs are still a major cause of personal bankruptcy in the United States).[22] As things have turned out, my friends (and many others) have been getting much more spent on them by our public healthcare system than I have. Although this could be interpreted as inequality between individuals in the net benefits received from Canada's public healthcare system, I am, personally, okay with it. I will be quite content if my current situation continues and other people continue to receive more healthcare services than me. Indeed, I hope never to receive any of the expensive heart operations which my taxes help pay for. The greater sense of security Medicare meanwhile provides is enough for me.

Aren't Public Services Received Also Part of a Person's Income?

The healthcare costs example illustrates some of the difficulties encountered when we try to calculate the impacts of government on inequality. Part of the impact of government on inequality is the change in household money income when government transfer payments are added and taxes are subtracted. Figure 1.4 provides an overview. In addition, governments provide services like healthcare, education, police, road maintenance, fire protection, subsidized public transportation, etc. — all of which benefit individuals. Since these services have value, it can be argued that the value of public services received should be counted as part of each person's income.

However, to me it makes no sense to assign to sick people, as an addition to their annual "income," the cost of any healthcare they have received in the past year; they are not "better off" because they got sick and needed and got expensive treatment. Fundamentally, we do not know in advance who will be healthy and who will be sick in any particular year, and we all benefit from the fact the healthcare system is there for those who need it. To my mind, the most reasonable way to think about the impact of public healthcare on inequality is to think of it as providing insurance, which implies that the economic benefit of public healthcare for each person is the per capita cost of healthcare delivery. Because this is an equal amount per person,[23] counting the value of public healthcare services as part of income tends to equalize the distribution of income.

In European debates, the value of the public services received by all citizens without charge, or substantially subsidized, from the government is often called "the social wage." Including it in measurements of a household's income has an equalizing impact on inequality in the distribution of annual income because the benefits are mostly per capita. The big dollars in public spending go to healthcare and education, whose benefits are received throughout the income distribution. Many other areas of public expenditure are also, at least approximately, per capita costs.[24] Because the dollar value of the social wage is much the same for all individuals across the income distribution, it is a much bigger fraction of household income at the bottom than at the top, so including it as part of income reduces measured income inequality. As a consequence, when the value of public services received is included in international comparisons of inequality, countries with a higher social wage have less inequality than countries with a smaller social wage.[25]

Income Inequality or Consumption Inequality?

Although some authors[26] have argued that inequality of annual consumption should be the focus of discussion, overwhelmingly the international literature on inequality has focused on inequalities of income. To understand why, we have to look a bit more closely at the underlying concepts. Income, in a broad sense, is usually defined by economists as "control over the use of society's scarce resources."[27] Since people can use their income to consume immediately or they can save some of it, add those savings to their wealth and consume it later, the conceptual basis for income measurement is that "income" is "the maximum value a person can consume during a period of time and still be as well off (as wealthy) at the end of the period as [they are] at the beginning."[28]

Of course, turning this general concept of income into a practical measurement requires many nitpicking decisions of detail. Despite general agreement on this concept, many countries measure household income a little bit differently (the international manual on how to reconcile the cross-country differences in household income measurements to make the data comparable is 218 pages long).[29] Nevertheless, the core concept used in income measurement is "potential consumption, holding wealth constant."

For the many households who live paycheque to paycheque and spend all their income as it comes in, annual income and annual consumption are the same. But in any given year, a household's consumption can be more than its income if that household is running down its assets and/or going into debt (which can also be called dissaving or "negative savings"). If a household's annual consumption is less than its annual income, the household has positive savings — assets are being acquired that can be spent later. In any given country in any given year, measurement of an index of the inequality of household consumption invariably produces a smaller number for household consumption inequality than for household income inequality, because richer people tend to save more while poorer people are often dissaving.[30] However, the difference in measured annual inequality arises only because some households are storing up more problems for their futures by dissaving while other households are adding to their future advantages by saving.

Of course, even if economists sitting in their offices change their preferred measures of inequality, nothing in the real world outside changes. However, a key advantage of focusing on annual income inequality rather than annual consumption inequality is that income provides a clearer focus on what is happening to people this year. Since the annual income of households is the amount of money that would maintain their wealth at a constant level, the income concept holds constant for each household the wealth that will enable consumption in future years. By contrast, analysis of consumption inequality does not reveal the changes in assets and debts which are accumulating in the background.[31] A practical example of the importance of the difference comes from the United States in the early 2000s, when low- and middle-income households maintained their consumption, despite their lagging incomes, by going deeper into debt. As a result, although income inequality increased, consumption inequality did not — a process that could not last, and indeed came crashing down in the financial crisis of 2008.

Housing — Income, Consumption and Wealth

Owner-occupied housing provides a particularly important example of the practical difficulties in distinguishing consumption, income and wealth — and why this sometimes matters significantly for understanding trends in inequality. In 2021, 66.5 per cent of Canadian households lived in a house that they owned.[32] For many people, paying down the mortgage while they are working so they can live rent-free when they retire is the most important way they provide privately for their retirement years. Homeowners have to pay municipal property taxes, cover the cost of insurance and maintenance and pay down their mortgage, but they save on rent. The difference between the total costs of home ownership and the rent they would otherwise have had to pay is their net rental savings from home ownership.

Saving rent is one reason for buying a house. Capital gains when you sell is another big reason. As Chapter 6 will discuss further, capital gains on home ownership have become the major way in which the middle class in Canada acquires wealth, partly because capital gains on an individual's principal residence are tax-free. And in principle, even if you did not sell your house last year, you could have done so, which implies that the unrealized capital gains on your house should be counted as an addition to your potential consumption — i.e., as part of annual income. Adding together the benefits of capital gains and the net rental savings from home ownership, owning a home can be seen as an invisible source of income, which economists often call the "imputed income from home ownership."

Unlike income from other sources, both the imputed net rental savings and any capital gains from owner-occupied housing are not considered taxable income, so they do not appear in income distribution statistics based on income tax records (such as the data used for Figure 1.2 or Table 2.2). Likewise, neither are measured in the statistics on the household distribution of income derived from survey data we considered in Chapters 1 to 3 (e.g., Figure 1.4). The returns to home equity thus disappear statistically from inequality analysis.

Nonetheless, the returns to home ownership do matter for economic inequality, because the benefits of home ownership are quite unequally received. Clearly, such returns are zero for those who cannot buy their own home. Young owners with big mortgages also get much smaller "imputed income from home ownership" than the mortgage-free elderly (whose other sources of money income may be quite limited). Hence, including the imputed income from home ownership in measured income, as part of the "command over economic resources" of families, would make a difference to the relative income of older households compared to younger cohorts and would alter our perception of the distribution of income among age groups. Additionally, since upper-income homeowners have more expensive houses than low-income families, their net rental savings from home ownership and their tax-free capital gains are greater. Including the imputed income from home ownership and adding capital gains as part of income would increase the relative income of upper-income households, thereby increasing the measured inequality of income among people of the same age.

Capital gains have an even larger impact at the very top of the income distribution. Because capital gains have been, and continue to be, taxed at considerably less than the rate applicable for wage and salary income,[33] capital gains on stock options have become increasingly important as a form of top executive compensation. If a series of transactions can be arranged such that capital income from interest or rental or dividend income can get reclassified as capital gains income, the tax rate similarly drops. The tax code thus has built-in incentives to relabel labour or capital income as capital gains, whenever possible (even more tax may be avoided if income can get attributed to a Canadian-controlled private corporation or trust (CCPC)).

The Statistics Canada data that are available indicate that capital gains roughly doubled between 2017 and 2021 as a percentage of the total income declared by the top 1 per cent. For the top 1 per cent as a group, declared capital gains increased from 22.5 per cent to 40.2 per cent of total income — both up considerably from 5.9 per cent in 1982. At the very top, for the top 0.01 per cent, realized capital gains increased even more (from 30.8 per cent of total income in 2017 to 62.2 per cent of total income in 2021).[34] Although income tax data includes the capital gains that are realized when assets other than owner-occupied housing are actually sold, that data does not record any of the increase in market value of assets that are unsold (i.e., unrealized). Neither unrealized nor realized capital gains are measured in the survey data on income distribution in Canada since the necessary questions are not asked. Data on capital gains in Canada is therefore quite patchy. However, since it is only possible to have capital gains if one owns an asset, income from capital gains is necessarily concentrated among the more affluent, so the omission of capital gains from measured household income produces an understatement of top income shares. And discussion of capital gains leads naturally to analysis of the inequality of wealth, which is the subject of Chapter 6.

Chapter 6
INEQUALITY OF WEALTH

How much difference does a billion dollars make? Wrapping one's mind around the inequality of wealth in Canada is not easy. Most people can imagine having $100,000 in assets but a billion is $1,000,000,000 — ten thousand times larger than $100,000 — and it is hard to attach concrete meaning to so many zeros added at the end of a number. However, everyone knows the cliché that "time is money" so perhaps one way of illustrating the magnitude of the differences of wealth in Canada in the 2020s is to imagine your lifetime's length if money were time.[1] Specifically, to help visualize the implications of the actual differences in wealth which we observe, one can ask the hypothetical question: "How long a life could Canadians expect if they had to use their wealth to buy their remaining lifetime, at a price of ten cents for each additional second of life?" Since an hour has 3,600 seconds, and a million seconds is 277.8 hours (about eleven-and-a-half days), at that price each $100,000 would buy a bit more than a week-and-a-half of life.

In 2021, the Thomson family had a net worth of $54.3 billion (see Table 6.2) while the top half of one percent of Canadian families in 2019 were the 80,000 families with a net worth of $10 million or more (see

Table 6.1).[2] A net worth of $10 million would buy thirty-eight more months of time, while the 2,700 families with $100 million or more of wealth could get a minimum extra life of thirty-two years. A billion dollars would enable additional life of over three centuries (317 years) while the $54.3 billion fortune of the Thomson family would come close to buying them eternal life (17,207 years).

Meanwhile, the least rich forty percent of families in 2019 had a net worth of $100,000 or less. If they needed a dime to buy a second, they could look forward to a maximum life of about eleven and a half days, but most would get much less than a week. The 8.4 per cent of households[3] (i.e., a bit more than one in twelve Canadians) who have a net worth of $500 or less would, at a dime a second, live for less than 83 minutes. Of course, the middle 40 per cent of Canadian families (those with a net worth between $100,000 and $1 million) would live somewhat longer — their wealth would buy an additional lifespan ranging from 11.6 days to 16.5 weeks. However, if a dime bought a second of life, 80 per cent of Canadians would be dead in less than four months.

This hypothetical calculation illustrates the fact that when quantitative differences are really huge, they become qualitative differences. If money were time, at ten cents per second 80 per cent of Canadians would get four more months or less to live and 99.5 per cent would be dead in a little over three years — their worldview and consciousness would be qualitatively different from those of the billionaires who could expect to live at least 317 more years or the 17,207 years that the Thomson family would enjoy. It is easy to see that if people could expect differences in their lifetimes of months or years or centuries, most everything about their consciousness would be qualitatively different. It is a bit harder to imagine what life would be like if your wealth was ten or a hundred or a thousand times greater than it now is. Nevertheless, billionaires have lives that are qualitatively different from other people's and since the inheritance of wealth means that present-day wealth inequalities echo down the generations, the impact on lives of differences in wealth of these magnitudes similarly echo down the generations.

Technically, economists typically define "wealth" as net worth — the amount that a person could hypothetically consume at a particular point in time, if they immediately sold all their assets (real estate, bank balances, stock holdings, bonds, houses, automobiles, etc.) and paid off all their liabilities, including mortgages and personal debts. However, that perspective does not really recognize that owning assets can imply much more than just potential consumption. Wealth generates income but over and above the annual income flow from the rent, interest and dividends that come from wealth there is also the insurance value of assets — the sense of economic security provided by the availability of wealth in case of emergencies — and for the bottom 40 per cent of families, whose net worth is very small, lack of wealth conversely means chronic economic insecurity.

The potential consumption perspective underlying "net worth" calculations also does not capture the economic power of the very wealthy, especially because what the very rich own may be far less than what they control through ownership of a minority controlling block of shares or preferential voting rights on a limited class of shares.[4] The very wealthy also get social status and political influence. Ordinary people are not, for example, courted by university presidents seeking donations and they cannot expect to get their phone calls returned immediately by provincial premiers. Billionaires get that sort of treatment daily.

Peter Newman's description, over sixty years ago, of the relationship between Pierre Trudeau and Paul Desmarais of Power Corporation still captures some of the enduring ego rush of billionaires: "The channels of influence that link Power Corporation and the federal Liberal party carry considerable two-way traffic. For Paul Desmarais, the ultimate expression of power is to feel history as it is being made. It's when he is being consulted by the prime minister and premiers on options before they become policies that he really begins to fulfill every great entrepreneur's dream."[5] The status and power which accompany great wealth are central to understanding the motivations and the behaviour of billionaires, who continue to acquire more wealth even when they already have far more than they could possibly consume personally within their own remaining lifetime.

For the middle class,[6] the economic security of the "nest egg" of family money reduces anxieties about unemployment, illness, retirement or the possible homelessness of the children when the parents are no longer alive. As well, the monetary value of the most important middle-class asset (the family home) only captures part of its importance for individuals. In addition to the security that comes from knowing that no landlord can evict you, owning a home implies residence in a particular neighbourhood and the relationships that produces. For low-income people, for whom home ownership may be a dream, the key asset that they may have is an automobile, which may determine their ability to get and keep a job and has huge implications for their personal autonomy, mobility and convenience.

Statistics about the inequality of wealth (i.e., net worth — this book henceforth uses the terms "net worth" and "wealth" interchangeably) therefore only capture some of the inequalities implied by an unequal ownership of property. Nevertheless, inequalities of wealth are far greater than inequalities of income: the Gini index of inequality of net worth in Canada is, for example, over twice as large as the Gini index of equivalent disposable income.[7] However, the "net worth" definition of wealth precisely defines the relationship between income and wealth. Both income and wealth are measures of a person's command over resources but wealth is a person's stock of command over resources at a particular point in time while income is the flow of command over resources over a period of time.

To distinguish stocks and flows, economists often use the bathtub analogy: at any point in time there is a certain amount of water in a bathtub — the level of water in the tub is the stock of bathwater. The water coming in from the tap is the inflow and the water going down the drain is the outflow. As water flows into a bathtub, the level (i.e., the stock of water) increases if the inflow is greater than the outflow and decreases if the outflow exceeds the inflow. All this is happening over time, so to measure flows one has to specify a unit of time — so many litres per second or minute or hour for bathtubs, so many dollars per hour or day or week or year for income.[8] Stocks (like wealth) and flows (like income or consumption) are thus closely related. In any given period of time, the inflow of income minus the outflow of consumption is the net addition to the stock of wealth — i.e., savings. Over time, savings add up to wealth — as summarized by the accounting statement (or "identity"):[9]

Income - Consumption = Net Savings = Change in Wealth

Income and wealth are therefore very highly correlated, but there are exceptions. Some senior citizens, for example, may have significant assets (e.g., a house or farm), even if their current income from pensions and interest payments may be quite modest. Somebody who has just started to make money (e.g., a doctor who has just graduated from medical school) has not had much time to accumulate many assets or to pay off student loans.

Typically, however, wealth and income are strongly correlated — partly because a higher income enables more savings, which add to wealth. Canada's top one hundred corporate executives, for example, with an average income of $14.9 million in 2022,[10] also have significant wealth because they have had high incomes for long enough to accumulate assets. Assets also produce income. Bonds pay interest, stocks pay dividends and generate capital gains and the owners of apartment buildings collect rent. At the top of the wealth distribution, that capital income dominates. As Table 6.1 shows, the top 0.5 per cent (i.e., one family in every two hundred) in the Canadian distribution of wealth had more than $10 million in net worth in 2019. Even a 5 per cent rate of return on $10 million would produce an annual income of $500,000, in perpetuity, which is well up in the top 1 per cent of annual incomes — and there is good evidence that the average rate of return on large portfolios is significantly greater than 5 per cent.

Concentration of wealth has become increasingly important because in Canada, as elsewhere, labour's share of total national output (GDP) has been shrinking.[11] The Federal Reserve in the US has pithily summarized the global decline in labour's share of national income as "Capital's gain is lately labour's loss."[12] As they note: "The share of labour compensation in GDP has been declining for several countries around the world. In the US, this share has declined by 5% between 1975 and 2017. The decline in other countries is even greater, with the largest occurring in Canada, at almost 11%."[13] As capital's share of national income increases, the importance of the inequality of wealth for the distribution of well-being also increases. Since the current owners of wealth will eventually die, and their assets will pass by inheritance to the next generation, inheritances increase in importance over time. Inequalities of inheritances are therefore becoming increasingly important for inequality of opportunity.

Billionaires are very few in number but they hold a significant fraction of total wealth — which does not show up in the numbers from household sample surveys. In presenting its estimates of the distribution of wealth, the Parliamentary Budget Office (PBO 2020:3)[14] commented that: "Statistics Canada's principal family wealth microdata product, the Survey of Financial Security Public Use Microdata File (SFS PUMF), reports families with wealth up to only $27 million. By contrast, the lowest entry on *Canadian Business* magazine's list of the 100 'Richest People' had a wealth of $875 million." The PBO therefore supplemented the survey data with estimates from *Canadian Business* magazine's Richest People List.[15] Table 6.1 is calculated from their Table 4-2 to show the average wealth holding and wealth share within each segment of the wealth distribution of Canada.[16]

The rent, interest and dividends from ownership of wealth are most of the annual income of the top 0.1 per cent, and in market economies such as Canada's, wealth has always been substantially more unequally distributed than income. Even before Covid-19 upended the world economy, wealth inequality had been increasing strongly, but the pandemic supercharged the growth of top-end wealth. Table 6.2[17] is based on the *Forbes* magazine database of the world's billionaires and shows how extremely well the top 20 Canadian billionaires did for themselves during Covid times. Their size of their wealth increase (44 per cent) implies that the 2019 data reported in Table 6.1 understates the concentration of wealth in Canada at the beginning of the 2020s.

Table 6.1

Family Wealth Distribution in Canada, 2019

Family wealth quantile	Wealth Threshold ($ Million)	Number of Families (thousands)	Total Wealth ($ billions)	Average Wealth ($ millions)	Share of Total Wealth (per cent)
Top 0.01%	143.1	1.6	654	408.75	5.6
Next 0.09%	29.3	14.4	773	53.7	6.6
Next 0.4%	9.7	65.3	983	15.1	8.4
TOTAL TOP 0.5%	**9.7**	**79.7**	**2,410**	**30.24**	**20.6**
Next 0.5%	6.1	79.6	600	7.5	5.1
TOTAL TOP 1%	**6.1**	**159.3**	**3,010**	**18.9**	**25.7**
Next 4 %	2.3	637.4	2,097	3.3	18
Next 5 %	1.6	796.8	1,522	1.9	13
TOTAL TOP 10%	**1.6**	**1,593.50**	**6,629**	**4.2**	**56.7**
Next 10%	1	1,593.50	2,004	1.26	17.1
Middle 40%	0.1-1.0	6,373.80	2,932	0.46	25.1
Bottom 40%	under 0.1	6,373.80	132	0.02	1.1

Source: Calculated from Table 4-2 Parliamentary Budget Office (2020)

Who are the people at the top of Canada's wealth pyramid?[18] Are they a revolving door of entrepreneurship or a fairly stable hierarchy of establishment wealth? When I wrote my first book on economic inequality in Canada way back in 1981, it was clear to me then that "the Canadian industrial structure is, to a very large degree, dominated by foreign ownership and a relatively small number of great family fortunes."[19] The Weston, Black, Thomson, Desmarais, Bronfman and Irving families then had billions in assets and dominated a wide range of industries. Forty-plus years later, the same families are mostly still there. The obituary of Paul Desmarais in 2013 pegged the assets of the Power Corporation conglomerate at $527 billion and detailed his intimate links with Canada's political elite.[20] Although Conrad Black managed to dissipate most of his inherited fortune (and indeed served a brief bit of jail time for corporate fraud), the other big families of 1981 are still at the top of the Canadian economic pyramid, another couple of generations on in the line of succession.

In many cases, big money in the 2020s remains based on the opportunities an ancestor seized in the 1920s or earlier. The Thomson fortune ($54 billion in 2021) got started in Ontario in the 1920s when radio stations were the big new thing in mass media. At roughly the same time, K. C. Irving was starting his family dynasty in New Brunswick, building gas stations to service the rapidly expanding number of automobile owners who needed fuel and repairs. Prohibition in the United States during the 1920s meant the Bronfmans could make big money exporting alcohol to the Americans. Although the Bronfman fortune was as large as or larger than either Thomson or Irving in 1981, a grandson exaggerated his abilities as a film producer and spent heavily in Hollywood, which diminished the family fortune to $3.2 billion by 2021. The Richardson family fortune in Winnipeg (estimated at $9 billion in 2017) dates from even earlier, going back to 1857 and surging during the Prairie Wheat Boom of 1880 to 1910.[21]

The data for Table 6.2 come from the *Forbes* magazine database for 2021, which is certainly incomplete and outdated. For example, the Rogers family does not appear in Table 6.2, perhaps because their shares in the Rogers cell network (worth $8.98 billion even prior to the 2023 merger of the Rogers and Shaw cellphone networks) are held through a family trust.[22] Although the Desmarais fortune was ranked by *Forbes* at the death of Paul Desmarais in 2013 as the fourth largest in Canada, the Desmarais Family Residuary Trust holds the assets and individual family members similarly do not appear in the *Forbes* billionaire list. The $9 billion Richardson family fortune,[23] which dates from 1857, is also unmentioned by *Forbes*,[24] but Fix and Cochrane (2023) have

Table 6.2

Canadian Billionaires in Pandemic Times

	Forbes Rank March 2020	Wealth ($ billions) March 18, 2020	Wealth ($ billions) April 7, 2021	Change ($ billions)	Change (%)
David Thomson and Family*	1	$39.90	$54.30	$14.40	36.10%
Joseph Tsai	2	$12.60	$14.50	$1.90	15.10%
Galen Weston and Family*	3	$8.80	$13.4 4	$4.50	51.10%
David Cheriton	4	$6.90	$11.90	$4.90	71.00%
Huang Chulong	5	$6.40	$8.50	$2.00	31.30%
Mark Scheinberg	6	$6.20	$6.20	$0.00	0.00%
James Irving*	7	$5.70	$5.40	-$0.30	-5.30%
Jim Pattison	8	$5.40	$12.60	$7.20	133.30%
Emanuelle Saputo and Family	9	$4.80	$7.60	$2.80	58.30%
Anthony von Mandl	10	$4.20	$11.00	$6.80	161.90%
Daryl Katz	11	$4.00	$4.70	$0.60	15.00%
Chip Wilson	12	$4.00	$6.30	$2.30	57.50%
Alain Bouchard	13	$3.90	$5.70	$1.80	46.20%
Tobi Lutke	14	$3.80	$12.60	$8.80	231.60%
Lawrence Stroll	15	$3.30	$4.00	$0.80	24.20%
Bob Gaglardi	16	$3.20	$3.70	$0.50	15.60%
Arthur Irving*	17	$3.20	$2.40	-$0.80	-25%
Jean Coutu and Family	18	$3.00	$3.70	$0.60	20.00%
Charles Bronfman*	19	$2.90	$3.20	$0.30	10.30%
Mitchell Goldhar	20	$2.80	$3.40	$0.60	21.40%
TOTAL WEALTH		$135.00	$181.70	$59.70	44%

Source: https://www.policynote.ca/the-rich-and-the-rest-of-us

** signifies identified by Newman (1975) as among richest 19 families in Canada*
Bold signifies continued top status since 1975

traced out their network of corporate control using Statistics Canada's Intercorporate Ownership data base.

Net worth at the very top fluctuates with the business cycle and the stock market — for example, in 2023 *Forbes* magazine increased their estimate of the Thomson fortune to $57.9 billion (US $),[25] up $3.6 billion from their 2021 estimate, just two years earlier, reported in Table 6.2. Nevertheless, Table 6.2 still gives a hint of the staying power of the great fortunes of Canada's financial aristocracy by noting those of the top twenty Canadian billionaires identified by the *Forbes* database in 2021[26] who are from families that Newman (1975) identified fifty years earlier as the richest nineteen families in Canada (clearly an underestimate of long-term stability since, for example, the Desmarais and Richardson fortunes are missing).[27]

As Table 6.1 reports, the poorest 40 per cent of Canadian families had average wealth of approximately $20,000 which implies total net worth of $127.5 billion for those 6,373,800 families. Meanwhile, as one can compute from Table 6.2, the total wealth of the richest eight Canadian families in 2021 was $132 billion — significantly greater. However, both Table 6.1 and 6.2 measure only the net worth implied by the market value of asset ownership, and thus understate the concentration of economic power in Canada. Small stockholders do not acquire with their shares any ability to influence corporate decisions. Upper-middle-class families who assemble a portfolio of stocks become entitled to dividend incomes and can hope for capital gains but they do not gain any ability to influence events. Large holdings are a very different issue. Since minority owners can effectively control a company without owning all of its stock, and since some stock may be issued with very different voting rights than other shares, the net worth of controlling families often understates their corporate power. In 2021, for example, Rogers Communication was ostensibly a public corporation, but it had a two-tier share system in which class A shares came with voting rights, but class B shares did not. The Rogers family owned about 10 per cent of the Rogers class B shares but had 97 per cent of the control-conferring class A shares[28] — the market value of their Rogers share holdings ($8.98 billion) understated their corporate power.

Indeed, it has long been part of Canadian reality that the concentration of corporate power is greater than the concentration of net worth. When, for example, the Black brothers inherited their father's shares in Argus Corporation in the 1970s, its minority shareholding control over Canadian Breweries Limited, Dominion Stores, Hollinger Mines, Crown Trust, Domtar, Standard Broadcasting, Massey Ferguson, Dominion Malting Co., Orange Crush Ltd., British Columbia Forest Products Limited and the St. Lawrence Corporation meant that their economic power vastly exceeded the market value of their investments.

The Black brothers were the third generation to control the family fortune but they sold off their diversified holdings in favour of investments in newspaper publishing, which turned out badly. In the Black family saga, Canadian jobs were collateral damage. Massey Ferguson (originally Massey-Harris) was, in the 1950s and 1960s, a major Canadian-based multinational[29] and by some calculations the largest manufacturer of agricultural machinery in the world, with major plants in Toronto and Brantford. When the Black brothers sold, it was absorbed by competitors. Canadian jobs disappeared as the head office and manufacturing moved to the US. The economic privilege of the Black family may have been transitory, but so too was their contribution to Canadian economic development.

Deciding the location of corporate head offices is a very visible demonstration of the power conferred by corporate control. Since the location of the corporate head office typically also implies the location of high-end jobs in accounting, information technology, legal and other support services, jobs and tax revenue for the local community will disappear if a head office is moved. Head office location often also influences the location of other "footloose" activities (like research and development laboratories) that could in principle be sited anywhere and which may be important for long-run technological change.[30] However, the head office location decision is only the most visible of the many decisions which the controlling shareholders of a major company get to make which matter for the rest of society — and the exercise of corporate power is usually much more discrete. Indeed, really powerful people do not often have to explicitly tell their underlings what to do — because everybody knows it is in their own best interest to anticipate the desires of the powerful. The political influence of the very wealthy finds expression only partly in getting their desired policies implemented — just as important are the policies (like wealth taxation) that are not seriously considered by governments, because "that would never fly."

Economic power also depends on context — being a big fish matters much more in a small pond than in a large one. The Irving family, for example, has assets around the world but their $7.8 billion fortune originated in New Brunswick (population 787,014 in 2023) where their holdings in a wide variety of industries continue to dominate the local landscape. Vertical integration of supplier firms, secretiveness and aggressive tax avoidance have characterized their management style. (For example, the family patriarch moved legal domicile to Bermuda in 1971 where an Irving-owned insurance company continues to receive premium income from Irving-owned businesses in Canada, thereby transferring corporate revenue to a jurisdiction with zero corporate tax.[31]) Nevertheless, Fix and Cochrane (2023) have recently traced the Irving corporate linkages within Canada using Statistics Canada's Intercorporate Ownership database.[32]

For the first generation of Canada's mega-wealthy (i.e., the people who actually made the money), being smart, ruthless and very hard-working was undoubtedly important — but that cannot be the whole story. There are many smart, ruthless and very hard-working Canadians who are not billionaires, or even millionaires. Luck — being in the right place, at the right time — always has been crucial. However, for the generations who inherit, hired money managers can take the work out of investment decisions and a portfolio of assets can be diversified so that its value does not depend on luck. It is much easier to avoid losing a fortune than to make it in the first place. Once the money has been made and succeeding generations inherit their portfolio of assets, they do not really need hard work, ruthlessness or luck. Whether they stay at the top depends on who they hire as financial advisers and who they employ as managers of the family companies — and on how much capital they may destroy by interfering personally in the hired manager's business decisions.[33]

Middle-Class Wealth

For middle-class Canadians, inequalities in the acquisition and inheritance of wealth take a very different path. The vast majority of Canadians know that they can never expect to live entirely off their inheritances, but they also know that even a small bequest can make a big difference to their quality of life. Historically, Canada's middle class has had a straightforward sequence of asset portfolios. The first big asset to acquire was the car, to get to work. The house was the next big purchase. Families who could get into the housing market would find their net worth increasing over time as the mortgage was paid down and the house was fixed up. Although a divorce, severe illness or a long layoff might derail the standard life plan, mortgage-free housing during retirement was a common aspiration — a plan which often implies some wealth will be left for the children to inherit (an important variable being whether ill health and long-term care costs in old age eat up the assets).

Owning a home provides savings in housing costs equal to rent avoided minus costs of ownership (i.e., property taxes, mortgage interest, insurance, repairs, etc.). As a mortgage is paid down, the mortgage interest component of payments declines. Home ownership in Canada has thus historically been partly a retirement saving strategy whose benefits are eventually received in the form of rent-free housing when the mortgage is paid off.

In Canada, there are also significant hidden advantages for the economic security of working-class people when they save in the form of home equity. If they have an unemployment spell longer than six months and exhaust any EI benefits and have to turn to social assistance, they will find that before they can make a social assistance claim they have to spend down almost all of their financial wealth. In 2022, for example, single people on social assistance could only keep $2,000 in liquid assets in Nova Scotia, $1,500 in Saskatchewan and $2,235 in Alberta.[34] But social assistance clients are not forced to sell their homes, so savings in home equity are protected. Also, people over sixty-five who have to depend on the Guaranteed Income Supplement (GIS) will find that their GIS payments are cut by $0.50 for each dollar of interest or dividend income they receive from any financial savings. If they had instead saved by paying down their home mortgage so they could be mortgage-free in their old age, there would be no cut in their GIS payments.

The Canadian system thus builds in major financial incentives to home ownership, but homes are much more than just economic assets for many people. Owning a home provides the security that the landlord cannot evict you and the autonomy to decide for yourself how to fix your place up. Home ownership also implies belonging to a particular neighbourhood and having membership in a particular community — what some would call social stability. Since even the best-laid plans can be derailed by life events such as divorce, a long spell of unemployment or a major illness, some people do "lose their homes" — and the connotations of that phrase reveal that home ownership has, for many people, much more than just monetary significance.

Because middle-class Canadians tend to have pretty straightforward financial affairs, surveys of the population can paint a fairly accurate picture of the net worth of the middle 90 per cent of Canadians. Figure 6.1 (taken from Statistics Canada's Survey of Financial Security) presents the net worth (in 2022 dollars, and including the value of pension equity) of households at the 10th, 30th, 50th, 70th and 90th percentiles of the distribution of net worth in 1999, 2005, 2012, 2016 and 2019.

Figure 6.1

Net Worth of Canadian Families, 1999–2019

(2022 dollars)

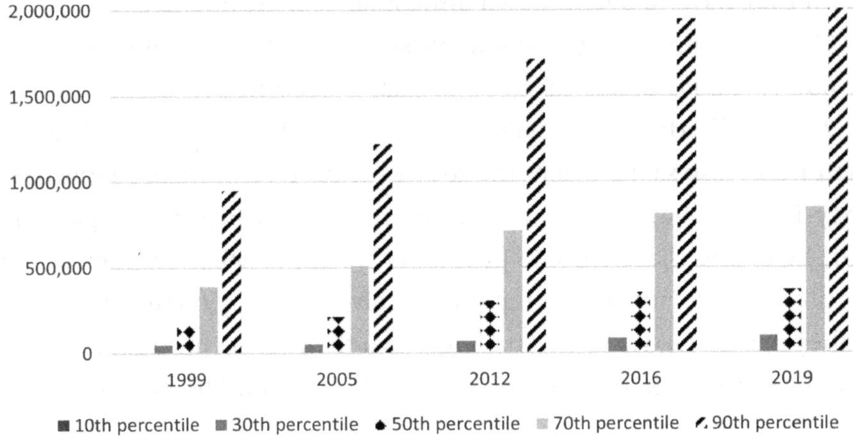

Source: Statistics Canada Table: 11-10-0049-01

As Figure 6.1 shows, from 1999 to 2019, there was a significant increase in the net worth of most Canadian middle-class families. However, that was in large part driven by the rising price of houses. In a rising market, financial leverage works to the advantage of borrowers: if you buy a house for $400,000 with a down payment of $40,000 and a mortgage of $360,000 and the house price then goes up to $500,000, your $40,000 investment has become net home equity of $140,000, for a capital gain of $100,000, which is completely tax-free. For years, middle-class Canadians have gotten used to making major, tax-free capital gains on their houses, which produce increases in their wealth far greater than anything they could conceivably save out of their annual salaries.

But there is a potential downside to mortgage financing of owner-occupied housing. If the market turns down, the homeowner eats all the loss. In the example above, if the market price of the house in the example above dropped to $350,000, all the down payment would evaporate and the borrower would be "under water," owing $10,000 more on the house than it was worth.[35] The fate of US homeowners during the Great Recession of 2009 to 2010 provided an important example of how this can happen. Just as in Canada, the family home is the main asset of the middle class in the US. The 2001 to 2007 boom in housing prices swelled the paper values of these assets but middle-class Americans were highly exposed to the subsequent bust in prices. As a result, between 2007 and 2009, the net worth of the median American household fell by 35.1 per cent, hundreds of thousands of homes were lost to foreclosure, the banking system came close to collapse and the world economy went into recession.[36]

For the many Canadians who bought their homes decades ago and just want to continue living in the same place, it is the use value of housing that matters. From one year to the next, increases in housing prices are seen by many people as just a paper gain — one that often appears somewhat surreal compared to their normal daily expenses. It is when the house is eventually sold or passes by inheritance to the next generation that capital gains have a real impact.[37] Indeed, the size of capital gains on housing relative to the savings out of salary that are remotely possible means that capital gains on housing have become the main source of family wealth acquisition for middle-class Canadians.

In 1952, for example, my parents bought (for $12,500) the house I grew up in. It was then on the eastern outskirts of Ottawa, but when it was sold fifty-five years later for $450,000, Ottawa had expanded so much further to the east that it was almost inner city. The new buyer bulldozed the house to the ground and built a monster home on the site. They effectively paid $450,000 for the land alone, which had increased in value as Ottawa's population grew from 282,000 in 1950 to over $1.1 million in 2007 when the house was sold. For my parents, who bought in at the start of this population growth, the total capital gain was considerably greater than the savings possible out of annual salary income.[38]

As a country urbanizes and the population increases, cities spread outward as they grow. Land in the city core increases in value, so the early generations of rural-urban migrants get the increase in land value that comes as early suburbs become inner city. In the next Osberg generation, when my brother and I left home, he went west and bought a house in West Vancouver and I went east and bought a house in Halifax.

He timed it just right and sold his place at a market peak for multiple millions, moving to Vancouver Island. Although my capital gains in Halifax (if I were to sell) would be under 10 per cent of his, neither he nor I could possibly have saved out of our annual incomes anything like the increase in the value of our houses. Wealth acquisition for Canada's middle class is now primarily about capital gains in the housing market.

However, on a day-to-day basis, the capital gains of housing wealth are, for many people, a somewhat unreal paper gain only vaguely connected to real life. Houses are not like financial assets, such as shares or bonds, whose only purpose is to store and accumulate purchasing power. Housing is a necessity of life, recognized as a basic human right since the 1948 Universal Declaration of Human Rights. When economists inform their friends and relations that they are now all millionaires due to the increase in house prices in their area, a common response is: "But I'd just have to buy another house, because I have to live somewhere. I'm no better off, if I sell this house and buy another similar one, because house prices have gone up everywhere." That response hints at an important problem with economists' calculation of net worth. If the calculation of total potential consumption at a point in time includes the market value of owner-occupied housing, what would one do the day after consuming one's net worth?

When, roughly eighty years ago, J. R. Hicks suggested that "income" should be defined as: "The maximum value a person can consume during a period and still be as well-off at the end of the period as at the beginning," he defined the perspective that remains dominant in economics. At dinner parties, economists can (and do) sometimes try to explain to their home-owning friends and relations how rich they now really are, due to capital gains on housing, because if they sold their houses they could buy many, many consumer goodies that they could not have remotely afforded several years ago. But when those friends and relations respond that they are just living the same life in the same place as they were years ago and to "be as well-off at the end of the period as at the beginning" means, for them, living in the same type of house in the same place, the dinner table discussion usually moves on to other topics.

In the aftermath of such a collision of perspectives, some economists may then start to compare the reactions of their professional colleagues and the sentiments of their friends and relations on the housing issue. Economist colleagues, all well-schooled in the importance of opportunity cost and the calculation of market values, universally take it as obvious that the market price of housing (net of any mortgage debt) should be counted as part of personal wealth and that capital gains on housing are indistinguishable in value from capital gains in the stock market. However, friends and relations who have not had the benefit of years of graduate education in economics often seem to think of housing a bit differently. They usually do have a clear idea of recent real estate price trends (perhaps because it's a standard topic of neighbourhood gossip) and it certainly is a source of security to them to know they could get a lot of money for the house if they ever really needed cash in an emergency. However, their houses are their homes, which carry their memories of family life, embed them in communities and securely provide a necessity of life. By exempting from taxation capital gains on owner-occupied housing, tax law in Canada recognizes, to some extent, this alternative perspective on housing.

As they age, middle-class people also usually acquire more consumer durables and sometimes RRSPs, but direct ownership of financial assets has never been all that common in the Canadian population. In 2019, for example, only 8 per cent of Canadian family units owned directly any stocks at all (and half of that 8 per cent owned less than $23,000).[39] Roughly three-eighths of the workforce have a job with a pension plan, and if they can stay in that job, their net worth also increases with job tenure as pension plan equity builds up. However, because home equity is by far the dominant form of wealth holding for most of middle-class Canada, wealth acquisition by the middle class is dominated by the housing market — a capital gains lottery whose prizes depend on where and when the house was bought and when it was sold.

However, only the people who can buy a ticket get to play the lottery. In recent years a major problem for the "typical" Canadian pattern of middle-class wealth acquisition is whether younger families can get together enough down payment for a house in a period of rapidly rising house prices. Since children typically have parents who are twenty or thirty years older, the people who are in their late twenties or early thirties and want to buy houses usually have parents who are somewhere in their fifties or early sixties. At this age, some upper-middle-class parents may have the cash flow and the retirement security to help their kids with down payments on desirable housing — but parents who have most of their wealth tied up in their own house and are worrying about their own retirement years are unlikely to be able to come up with much cash, especially comparing their savings to current house prices. Many adult children are thus out of luck.

The escalation of housing prices in Canadian cities means that in Toronto or Vancouver, and increasingly in cities like Halifax and Montreal, dual incomes and significant family money are now required even for a starter home. People without family money to help can sometimes still get into home ownership if they are willing to buy a small enough house or drive far enough into the suburbs. But particularly in big cities, the quality and commuting time associated with lower-cost housing makes a huge difference to well-being. Inequalities in commuting time and available living space do not show up in statistics on household money income. The capital gains from getting into the housing market earlier also are not measured in household income.[40] Hence when house prices are high and rising, family money, which helps with home ownership and enables an inheritance of well-being, does not show up in statistics on inequality, even if the growth of Canadian cities means that having serious family money has become far more important than it used to be.

Poor People and Their Assets

As Figure 6.1 illustrates, between 1999 and 2019 the net worth of families in the top half of the wealth distribution grew strongly, while wealth at the bottom grew far less. Indeed, in Figure 6.1 it is hard to even see the net worth of families at the 10th percentile of net worth ($1,668 in 1999 increasing to $3,300 in 2019). Most people in the bottom 20 per cent of the wealth distribution do not have much in the way of either assets or debts. Rent, food and other monthly expenses soak up their incomes. Both liabilities and assets are low because poor people often cannot get credit, either because they do not have any security to pledge for loans or because they have acquired a bad credit rating.

The big asset that poor people in Canada most commonly possess is an automobile, which in rural and small-town Canada, where some sort of transportation is a practical necessity of life, is not really a discretionary choice. In urban areas, even a beaten-up, old junker of a car can save a lot of the time and hassle of buying groceries and getting to work or enabling employment in the first place. In general, the "use value" and the "exchange value"[41] of the assets of poor people diverge significantly because although the dollar market value of their consumer durables is not much, the ownership of even a few assets makes a big difference to quality of life. Poor people are often strong defenders of property rights, which is not surprising when you realize that property matters most when you have least of it. Precisely because poor people have so few assets, the things they do have matter a lot for them.

Wealth at the Top: The Instability Implications of Increasing Inequality

> *To turn $100 into $110 is work. To turn $100 million into $110 million is inevitable.*[42]
>
> — *Edgar Bronfman*

At the very top of the Canadian wealth distribution, one finds both inherited wealth (e.g., the Thomson, Weston, Desmarais, Rogers, Shaw, Richardson, Bronfman and Irving families) and some new money. Residential real estate is part of their asset picture, but most of the portfolios of very affluent people are business equity, stocks, bonds and other financial instruments. Because wealth generates income, the very wealthy are also at the top of the income distribution.

Large investors in private equity investments historically have had returns in the 10 per cent or more range (which implies that a one-billion-dollar portfolio would generate $100 million or more in annual income).[43] The very wealthy can afford to hire the best investment advisors and they have financial opportunities that are unavailable to small savers. Even after financing extravagant levels of consumption, the higher rates of return on very large portfolios produce a flow of savings each year that grow those portfolios even larger.[44] As Chapter 1 shows, when the rate of income growth in Canada has been higher, the higher one climbs in the income distribution. As the incomes of the top 1 per cent increase (and as the incomes of the top 0.1 per cent and top 0.01 per cent increase even faster), there is an increasing flow of their savings into financial markets.

Meanwhile, middle-class families are going deeper into debt,[45] often to finance increasingly expensive housing. But increasing financial assets at the top and increasing financial liabilities in the middle are really two sides of the same coin. Financial instruments are always inherently both an asset to the holder and a liability to the issuer. In order for the increasingly affluent, as a group, to acquire ever more net financial assets, somebody else has to acquire ever more net financial liabilities (either directly as greater household debt or indirectly as taxpayers who eventually will have to pay for increased government debt).

Indeed, macroeconomic balance requires it. In economics, every market transaction can be seen from two sides: every market transaction is both a sale to the seller and a purchase to the buyer. Total spending therefore always has to equal total receipts.[46] But for total income and total expenditure to balance, whenever the increasingly affluent abstain from spending some of their increased income and save more, somebody else has to spend more than their income and save less. By borrowing and spending, debtors — both households and governments — balance the behaviour of creditors and maintain the real flows of the economy. Over-spending by debtors is always the flipside of under-spending by creditors.

If greater borrowing and spending are insufficient, at a given inflation-adjusted rate of interest, to balance greater savings and maintain total income and expenditure, downward pressure on interest rates and aggregate output results. A growing chorus of economists[47] has argued that increasing inequality implies that Western economies have a structural tendency to secular stagnation, due to an excess and ever-increasing flow of savings coming from the rising incomes of the very affluent. The result has been a decline in the world real interest rate, particularly since 2000.[48] When the general level of interest rates declines, investors seeking a target rate of return must assume increasing risk in their asset portfolios to generate any given income target.

The financial crisis of 2008 and the Great Recession which followed were facilitated by financial innovation in the United States and by a facilitative regulatory environment, which papered over increasing risk by allowing banks to repackage risky mortgage loans and sell them as safe financial assets. But the key underlying driving force was the flow of savings into financial markets. Since top incomes were rising robustly, middle-class aspirations to try to "keep up" in consumption meant that willing borrowers were available to absorb the increase in credit available. Higher housing prices (driven by the expectation of yet more increases in house prices) allowed households to support increased consumption through refinancing of their mortgages, so household debt rose even as household incomes stagnated. This combination of factors successfully maintained high aggregate demand and relatively low unemployment in the United States through 2007 but continued stagnation in the incomes of poor and middle-income households meant loans and leverage (the debt/income ratio) kept rising.

Both the Great Depression of 1929 and the Great Recession of 2008 were preceded by a sharp increase in income and wealth inequality and by a similarly sharp increase in debt-to-income ratios among lower- and middle-income households. But debt-to-income ratios for the middle class cannot increase forever. Slow income growth for middle-income households means that with continued borrowing, their loan leverage keeps growing. Eventually, debts begin to be perceived as unsustainable, and a financial crisis, with severe implications for the real economy,[49] becomes inevitable — only needing a trigger.[50]

Residential construction has long been an important, and quite volatile, component of total investment and the business cycle. Indeed, "housing starts and the change in housing starts together form the best forward-looking indicator of the cycle."[51] Periodic housing booms are fed by the cost and availability of credit and by self-reinforcing expectations of future increases in house prices. Since owner-occupied housing is the main asset type held by middle-income households, home mortgages mean financial leveraging has become a normal middle-class phenomenon and middle-class net worth has become very sensitive to house price changes and interest rates. But as households become more indebted, their probability of default increases — which means that financial assets become increasingly fragile.

Chapter 2 discusses the problem of "debt stability" in the context of public sector debt. Its logic is equally applicable to households and the private sector. And it is as true for individuals as it is for governments that the burden of debt depends on the size of debt relative to income and on the interest rate paid on that debt. If the interest rate is zero or near zero (as was the case during the Covid-19 pandemic)[52] then even a mountain of debt has very little immediate cost. However, if interest rates increase when the debt is large (as in 2023 and 2024), an ever-increasing fraction of revenue must go to servicing the debt rather than paying for current consumption, a process which is eventually unsustainable.[53] For governments facing a collapse in real output and employment — such as caused by the financial crisis in 2008–09 or by Covid-19 in 2020–22 — a large stock of government debt outstanding adds enormously to the macroeconomic demand management problem because increases in tax rates and/or cuts to program expenditures would reduce total demand and collapse income growth, thereby worsening the debt situation.

If governments, firms and households all simultaneously spend less and try to pay down their debt, that decrease in spending means there is less total demand for goods and services. A shrinkage in total purchases necessarily implies a corresponding shrinkage of total sales and total income. Hence, if all sectors — households, firms and governments — were to attempt to pay down their debts simultaneously by spending less than their incomes, a recession would be the inevitable result. From a macroeconomic perspective, unbalanced income growth rates and ever-increasing income inequality therefore mean that one instability leads to another — and pressures intensify over time as the increasing income share of the top 1 per cent implies their savings flows are an increasing fraction of national income.

Because financial and real flows are interdependent, unbalanced income growth rates produce rising stocks of financial assets at the top and greater stocks of financial liabilities elsewhere. Increasing financial fragility then produces an increasing probability of a financial crisis, with big impacts on real economic activity. When governments respond with deficit spending, this accumulates as public debt, which itself becomes increasingly fragile whenever interest rates exceed the growth rate. But if interest rates are kept low to stimulate consumer demand, households acquire levels of private debt they can only continue to finance if ultra-low nominal interest rates continue indefinitely. And so the global economy has limped along, never fully recovering but staggering from instability to instability.

Implications

Increasing macroeconomic instability is a long-term implication of unbalanced growth, increasing top-end income inequality and highly unequal wealth distribution. Because large fortunes produce large incomes, incomes and savings grow fastest at the top and the growing imbalances of financial assets and liabilities produce a tendency for recurrent financial crises, which feed the risk of long-term and recurrent recessions. Chapter 3 discusses the increased social stresses produced when elite incomes grow much faster than those of the middle class. Those social stresses are magnified in impact when economic growth slows and becomes more unstable.

The importance of increasing wealth inequality is also heightened by the fact that in all the advanced countries capital income has been increasing as a share of total national income. When the interest rate on capital exceeds the rate of economic growth, capital grows at the rate of interest while income grows at the (slower) rate of economic growth. The capital/income ratio therefore necessarily rises.[54]

These trends are likely to be reinforced by future technological change. In its 2024 study of the economic impacts of artificial intelligence, the IMF noted that in addition to its impacts on the inequality of labour incomes, "AI adoption also leads to increases in the return on capital, raising capital income, which in turn increases wealth and wealth inequality consistently with the initial distribution of asset holdings."[55] As capital income becomes a larger and larger share of total income, the mechanisms which determine wealth holdings necessarily become increasingly important.

For the middle and upper-middle class, the lottery of real estate price fluctuations is, in practice, far more important than savings from salary in determining the wealth of the family line. Luck takes a different form in the business world, where being in the right sector at the right time with the right product has been crucially important in the origins of the great family fortunes that dominate the top of Canada's wealth distribution. Once great fortunes have been created, professional management and diversification of the portfolio can ensure the perpetuation and growth of the family fortune over time. Since Canada, unlike most other developed nations, does not have inheritance or estate or wealth taxes, successive generations of Canada's financial aristocracy can inherit and accumulate even greater wealth without impediment. The great family fortunes of Canada's economic elite thus continue to dominate the top end of our distributions of income and wealth, even as recurrent financial crises destabilize economic growth.

Chapter 7
OUTCOMES AND OPPORTUNITIES

Back in the 1950s and 1960s in Canada, average real wages grew strongly while balanced economic growth meant the inequality of annual incomes was stable. The introduction to this book starts with the observation there is considerable nostalgia for that economic recipe. But were those times, from the point of view of women, Indigenous Canadians and people of colour, really the "good old days"? Back then, people concerned about social justice fought for minimum wage laws to prevent the exploitation of labour, but those laws set a different floor on hourly wages for men and for women. (For example, in Ontario in 1964, the minimum wage was $1.00 an hour for men and $0.85 per hour for women.) In those days, gender inequality was part of the landscape, from the top to the bottom of Canadian society. It was, for example, taken as normal in 1981, as earlier, that all the justices of the Supreme Court of Canada would be male.[1] Stark differences in average incomes, unemployment and educational attainment for First Nations and people of colour were then similarly thought to be unremarkable. First Nations people did not even have the right to vote until 1960. One could go on and on about the ignored injustices of the "good old days."

Today, the Canadian Charter of Rights and Freedoms[2] clearly outlaws "discrimination based on race, national or ethnic origin, colour, religion, sex, age or mental or physical disability." Gender balance in senior public appointments (e.g., to the federal cabinet) has become a major issue — always talked about, even if not always actually attained. In 1959, women accounted for 6 per cent of medical school graduates, but since 2004 women have been the majority.[3] Women are also now the majority of new lawyers.[4] Although today few people would claim discrimination and bias have been eliminated from Canadian life, progress has been made in breaking down old barriers to individual success — for example, in reducing the inequalities between men and women in access to high-paying professions.

But how can these improvements in equality of opportunity be reconciled with the increasing inequality in income shares documented in Chapter 1? What exactly is the connection between inequalities of outcome and inequalities of opportunity? There are entire books on "inequality in Canada" that discuss inequality in average incomes between groups of people, as defined by gender, race, religion, ethnicity, country of origin or some other characteristic.[5] But suppose all inequalities in average income between such groups were eliminated. Suppose discrimination in access to top positions was zero. Logically speaking, when all members of all groups have equal opportunity to obtain high positions, this also implies all members of all groups also have equal opportunity to get low positions; after all, the people belonging to previously favoured groups who do not now get into the top positions have to end up somewhere else.

A world where all equity-seeking groups have equal opportunity and are, like all other population groups, proportionately represented among corporate executives and company directors, doctors, lawyers and all other desirable social positions is also a world where equity-seeking groups and all other population groups achieve equal opportunity in being proportionately represented among the homeless. In the same way that pouring enough water into a glass to make it half-full will simultaneously make it half-empty, one can describe equal opportunity either in terms of its impact at the top of the income distribution or in terms of its impact at the bottom — the one logically implies the other.[6] So what does greater equality of opportunity for access to high-paying professions or positions imply for the inequalities of labour incomes? And even if opportunities for earning labour income were equalized, total compensation of employees was only about half (50.8 per cent) of GDP in Canada in 2023.[7] What about the other half of national income? How important are inequalities of opportunity for the inheritance of wealth?

Adanac: Equality of Opportunity and the Inequality of Labour Incomes

As a starting point for discussion, let's imagine a very simple economy (we can call it "Adanac") in which there are only two types of jobs and two pay rates. Executives make $200,000 per year, and secretaries make $40,000. Let's assume we start with a situation in which there are four men and four women and all the executives in Adanac are male and all the secretaries are female.[8] Gender inequality is thus total. All women make $40,000. The men make $200,000 each, five times as much as each woman. In this imaginary economy, the bottom 50 per cent of people make $160,000 in total, which is 16.6 per cent of the economy's total income ($960,000). It can be shown that the Gini index of inequality of income in Adanac would be 0.334 — not so very different from the Gini index for Canada today.[9]

How important is gender in determining the inequality of income in Adanac? If we want to ask how much of total inequality of income in Adanac is due to inequality between groups (i.e., between males and females) and how much of total inequality of income is due to inequality within groups (i.e., inequality among males and among females), the answer may appear to be easy. Since there is zero income inequality among men and zero income inequality among women in Adanac, an analyst who starts from the assumption that personal characteristics are what cause income will conclude that all income inequality in Adanac is due to between-group inequality.[10] An analyst who makes such an assumption might then jump to the conclusion that gender-based discrimination is what causes income inequality and that reducing discrimination would therefore reduce income inequality.

Table 7.1

Illustrative Example of an Occupational Structure

$200,000	[EXEC 1]	EXEC 2]	[EXEC 3]	[EXEC 4]
$40,000	[SEC 1]	[SEC 2]	[SEC 3]	[SEC 4]

But would income inequality decrease if there was greater equality of opportunity? If we could reduce or eliminate male/female inequality of opportunity in Adanac, what would happen to income inequality?

Imagine that Executive 4 trades places with Secretary 4. Executive 4 is now female and earns $200,000 while Secretary 4 is now male and makes $40,000 so the distribution of incomes among men changes from {200,000, 200,000, 200,000, 200,000} to {200,000, 200,000, 200,000, 40,000}, and the distribution of incomes among women changes from {40,000, 40,000, 40,000, 40,000} to {40,000, 40,000, 40,000, 200,000}. This change introduces within-group income inequality among men and women but the total inequality of incomes among all people remains the same: of the eight people in this example, four are still making $200,000 and the other four are still making $40,000. The Gini index, or any other index, of inequality of income among all people is completely unchanged. The occupational structure of the economy has not changed: executives still make five times the salary of secretaries. The only thing that has changed is the assignment mechanism for highly paid and poorly paid positions. Although increasing equality of access to highly paid jobs does not necessarily have any impact at all on the total inequality of incomes, in an accounting sense, part of total inequality can now be associated with within-group inequality and part can be associated with between-group inequality, so the proportion of income inequality associated with within-group and between-group differences changes.

When males occupy three executive positions and one secretarial position, the total income of all men is $640,000, so the average income of men declines to $160,000. With three secretaries and one executive, the total income of women is now $320,000 so the average income of women rises to $80,000. The male/female ratio of average pay thus falls from 5:1 to 2:1. This would be an improvement, but a 2:1 gender pay ratio would also often be seen as an indicator of continuing inequality of opportunity.[11] If one more male executive (#3) and female secretary were to trade places, men would then earn {200,000, 200,000, 40,000, 40,000} and women would make {40,000, 40,000, 200,000, 200,000}. Men and women would then be equally likely to become an executive or a secretary, and average wages would then be equal for men and women. All the inequality of incomes would be associated with within-group inequality while between-group inequality would fall to zero. Discrimination between men and women in access to employment would completely disappear in this final case. Nevertheless, the Gini index would still be 0.334 and inequality in the distribution of income among all people would be unchanged.

These Adanac examples are intended to illustrate the importance of the demand side of labour markets — the hierarchical structure of jobs that generate earnings for individuals and the pay differentials that go with these jobs. These examples do not imply that eliminating gender discrimination, or other forms of discrimination, in access to jobs is unimportant. Non-discrimination and procedural equity in access to positions of economic advantage are important social objectives in and of themselves. What these examples do show is that improving procedural equity and the fairness of the mechanisms of allocation of people to positions with unequal rewards does not in and of itself change those unequal rewards — i.e., change income inequality. Non-discrimination in access to jobs with unequal wages does not reduce the inequality of the salaries of the jobs which employers offer.

As well, reducing inequality in opportunities for labour income does not affect income from capital — which is roughly half of GDP in Canada. The Adanac example talks only about the pay received by workers in different jobs. Who owns the firms that they work for, and who will inherit that ownership, is unmentioned. Inequality in the opportunity to receive capital income is unexamined.

Of course, gender identities are more complex than a simple male/female binary and in using male/female differences to illustrate unequal opportunities for labour income, the Adanac examples have only looked at one of many possible dimensions which can be used to divide Canadians into groups on the basis of individual personal characteristics. The average incomes of Canadians of different ages, genders, races, religions, ethnicities, regions of residence, countries of origin, years of education, Indigenous status, sexual preference or other characteristics could also be compared. Along all these dimensions, one will find differences in average income. Some of the characteristics associated with income differences (like region of residence or years of education) can be changed by individuals during their lifetime, while others (like country of origin) are more immutable.[12] How much does it matter if these differences depend on individuals' choices?

The Roles of Education

Thus far, the Adanac example has been framed as an example of the differentials in pay associated with being male and female. But Adanac would have the same Gini index of inequality of incomes if gender did not matter and access to executive positions paying $200,000 and secretarial jobs paying $40,000 was determined solely by who had more years of education. The question for individuals would then become "How much education is enough?" to get the best jobs — and the answer has changed over time in Canada. A century ago, when high school graduation was relatively rare in Canada, one could get started on the path to top management with Grade Twelve (i.e., in most provinces, Grade Thirteen in Ontario). In the 1960s, a Bachelor of Commerce degree was enough to get hired as a management trainee. Today, an MBA is often the minimum credential needed to get in the management door.

But why might firms want to reserve their best positions with the best pay for the people with the most years of education? Why might the level of education needed for top jobs change over time? One possible explanation is that the distribution of innate intelligence probably has not changed much for many centuries. Really smart people are probably just as rare today as they ever were. If technological and market change is rapid and if the specialized skills and knowledge which people need to do their jobs well are largely learned on the job, it makes sense for firms to try to hire the smartest people, who can learn the fastest, for their most important jobs. Since everyone would like to be thought to be smart, firms have to look for a reliable signal of relative ability. Success in school is that sort of credential; it signals a person's underlying ability to learn. Even if job candidates studied irrelevant subjects, somebody who got an A-plus in ancient Greek or medieval history or differential calculus is probably a better bet for a top job than somebody who got a C-minus on the same exam.

In this "signalling" or "credentials" perspective, education is a signal of ability and the role of educational institutions, like universities,[13] is to provide credentials to enable the relative ranking of individuals in the queue for desirable positions — but the distribution of earnings is determined by the number and relative pay of positions in the hierarchy of jobs, that is, by the demand side of the labour market. The average level of education increases over time because whenever one individual tries to get ahead by getting more schooling to signal that they are smarter than average, it is in everyone else's interest to also get more education to avoid falling behind. Increasing years of education therefore becomes a competitive necessity in the labour market.

In the Adanac examples, it is the structured hierarchy of positions in a market economy, and the pay rates which accompany those positions, which cause the overall level of labour income inequality. Individual personal characteristics (like gender or education) just determine each person's relative rank in the queue for desirable positions. In these hypothetical examples, the overall distribution of income is determined by the distribution of jobs and the pay rates that go with those jobs; income inequality comes entirely from the structure of jobs and their associated incomes (i.e., from the demand side of labour markets). Institutional changes may alter the wage structure — if secretaries were to unionize and successfully demand higher wages, inequality would decrease. Technological change, such as artificial intelligence, which eliminated the need for most of the executive jobs would also change the inequality of earnings. The key issue for labour income inequality is the number of different types of jobs and the rate of pay attached to each job.

Real-world Canada is, of course, a much more complicated place than hypothetical Adanac. The Adanac example is drawn starkly, to make the point that income determination and income distribution are two different issues. Income determination is about *who* gets higher earnings. Income distribution is about *how many* people get high-paying jobs, *how many* people get low-paying jobs and *how far apart* their salaries are.

Much economic analysis has, however, made the assumption that people's personal characteristics are all that matters for pay determination. In the "human capital" model of the supply side of labour markets, it is assumed that people with more education get higher pay because education increases the productivity of their labour time.

At one level, for the self-interested decisions of individuals, the arguments between the "human capital" and the "credentials" perspectives do not matter much. For any individual, the calculation of whether or not it is financially worthwhile to get more education is not really affected at all by *why* one can expect to get a higher salary with more education. The investment motivation to get a university degree is the same, regardless of whether or not the higher pay of graduates is because a degree causes an improvement in productivity or because a degree is a credential that successfully signals higher ability.[14] For individual decisions, it is also reasonable to assume that since there are millions of other people in the labour market whose decisions will likely remain the same, the existing general level of wages and employment will likely remain unchanged.

When, for example, I initially thought about the possibility of getting a PhD myself, the relevant issue for assessing the financial returns to my personal decision was the fact that one needs a PhD to be a university professor. Why a PhD is needed for an academic job — whether the degree represents human capital or a credential — is not particularly important for personal decision-making. As an individual, I could also be pretty sure my decision, one way or another, would have no effect at all on the general level of wages and the job characteristics of people with PhDs. Hence, I could reasonably assume the type of job and the wages that PhDs were then getting was a good predictor of the pay that I could expect in the future if I got a PhD.

But those would not be reasonable assumptions to use in predicting what would happen if everyone were to get a PhD. If we are trying to figure out whether educational policy can reduce income inequality, we are trying to predict what is likely to happen if there were a general change in people's education. It is not a reasonable assumption to think that if everyone got a PhD, all the new PhDs would get exactly the same types of jobs as PhDs now do and that the current returns to a doctorate would remain unchanged.

For public policy decisions, the arguments between the human capital and the credentials perspectives matter, a lot. If the credentials model is correct, then the real world looks a bit like Adanac, where a person's relative rank in the job queue is what matters for their individual earnings and the distribution of earnings is largely unaffected when the general level or the inequality of education changes. If the human capital model is at least partially correct, more equal education would reduce inequality in the distribution of earnings. Many economists think (like me) that there is some truth in both perspectives. But saying that is not saying much, since the precise implications for the overall inequality of wages and employment of a general change in the supply of schooling depend on what is also happening to the structure of demands for skilled labour, and structural shifts in labour demand are very hard to predict — as our current uncertainty about the long-run impacts of artificial intelligence on the structure of employment exemplifies.

Education and Inequality of Opportunity

Nevertheless, it is clear that education matters for *who* gets ahead in the labour market — i.e., for earnings determination. There is little uncertainty in the data about the fact that the inheritance of educational advantages is one of the chief mechanisms for the intergenerational transmission of occupational status. Countries with more inequality of income also have more inequality of opportunity, partly because when parents have unequal incomes and can spend what they want on the education and other forms of the human capital of their own children, the inequality of income among adults inevitably helps determine the inequality of opportunity among children.

In all countries, childhoods differ and childhoods matter. In early childhood, people get different levels of nutrition and different life lessons about values and habits from their parents. When they are a bit older, children attend the schools and live in the neighbourhoods that their parents choose. Inequalities in primary and secondary education and whatever after-school preparation for life children are going to get all happen while their parents are making the choices — choices which determine the later options available to people (e.g., for post-secondary education).[15]

Because richer parents can afford to spend more on their kids, "countries with a higher degree of income inequality are also characterized by greater inequality of opportunity — less unequal countries are also those that have a higher degree of intergenerational mobility."[16] The observation that earnings inequality deepens through inheritance of human capital over generations is hardly new. As the great English economist Alfred Marshall remarked in 1913, "the professional classes especially, while generally eager to save some capital for their children are even more on the alert for opportunities of investing it in them" while the children of the working classes "go to their graves with undeveloped abilities and faculties." Marshall insisted especially that "this evil is cumulative"[17] — and for decades sociologists and economists have studied the intergenerational transmission of socio-economic status.[18]

In the human capital model, the intergenerational inheritance process has been formalized by including parental altruism and intergenerational bequest in the determination of human capital. When parents care about both their own lifetime consumption and the well-being of their children and when the children similarly care about both their own lifetime consumption and the well-being of the grandchildren, altruism within the family links wealth, income and well-being over generations. From the human capital perspective, the unequal distribution of income of each cohort of parents is partly due to their own unequal inheritances from the grandparents' and great-grandparents' generations, and the unequal incomes of parents enable unequal bequests to their own children.[19]

For parents, the key constraint on the size and composition of their bequest to their children is their own lifetime income.[20] The children of low lifetime-income parents may get some human capital while children of high lifetime-income parents get both more human capital and a financial inheritance. Because the parents' lifetime incomes enable the bequests received by their children and the incomes of the parents depend on the inheritances they got from the grandparents, whose lifetime incomes depended in turn on the inheritances received from the great-grandparents, each family line is linked through the generations to those coming before and those going after.

A pure market economy therefore is a dynastic society.[21] Bad luck in investments may imply that, in the long run, rich families may become poorer, but this is no consolation to children from poor families in any given generation. Inequality of outcome in one generation necessarily begets inequality of opportunity for the next, but that inequality of opportunity is also socially inefficient. Because the smart children of poor parents are not able to increase their human capital as much as the dull children of rich parents, talent is wasted and total output is lower than it could be with equal opportunity.

In this framework, public schools can increase both equity and efficiency. Equity is increased because public schools provide more equal resources for the education of all children, irrespective of the income of their parents, thereby increasing equality of opportunity. Efficiency is enhanced because the talents of poor children do not go undeveloped when their parents do not have the resources to invest adequately in their children's education. By taxing the income of all adults in order to provide a more equal education[22] to all children, the public school system redistributes opportunities. If this taxation and public spending on education did not occur, each child's education would depend solely on the private resources of their own parents, and the more unequal the distribution of income is among parents, the more unequal the distribution of opportunity among children will be.

Increasing Inequalities: Outcomes and Opportunities

Chapter 3 discusses the long-term increase in the income share of the top 1 per cent and some of the implications of increasing top-end inequality for the other 99 per cent of Canadians. In addition to escalating norms of ostentatious consumption, the increasing manufacture of envy through aspirational advertising of luxury goods and the increasing political role of socially disconnected elites, there is the impact of Canada's increasing top-end income inequality on the inequality of opportunity. Because top 1 per cent parents care about their children, they can be expected to try to pass on their advantages to their children — which means purchasing as much influence over the social mobility process as they can. But when the parents are already at the top, the only possible future mobility for their children is down. And as the top of the income distribution pulls further away from the middle, the costs of any such downward mobility increase. So how can one expect Canada's affluent to react as the "drop from the top" increases?

As top incomes increase, affluent parents can spend ever more on enrichment activities for their children like summer camps and after-school coaching. They also can pitch in for extra fundraising, if their children are still in the public school system, or they can move their children into private schools. Since middle-class parents cannot afford to spend nearly as much on such activities, their kids have to depend more heavily on what is on offer in the ordinary public school system. So good neighbourhoods have good schools with "extras" like school excursions and music programs, while low-income neighbourhoods have schools with many problems, but no "extras" — different starting points for kids in the race of life.

The children of high-income, university-educated parents in Canada have always had a better chance of going to university and earning high incomes than the children of low-income, high school (or less) educated parents. That is true everywhere. However, historically Canada has prided itself on having had a public school system that did a better job of equalizing children's chances of higher income than the US or the UK. Comparative analysis of data on school achievement and later occupational success indicates that the difference which socio-economic origin makes to children's chances of university attendance and decent jobs has not been as great in Canada as has been observed in the US or the UK (although equality of opportunity in Scandinavian countries is even higher).[23] Partly this is due to our history: in most parts of Canada, private schools have historically only served a small percentage of families. These results are also a picture of the way things used to be; the data on intergenerational social mobility come from surveys of children who went to school in the early to mid-1980s, before the cutbacks to public expenditure that have since dominated school funding.

Nevertheless, Canada's past record of reducing inequalities of opportunity is, in my view, something to be proud of. The issue for today is whether Canadian governments will in the future fund the public school system at a rate that minimizes the achievement gap between children from affluent backgrounds and from poor families.

And unfortunately, the "human capital" model of labour markets omits an unpleasant reality of intergenerational social mobility: that top positions are scarce. Every year, for example, law schools, business schools and medical faculties deny admission to some applicants. Within firms, as the Adanac examples highlighted, there are a limited number of top slots; only some people get promoted. Parents, of course, care about whether it is their child who will get ahead. But when there is competition for a limited number of top slots, there is also an unavoidable reality: winning for some implies losing for others. If your chances of winning a foot race increase, my chances of winning the same race must necessarily decrease — and if there are only a hundred places available in law school, when your child fills one of those slots, my child's chances of getting in decrease. In intergenerational mobility, an improved probability of success for other people's children necessarily implies a poorer chance of success for your own child.

Although competition for top slots necessarily depends on relative rank, how much that matters depends on how unequal the outcomes are. If being an electrician, a teacher, a lawyer or a bus driver all imply, at the end of the day, a reasonably comparable lifestyle, then parents know their kids will be all right even if they do not get into the "best" law or medical school. When income differentials are small, a well-funded public school system which equalizes the chances that kids from richer and poorer backgrounds will do well in school is not much of a threat to upper-income families.

However, increasing inequality means the gaps between the payoffs to different positions widen. As the consequences of "falling behind" worsen, affluent parents feel more pressure to ensure their own child will "get ahead" — and they now often pass that pressure on to their children. For kids, one cost of increasing income inequality therefore is the "loss of childhood." As a university teacher, I now see much higher levels of stress among students than ever used to be the case, but I realize that their stress understates the problem because I am meeting students who are already in their late teens or early twenties and already got this far. The pressure parents apply to their school performance starts much, much earlier.

In daycares and primary schools, "intensive parenting" now sends the relentless message that life is a competitive struggle. Incessant extracurricular enrichment activities now soak up the time that kids used to have just to play and hang out with friends. In an age of increasing inequality, parents have strong reasons to emphasize good grades more than they used to because increasing inequality has raised the stakes for childhood educational achievement. But children bear much of the costs. As parents increasingly pressure their children, at ever-earlier ages, to excel in school, the children lose in playtime, in the additional stress associated with school success (or failure) and in the increased costs of dysfunctional teenage rebellion against these greater parental pressures.

Canadian parents have always had conflicted aspirations for their children. We want our child to win, in a fair race. We are, at least rhetorically, in favour of "equality of opportunity" and we simultaneously spend heavily on after-school enrichment activities to advantage our own children. In a low-inequality world, we would never really have to face the difficult question: which part of our values is, in the end, more important — is it the "fair race" part? Or is it the "my kid does not lose" part? When income inequality is low, the potential conflict is not as important, but as the inequality of outcomes increases, the incentives to ensure an advantage for your own child inevitably also increase.

For affluent parents, the dark side of more equal opportunity is that it increases the chances of downward intergenerational mobility. Equal opportunity social mobility would imply that everyone's chances are the same for every position, so the higher up a parent now is in the occupational hierarchy, the higher also are the chances of downward intergenerational mobility for their children. If the parent's income is now at the 95th percentile of the earnings distribution ($148,000 in 2021), equal opportunity for all children would mean that their child would have a 5 per cent chance of doing better than them in the labour market and a 95 per cent probability of doing worse. The big question for parents then is: what are the consequences for my children of downward mobility in income rank? In a relatively equal society, the answer is "not much," because differences in income rank do not imply large differences in standard of living. However, the greater the gaps between income ranks, the more downward mobility matters — and the closer the parents are to the top of the income distribution, the more likely it is that their children will lose from greater equality of opportunity and more social mobility.

Larger income gaps therefore increase the cost of a "drop from the top" for the children of the advantaged. When top-end inequality is increasing over time, the costs of potential downward intergenerational economic mobility for the children of affluent families are increasing over time. High-income parents then have to worry more about their children's potential competitors, and it becomes ever more important for high-income parents to give their own children every possible advantage. As a consequence, since there are always two ways to win a race — running faster yourself or ensuring that your competitors run slower — increasing inequality accentuates the reluctance of the top 1 per cent to pay the taxes that could help equalize opportunity by adequately funding public schools, because their own children now have more to lose from the competition of poor children.

In Canada, of course, everybody pays lip service to wanting greater equality of opportunity. And when the affluent back away from paying for the education of their children's competitors, it is usually in small increments as, for example, when they lobby for taxpayer support for private schools (as already exists in Alberta). But the bottom line is whether, in the long run, the affluent will actually pay for a good education for other people's children. In the longer run, as memories of a somewhat shared common childhood background in the public school system recede into stories about grandparents, it will become harder to maintain the myth of equality of opportunity. And the greater the success of the top 1 per cent in ensuring continued high socio-economic rank for their own children, the smaller the chances of upward mobility for children from poorer households. For the 99 per cent, increased inequality of opportunity is thus another cost of increasing income gaps.

Could Educational Reforms Possibly "Solve" the Inequality Problem in Time?

Probably partly because education is such an important determinant of individual earnings, a recurring feature of debates on increasing economic inequality is the suggestion that improving the education system can solve the problem of increasing inequality. But is this at all plausible?

Personally, I think there are many reasons to agree wholeheartedly that improving Canada's systems of education would be a "good thing" to do. A good education is important for many reasons, including (but not limited to) the positive impact of education on health, length of life, civic engagement, voting, volunteering, decreasing criminal activity and much more.[24] Many philosophers, over many years, have also remarked on the importance of a well-rounded education for the skills and the wisdom required to live a rich and well-considered life. In my view, better education is definitely something public policy should try to achieve. But I highly doubt that better education could "solve" Canada's inequality problems in anything like the timeframe required.

Firstly, as already noted in Chapters 2 and 3, Canada's trend to increasing inequality has been concentrated at the very top. The incomes of the top 1 per cent have been growing dramatically faster than those of the middle class — and most of their income is from capital, not labour. Even if improving the educational system reduced inequality of opportunity between the disadvantaged and the middle class and reduced wage differentials within the middle class (e.g., the university/high school average wage ratio), this would not solve the problem of how to equalize the growth rate of incomes of the bottom 99 per cent and top 1 per cent. Indeed, Canada's experience already offers a guide. For the working-age population (twenty-five to sixty-four), Canada's tertiary education attainment level (62.7 per cent in 2022) has been the highest of all OECD nations for many years.[25] Canada's investment in education has been a "good thing" for many other reasons, but it has not produced an equalization of income shares.

Initiatives to improve educational quality also inherently operate with long time lags. Even if an all-powerful leader could wave a magic wand and instantaneously and totally revolutionize primary and secondary education in 2025, they would have to wait twelve years to see, in 2037, the full impacts of these reforms on high school graduates. To improve education over current Canadian levels, some tertiary education would be needed, pushing the earliest possible labour force entry to 2041 or later. Even then, the impact on earnings inequality would initially be small, because every year only about one-fortieth of the workforce changes. Every year there is an inflow of new graduates entering the workforce and an outflow of people retiring. The impact on average labour force skills each year of changes in education is the differential between the education of the people who are entering the workforce and the education of those who are retiring. If people normally work for about forty years, it would be roughly twenty years before graduates of an improved education program became the majority of workers (i.e., around 2061, or about thirty-six years after the initial educational policy change). Until about then it would also be hard for researchers to detect any measurable impacts on the inequality of annual earnings (if they then existed and if they could be distinguished from the impacts of technological changes such as the introduction of artificial intelligence).

The beneficiaries of educational reform would, of course, also be the children who will be going to school and not their parents, who have already left school. But in 2022 roughly a third of Canadian adults did not intend to have children[26] and Chapter 2 reports polling data which indicated that many Canadians are quite unhappy, right now, with income inequality trends. Is it at all plausible to think that Canadians will put up with things as they are for the next thirty or forty years and be satisfied with waiting until 2060 or later to see the possible impacts of educational reforms on the income inequality of future generations?

Years ago in my high school English class, one of the plays we studied was Arthur Miller's classic, *Death of a Salesman*. The way I remember it, an unsuccessful salesman, Willy Lomax, comes home repeatedly from another day of failure but never surrenders the hope that one day he will succeed. I often think of that play, and the importance of hope, when I see yet another academic paper relentlessly emphasizing the importance of a good education for success. Whether or not a person will do well in formal education is something that is determined very early in life. Well before the age of twenty-five, most of us come to know what level of education we will attain — but there is a lot of life yet left to live. Although over 60 per cent of Canada's youth now go on to post-secondary education, that means roughly 40 per cent do not. Telling that large a fraction of the population that their chances for success in life are over before the age of twenty-five is not a recipe for social stability.

The Inheritance of Capital

A few years ago, I was attending a session on inequality of opportunity[27] at an international economics conference in Copenhagen. The academic papers being presented used all the best methodologies of modern economics, with state-of-the-art data and lots of sophisticated econometrics, to explain the intergenerational linkage between the earnings of parents and the earnings of their children. But as I was listening to the papers, my problem was that the day before I had gone on a city tour which had included a visit to the royal palace. The tour guide had explained that the king's palace in Copenhagen was relatively modest because during medieval times real power had resided with the five noble families who owned most of rural Denmark.[28] Their vast estates in the countryside, passed on by inheritance for many generations, gave them the wealth to dominate politics in Denmark for centuries (and thereby ensure their own continued wealth). So as I was sitting in the audience the next day at the conference, the question that occurred to me was: "If we could have used all these modern statistical methods to analyze inequality of opportunity during medieval times in Denmark, would we have found the Five Families?"

And the answer is NO. As already emphasized repeatedly, sample survey data can paint a reasonable picture of the behaviour of the bulk of the population but the very, very wealthy are not in the data. Even more fundamentally, when the only questions being asked by researchers concern the intergenerational transmission of earning power in the labour market, the importance of inherited wealth and income from capital will be ignored entirely.

We would be missing a big part of the inequality picture in medieval Denmark if we ignored the aristocracy and the inheritance of great landed estates — and when we ignore the billionaires and the inheritance of great family fortunes in modern Canada, we are also missing important parts of our modern reality. But a word search for "capital," "wealth," "dividends" or "interest" in academic papers on inequality of opportunity usually yields zero hits[29] — these aspects of social reality are simply not mentioned. (Words like "interest" do sometimes show up with other meanings — as in "interesting" or "object of interest.") Capital has somehow disappeared from the analysis of inequality of opportunity in capitalist societies. But when the productive capital stock, land or financial wealth and the incomes that derive from their ownership in rent or capital gains, interest, royalties or dividend payments just disappear from the discussion, one is ignoring the inequality of roughly half of the national income. Although the ownership of large, landed estates lost much of its social significance many years ago, the ownership of property retains its importance — at the very top of the income hierarchy ownership of property and income from capital are the main events.

Furthermore, in the twenty-first century, as ever before, capital outlives its owners, so great inequality of wealth in one generation necessarily implies greatly unequal inheritances of property received by the next generation. The relative importance of inheritances also increases when the capital stock grows more rapidly than GDP —

i.e., when the interest rate exceeds the growth rate of the economy.[30] Discussion of wealth inequality and inheritance is therefore central to any realistic discussion of inequality of opportunity.[31]

Furthermore, suppose that Canada really did, for all identity groups, equalize opportunity to earn income in the labour market and as a result, everyone ran harder in the race for success but the same number of people got promoted to the same positions. In a fairer world with more equal opportunity, more types of people would perceive the possibility of promotion. More people would be incentivized to put in the extra effort in their current job that would demonstrate that they deserve promotion. A fairer world is inherently a more competitive world for workers because the privilege that now partially protects advantaged groups (e.g., white males) would be gone.

However, although more equal chances in competitions for promotion would encourage more people to try for promotion, there are always two winners in any promotion competition: (1) the person who is promoted, and who thereby gains additional authority, pay and benefits; (2) the employer, who gets the benefit of additional unpaid work effort by the unsuccessful internal candidates who worked harder, but not harder enough, trying to get promoted. If discrimination has meant that in the past some people did not bother to try for promotion because they thought they would not have a fair chance, then more equal opportunities will produce a larger number of plausible candidates for promotion — but there is not necessarily any change in the number of promotions. A promotion competition with, for example, five internal candidates will end with one winner getting promoted and getting a higher wage and four losers whose unpaid extra efforts are a gain to the employer, but when ten internal candidates apply, the employer benefits from the extra efforts of nine losers.

If one thinks of the Canadian economy as being like a factory which employs a CEO, shift supervisors, a few accountants and salespeople and many shop floor workers, discussions of equality of opportunity in the labour market are about fairness in who gets what job in the factory, regardless of their gender, race, ethnicity, Indigenous identity or other characteristics. Equal opportunity for all types of people to be shop floor workers, supervisors, accountants or CEOs is an important issue because the salaries of these jobs differ significantly, and the vast majority of Canadians depend for their livelihoods on their labour earnings from their jobs. Equal opportunity for labour earnings would therefore be a very good thing for ethical reasons. And one should also recognize that equal opportunity for labour earnings would also probably elicit more work effort by the greater number of employees who then try for promotion, which would benefit the current owners of the factory and the heirs to their estates.

Conclusion

Many years ago, Anatole France remarked on "the majestic equality of the laws, which forbids rich and poor alike to sleep under bridges, to beg in the streets and to steal bread."[32] His point was that procedural equality does not at all imply substantive equality. This does not mean procedural equality in the application of rules and laws is unimportant; fairness in the application of rules and eliminating discrimination and inequalities of opportunities in access to desirable positions are important objectives in themselves — but substantive equality may be the more fundamental issue.

In my view, greater procedural fairness is important, but it will not necessarily reduce the inequalities of income and wealth that we now observe in Canadian society. We should face squarely the fact that equalizing opportunity to be at the top necessarily implies equalizing chances to be at the bottom, and thereby increases the economic insecurity of those who now have to worry more about downward mobility. Reallocating the probability of homelessness so that it becomes an "equal opportunity" life outcome does not solve the substantive problem of homelessness. Furthermore, since previously favoured groups will, on average, always lose from greater equality of opportunity, larger gaps in incomes between the top and bottom increase the incentive of now-advantaged groups to oppose greater equality of opportunity.

Fundamentally, I think greater equality of opportunities depends on greater equality of outcomes. Since education remains a highly important determinant of individual earnings, and a crucial mechanism for the intergenerational transmission of economic status, the quality of the public school system is a particularly important example. Increasing income inequality implies a decreasing willingness of top-income earners to pay the taxes that will adequately fund the public school educations that will enable other people's children to compete more effectively with their own kids. Only a low inequality society can minimize the unavoidable tension between parents' desire to do the best for their children and their simultaneous desire to live in a fair society, with meaningful equality of opportunity.

Chapter 8
WHY DO ECONOMIC INEQUALITIES MATTER?

This chapter is about why and how I think economic inequalities at the bottom, in the middle and at the top will affect the Canada that we would like to live in, and why that matters. My bottom line is twofold: that economic inequalities matter crucially for human rights, (in different ways at the top, in the middle and at the bottom) and that economic inequalities undermine the social cohesion that Canada needs if we are to deal adequately with our big common problems, like climate change or periodic pandemics. In my view, Canada needs a shift in policy direction, and I outline some specific proposals in the final chapter.

But before getting to that, there is a prior question: what's wrong with the same old "solution" to Canada's inequality problem? The stability of Canadian political economy has long depended on economic growth to paper over the social stresses created by economic inequality, and for many years — most recently from 1946 to 1981 — this largely worked. In the bygone days of balanced growth, incomes grew at roughly the same rate for rich and poor alike so the inequality of income shares remained roughly constant. That changed in the early 1980s and for over forty years now it has not been possible to say that inequality is the price that Canadians pay for everyone's income increasing over time — the gains from the growth of national income have been disproportionately received by those already at the top of Canada's income distribution.[1]

So does Canada just need more rapid growth? A skeptic might note that Canadian governments have been promising faster growth for decades now, without delivering much to Canada's middle classes. But the "more growth" mantra has a continuing political allure because it promises that an important social problem (inequality) will just go away if we tweak the existing policy framework a little, avoiding talk of any deeper structural change. But is a growth solution feasible? Could it solve the inequality problem? Should it?

Could Faster GDP Growth "Solve" Canada's Inequality Problem?

Chapters 1 to 4 note that since 1980, economic growth has been very different for Canadians at the top, in the middle and at the bottom of Canada's income distribution. The pursuit of more rapid growth of total GDP has been, since the early 1980s, the rationale given for the package of public policies sometimes described as "Neo-Liberal" (i.e., inflation targeting, balanced budgets, privatization, deregulation, reduced social spending and lower taxes on top incomes, expansion of "free trade" agreements, etc.). True believers in that policy package argue Canadians should now just double down and do even more of the same and faster GDP growth will surely arrive someday to solve our problems. Is that plausible?

A first step in analyzing this argument is to distinguish clearly between "growth" and "growth per person" — i.e., between the growth of GDP and the growth of GDP per capita. Canada's population growth — from 12.4 million in 1946 to 24.9 million in 1981 and 40.5 million in 2023 — has always been a significant driver of the growth of national income. However, population growth also increases the number of people who share economic output. If average income is to rise, GDP has to grow faster than population. While there have been surges and pauses in population growth in Canada, until recently population growth was slow and fairly steady — between 1980 and 2015 the average annual rate of Canada's population increase was 1.1 per cent, with little variation from trend.[2] Since the birth rate in Canada has been low for decades, almost all of Canada's population growth in recent years has come from immigration. The rate of population growth in Canada has therefore become something determined by federal government policy choices about the number of permanent and temporary immigrants to be admitted.

From 2015 to 2019, Canada's population growth rate edged up to 1.6 per cent, and after a pause during the Covid-19 years 2020–21, it surged to 3.2 per cent in 2023 (i.e., a population increase of 1.3 million between Q4 2022 and Q4 2023). When that many new people try suddenly to find a place to live, new homes and apartments just cannot be built fast enough to meet the increased demand.[3] In 2024, Canada's urban skylines were dotted with new apartments under construction, but many of Canada's urban parks were also filled with tent encampments of the homeless. Although total GDP increased from $2.54 trillion in 2022 to $2.57 trillion in 2023, that gain of 1.1 per cent did not keep up with population growth. GDP per capita declined by 2.01 per cent, from $55,707 to $54,588.[4]

So what are the chances of a future acceleration of growth which is both sufficiently large to keep up with population growth and sufficiently balanced to stabilize income inequality? As Chapter 2 notes, economic growth between 2000 and 2014 depended heavily on the oil boom, which has now ended. Income growth for Canada's middle class depends very much on how fast the economy as a whole will grow, and recent Canadian forecasts agree in predicting a growth slowdown. As Canada's baby boom generation moves further into their retirement years, labour force participation is expected to decline — and health care and old-age pension costs will increase. Finance Canada bases its projections of future growth on an average of private sector forecasts and on that basis, as of April 2024 real growth of total GDP was expected to be approximately 1.8 per cent annually until 2028 and 1.6 per cent per year from 2029 to 2055. If future population growth averages 0.9 per cent annually,[5] this implies real national income per capita growing at 0.9 per cent annually until 2028 and 0.7 per cent per year thereafter (assuming no recessions occur). Since this would be roughly half the average 1.39 per cent annual growth rate in real per capita GDP which Canada enjoyed over the 1981 to 2008 period, a substantial slowing of economic growth is anticipated.

Are these forecasts about future GDP growth rates too pessimistic? They ignore the probability of a recession or a global slowdown in trade (perhaps driven by geo-political conflicts), and they also discount the terms of trade impact of continued low resource prices. The "secular stagnation" argument[6] that global growth rates are slowing as excess global savings confront a dearth of profitable investment opportunities is also ignored. The assumption that productivity growth will continue at a constant rate forever also ignores the argument that technological change inevitably hits diminishing returns at some point — there have been recent declines in multi-factor productivity growth in many advanced economies, not just Canada's.[7]

What would it take for middle-class incomes to "keep up" with the growth of top incomes? Compared to their past income growth rates, if top incomes in Canada were to grow at roughly 1.5 per cent annually going forward, that would be a significant slowdown for many of the top 1 per cent (see Table 2.2). Nevertheless, to maintain the same income ratio and prevent proportionate inequality[8] from increasing further, a similar growth rate of 1.5 per cent for the median income taxpayer would be required.[9] But although 1.5 per cent growth would be slower growth for top incomes, for the middle class it would be a very considerable acceleration. The long-term growth rate of median real hourly wages between 1980 and 2010 was less than a quarter of that (i.e., 0.36 per cent annually). Even during Canada's oil boom period, median real hourly wages only grew by 1.3 per cent annually.

The average private sector forecast that informs the 2024 federal budget is for even slower growth — real national income per capita growing at 0.9 per cent annually until 2028, and less thereafter — but growth optimists may object that the "Third Industrial Revolution" of computers, telecommunications and the internet will produce a larger productivity impact than is predicted in current forecasts. However, if machine learning, new sensors and "big data" computer technology are only now just beginning to have their full impacts, the problem for a "growing the middle class" scenario is that these technologies also mean "it is largely already technologically possible to automate almost any task, provided that sufficient amounts of data are gathered for pattern recognition."[10] If so, many middle-class occupations from truck driver to graphic artist to lawyer once thought to be "safe" from replacement may soon be obsolete.

Nobody has a crystal ball that can predict for sure what technological change will happen in the future. But economists can make different "plausible" assumptions about which occupations will be affected, and then add up the numbers. Early estimates of the possible disruptive impacts of robots, artificial intelligence and machine learning on employment have varied widely, from 9 to 47 per cent of all jobs.[11] Those estimates were revised sharply upward in 2024 by the IMF, which argued: "In advanced economies, about 60 percent of jobs are exposed to AI."[12]

In the past, the highly skilled and the well-educated were less affected by technological change. But it is unclear whether the future impacts of artificial intelligence on jobs for low-education blue-collar workers, such as truck drivers, will be greater or less than impacts on more-educated white-collar workers like call center employees or insurance adjusters or lawyers or investment advisers. Both manual and cognitive jobs are at risk, but net impacts on labour income inequality depend on how AI is developed — whether it will be complementary to, or competitive with, human skills. If more rapid productivity growth implies even faster shrinkage of employment opportunities for the poorly educated (and particularly for poorly educated men), this will imply declining incomes for displaced lower middle-class workers. If artificial intelligence replaces many well-educated workers, increased income inequality within the middle class and increasing insecurity for all those who fear displacement will be the result. However, the uncertainty of scenarios for labour income inequality contrasts with the clarity of forecasts for capital income: "Unlike labor income inequality, capital income and wealth inequality always increase with AI adoption."[13]

Meanwhile, the people at the top of Canada's 1 per cent have become accustomed, over the past forty years, to their incomes growing much more rapidly than 0.7 per cent annually. Even a 1.5 per cent future growth rate would be a significant slowing of income growth for many of Canada's elite, so it will be hard to convince them that they should pay more in taxes to reduce inequality and lessen insecurity. The allure of a slogan like "growing the middle class" is that it makes economic policy sound painless — if the middle class can just have its income grow a bit faster, tax rates on top incomes could continue as they have been for the last forty years, and nobody at the top would ever have to give anything up.

During Canada's oil boom period, one could often read newspaper columns and articles which compared Alberta's economic growth rate to growth in Ontario, Quebec or Atlantic Canada, often with the theme of "what's wrong with these laggards." For years, many Canadians clearly mistook the oil boom in Alberta as economic growth that could be "normal." Partly as a result of this history, a mirage still dominating our national discourse is the seemingly painless proposition that if Canada's economic pie could just grow really fast, nobody needs to worry much about how it is divided. But if Canada, like other rich nations, is entering a period of slower GDP growth, that implies income distribution now matters more than it used to and will matter even more in the future. Especially when the total economy grows more slowly, it is just not plausible that middle-class income growth can accelerate enough to restore the level of equality that Canada used to have. In fact, if income growth at the top continues at anything like its recent rates, unrealistic rates of growth are needed for median income growth just to "keep up" with the recent income growth rate of the top 1 per cent. Of course, even if income growth rates were to equalize and income shares were to stabilize, the absolute size of income gaps would continue to increase. As Table 2.2 shows, in 2021 the midpoint income of the top 1 per cent (the 99.5th percentile) was $522,000 and the midpoint of the 99 per cent (the 49.5th percentile) was $45,000, so an annual growth rate of 0.8 per cent produces an annual increase of $4,200 at the top and $360 at the middle — i.e., the dollar income gap widens by $3,800 annually.

Slower growth of GDP per capita, in a country as rich as Canada, need not be considered a catastrophe so long as we can solve the problem of how that national income is shared. Given where Canadians now are in material affluence, slower growth of national income has a completely different meaning than slower GDP growth in very poor countries, such as in sub-Saharan Africa. However, slower growth does make it more urgent for Canadians to think carefully about the difference between national income per capita and economic well-being and about how our material affluence is shared.

Robots, Artificial Intelligence and the Age of Green Abundance

Many people, over many years and from different sides of ideological divides, have questioned whether economic growth should always continue to be the focus of economic policy in rich nations. Over ninety years ago, one of the founding members of the "Chicago School" of economics wrote, "Our thinking about life values runs too much in terms of material prerequisites and costs. It is an exaggeration which may be useful to say that economic goods as a class are predominantly 'necessary' rather than truly valuable. The importance of economic provision is chiefly that of a prerequisite to the enjoyment of the free goods of the world, the beauty of the natural scene, the intercourse of friends in 'aimless' camaraderie, the appreciation and creation of art, discovery of truth and communion with one's own inner being and the Nature of Things."[14]

Frank Knight wrote these words in 1933, in the depths of the Great

Depression, when material affluence in both Canada and the United States was far less than it is today. To be specific, in Canada, real national income per capita in 1933 was 10.3 per cent[15] of its level in 2022. In aggregate material output, Canadians today have about ten times more marketed goods and services per person than Canadians had in 1933 — but even back then Knight wanted to be clear on the distinction between means and ends in life. He thought economics could be a useful thing to study because it can help enable people to have the material underpinnings of the good life, but he insisted that more material consumption is only a means to an end and not the end in itself. He went on to say:

> Civilization should look forward to a day when the material product of industrial activity shall become rather its by-product, and its primary significance shall be that of a sphere for creative self-expression and the development of a higher type of individual and of human fellowship. It ought to be the first aim of economic policy to reduce the importance of economic policy in life as a whole. So it ought to be the highest objective in the study of economics to hasten the day when the study and the practice of economy will recede into the background of men's thoughts.

Writing at roughly the same time, John Maynard Keynes argued:

> the needs of humans fall into two classes — those needs which are absolute in the sense that we feel them whatever the situation of our fellow human beings may be, and those which are relative in the sense that we feel them only if their satisfaction lifts us above, makes us feel superior to our fellows. Needs of the second class, those which satisfy the desire for superiority, may indeed be insatiable; for the higher the general level, the higher still are they.[16]

Keynes was impressed by how much the development of labour-saving technologies, in combination with the accumulation of capital over many years, could add to the productive capacity of an economy. He asked his readers in 1930 to imagine "that a hundred years hence we are all of us on the average eight times better off in the economic sense than we are today" (which turned out to be an underestimate). Although he thought competitive consumption (what he called the "needs of the second class") was a pointless, hedonic treadmill leading nowhere, he foresaw the potential for growing productive capacity to satisfy absolute needs, which he believed means "that in the long run that mankind is *solving its economic problem*" (emphasis in original).

Keynes defined technological unemployment as "unemployment due to our discovery of means of economizing the use of labour outrunning the pace at which we can find new uses for labour." His worry was that after having satisfied absolute needs and having solved the economic problem of scarcity, the habits and instincts bred into people for countless generations of scarcity would produce a sort of nervous breakdown when confronted with humanity's "real, permanent problem — how to use freedom from pressing economic cares, how to occupy the leisure, which science and compound interest will have won, to live wisely and agreeably and well."[17] Given the difficulty of surmounting these ingrained habits, Keynes believed that "for many ages to come, everybody will need to do some work to be contented," and he suggested that about fifteen hours a week would do.

Although Keynes was impressed by the labour-saving nature of the technologies of his day, he lived at a time when telephone operators still manually connected every call and elevator operators were needed to move people from one floor to another in offices and apartment buildings — jobs most Canadians now alive have never even seen. He clearly had no conception of the world of artificial intelligence, robotics and driverless vehicles which we are now actually entering. But his optimism should still serve as a bit of an antidote to the gloom and doom and anxieties about the future which now often surround our discussions of robotics, artificial intelligence and the potential of technological change to eliminate millions of jobs in affluent nations.

Keynes was pointing out that when technology and capital accumulation have advanced to the point where machines are able to do most of the jobs which people now have to do, this is, at least potentially, very good news. When robots can make the robots that can do most of our current jobs, robots will also be able to do the new jobs required for decarbonization and the mitigation of environmental damages. The "Age of Green Abundance" will then be technically possible. It will then be technically feasible for all people to enjoy a full material standard of living and also protect the environment and also enjoy many more hours of leisure in which to develop the full potential of their unique personalities. The "Age of AI" could in principle be the "Age of Green Abundance" or perhaps the "Age of Green Leisure."

The big problems in getting from here to there are not technological but social. If the Age of Green Abundance is to actually arrive, we will have to change the distribution of work and of rewards: the humans who are displaced by robots and artificial intelligence will still need something to do and some source of income. The big question is whether human societies can manage to reorganize themselves in time so the positive potentials of this "Age of AI" actually become realities — or whether the gains from technological change will continue to be appropriated at the top as the "Age of AI" becomes the "Age of Ever-Increasing Inequalities."

The Social Choices of the 1930s

What can we learn from history about the consequences if economic inequalities continue to increase? Western nations all had to grapple with the implications of the massive economic inequality which emerged during the 1920s and the subsequent economic instability and the Great Depression of the 1930s which that produced, but they took very different paths. Writing as they were in the early 1930s, neither Knight nor Keynes could have foreseen the full implications of the divergent paths that rich nations later took. But as we read today what Keynes and Knight wrote in the early 1930s, we know how history actually did turn out.

In the United States, President Franklin D. Roosevelt's New Deal had many interlocking parts: public spending to stimulate output and employment, plus regulatory reforms to stabilize financial and labour markets, plus more progressive taxation plus social security. The New Deal restrained top-end income growth with increased taxation, assisted middle-class income growth by facilitating unionization, increased economic security with unemployment insurance, welfare and old age pensions, recycled financial flows by redistributing income and regulated financial markets to avoid excess speculation. Taken together, these reforms stabilized American inequality dynamics for nearly fifty years — but started to come unstuck in the 1980s as market liberalization took precedence.

In Europe, the emergence of stable social democratic welfare states in Nordic countries also dates from the 1930s. And it was a major achievement. A bitter history of class conflict preceded the Nordic social democratic consensus. In Finland, the civil war of 1918 between "reds" and "whites" has been estimated to have killed more than 1 per cent of the population, mostly in mass executions and concentration camps (the equivalent in Canada today would be over 400,000 dead within a six-month period). By the criterion of days of production lost to industrial dispute, "up to the middle of the 1930s Sweden, together with Norway, had the highest measured 'relative volume' of industrial conflict in the Western world."[18]

However, in the mid-1930s, business and trade union leaders in Scandinavia did not have to look very far to see — in Russia, Germany, Austria and Spain — the potential costs for everyone if class conflict spiralled out of control into civil war. In 1935 in Norway and in 1936 in Sweden, business and labour signed historic agreements establishing centralized wage bargaining within a welfare-state framework. Scandinavians were able to step back from the brink and reap the benefits of mutual accommodation and social compromise while others such as Spain experienced civil war and fascism.[20] Those big compromises of the 1930s produced a social model that continues to deliver substantial social equality, very high levels of material affluence, robust civil liberties and democratic governance.

But the turmoil of the 1930s also produced fascism in Italy and Spain and Nazism in Germany. What the media now call "right-wing populism" and what political scientists now categorize as "xenophobic authoritarianism" came to power. Surfing on a wave of insecurities about the future and resentments about the past, the Nazis plunged Germany, and Europe as a whole, into disaster. Estimates of the death toll of the Second World War range between fifty and eighty million people.[20]

In all these events, economics mattered — something that was absolutely top of mind for the generation of economists who had grown up watching the galloping inequality[21] of the 1920s be followed by the mass unemployment and rise of Fascism and Nazism of the 1930s and then World War II and the Holocaust in the 1940s. When Paul Samuelson published the first edition of his introductory textbook — *Economics: An Introductory Analysis* — he was a young Assistant Professor at MIT. His text went on to over nineteen editions in English and twenty-six more in translation (and had many imitations). Samuelson dominated the discipline of economics for decades and in 1970 won the first Nobel Prize in Economics. But in 1948 he began his text by noting:

> The fact — clearly to be read from the history of the twentieth century — that the political health of a democracy is tied up in a crucial way with the successful maintenance of stable high employment and living opportunities. It is not too much to say that the widespread creation of dictatorships and the resulting World War II stemmed in no small measure from the world's failure to meet this basic problem adequately.[22]

His generation of economists dominated policy-making through the 1960s and into the 1970s but when they retired, they were succeeded by a generation whose lived experiences were very different. Baby Boomers grew up experiencing the social stability that a shared prosperity of balanced growth and full employment enabled — and took it for granted. Social and political stability morphed from a core objective of economic policy to a casual background assumption of economists.

Clearly, history never repeats itself exactly. The world of the 1930s and 1950s was a very different place — among other things, it had low atmospheric CO_2 concentrations and was largely divided among European colonial empires. The world today is a multi-polar mix of nations which has to deal with a global climate change problem. Dealing effectively with collective problems is arguably now both more difficult[23] and more urgent than it used to be. This brief summary of long-past events is only meant to indicate why my reading of history says there is a lot at stake in confronting the implications of increasing economic inequality. I think we should learn the lesson that increasing economic inequalities undermine social cohesion and create economic instabilities and social resentments that interact strongly in their impacts, are unsustainable in the political economy sense and can lead to disastrous outcomes. The key question is what we do about it.

Where Am I Coming from? — A Human Rights Perspective

Personally, in thinking about what sort of society I would like to live in, I start from the human rights perspective that says that all individuals should be able to pursue freely their own conception of a good life, and we should organize our society so each person can do so to the maximum feasible extent without interfering with the freedom of others to make their own choices about their own lives. Since humans are social animals and our world is complex and interdependent, we need a system of laws and norms of social behaviour to define our rights, freedoms and responsibilities, and to set the frameworks for our interactions. Because individuals must actually have their basic human rights if their choices are to be meaningfully free, the actual achievement of basic human rights for all citizens is the primary responsibility of a democratic government. National constitutions, international human rights covenants and the systems of law they establish are there to give concrete definitions to "rights," "responsibilities" and "freedom."

To be specific, the Universal Declaration of Human Rights (1948) of the United Nations (which Canadians were instrumental in drafting and which Canada signed[24]) and Canada's Constitution Act (1982) define an important list of basic human rights, which include both civil liberties and social and economic rights. Since governments are the signatories of human rights conventions on behalf of their national communities, there is an implied onus on public policy to respond and an implicit specification of concrete objectives. Once basic human rights have been actually achieved by all citizens, thereby enabling autonomous individuals to make free and informed choices, the government still has the responsibility of establishing the framework of laws and policies most likely to enable maximum economic and social well-being, but this is the secondary priority[25] of public policy.

Why Increasing Inequality at the Top Matters for Human Rights and Democracy

Chapter 3 notes how increasing top-end incomes reset social norms of competitive consumption and how the advertising industry provides the accelerant for increasing materialism and envy. Because increasing top-end income shares create growing markets for luxury goods, which depend on aspirational advertising, the 99 per cent are increasingly told about the pleasures and the importance of things they cannot possibly afford.

If middle-class people in Canada were just getting the same real incomes, and the same satisfactions from those incomes, this year as they were forty years ago, and if they could securely expect that to continue, middle-class income stagnancy might not be as big a deal. If incomes were securely predictable and therefore something they did not have to worry about, people could get on with the more important rest of life. But when the advertisers and the media tell them continuously how they are not keeping up and income stagnancy is combined with greater economic insecurity and inequality, it does matter. Unbalanced growth means the gaps between aspirational consumption norms and the achievable realities of normal lives are continually growing, so the life satisfaction which ordinary people get from their consumption shrinks as the income share of the top 1 per cent increases.

I do not think it is reasonable to expect that the majority of the electorate will accept forever that their level of economic well-being has declined, and will always continue to decline, relative to that of the elite. MAGA in the United States, Brexit in the UK and far-right xenophobic movements throughout Europe have shown that if mainstream political parties do not solve this problem, doubling down on mirages — as in empty promises to "grow the middle class" — will not cut it. Eventually, voters whose needs are not met in the political mainstream will turn to the extremes for solutions.

The dark scenario, as we have already seen in some countries, therefore is that as increasing inequality causes increased economic instability and greater social stress, authoritarian social movements emerge, selling dreams of a return to mythical "good old days" and looking for scapegoats when that does not materialize. Since the easiest policy to promise is "more growth" but that promise cannot hope to deliver enough growth for those who need it, there will be a relentless search for new scapegoats to blame.

In an EKOS poll of 1,003 Canadians in July 2016, 57 per cent of respondents agreed, and only 25 per cent disagreed, with the statement "If the current patterns of stagnation among all except those at the very top continue, I would not be surprised to see the emergence of violent class conflicts."[26] Canada is a country that has always been remarkably able to solve its problems peacefully, so when a majority of citizens can foresee violence, I think this is very, very bad news. My own opinion is that "the emergence of violent class conflict" is actually highly unlikely in Canada in the 2020s, because modern computer technologies, such as artificial intelligence combined with facial and voice recognition, now enable a level of real-time surveillance of the population that used to be unimaginable. However, I am not cheered by the ever-increasing ability of security agencies to watch all of us, all the time. Personally, I abhor the prospect of continued expansion of the surveillance state, and the reduction of the privacy and civil liberties of all citizens which that implies.

I believe strongly in the importance of civil liberties, such as freedom of thought, speech and association, for all citizens. It also seems to me that we can never take these freedoms for granted and that it is an illusion to think their continued existence can be independent of economic trends — specifically, trends in the economic insecurity and relative deprivation that large numbers of people now experience in their day-to-day lives. So I think we should recognize that the ability of the body politic to maintain political and civil rights depends in part on trends in economic inequalities, specifically, on the growing gaps between elite and middle-class incomes and the sense of exclusion and disrespect which that feeds.

As discussed in Chapter 7, increasing economic inequalities also threaten our aspirations for greater equality of opportunity. The democratic political process is also threatened by the increasing concentration of wealth and economic power in Canada and the political influence of an economic elite whose lived experiences are increasingly disconnected from the realities of ordinary people. There are many good reasons for reducing top-end inequality, and a running theme of this book is the idea that inequalities matter differently, at different parts of the distribution of income.

Why Inequalities at the Bottom Matter for Human Rights and Democracy

The linkage between social and economic rights and political freedom starts from the perception that, as Franklin Roosevelt put it in 1944, "true individual freedom cannot exist without economic security and independence. 'Necessitous men are not free men.' People who are hungry and out of a job are the stuff of which dictatorships are made."[27] The United Nations' Universal Declaration of Human Rights is based on this perception. Increasing inequality at the bottom — growing income gaps between the middle class and the poor — is a human rights issue, because the denial of social and economic rights implies deprivation of the functional freedoms which those rights entail.

Roosevelt's phrase "necessitous men are not free men" was actually taken from an English court case of 1762, which ruled that a contract to purchase could be set aside because it was entered into under duress.[28] Because free and informed consent is a prerequisite for the validity of a contract, and because the economically desperate have no choice but to submit to any contract terms which are proposed to them, onerous contracts made under such duress can be set aside. Roosevelt built on this idea to argue that individuals must actually be in possession of a basic level of economic security and well-being if they are to exercise meaningful free will in their economic and political choices. He went on to propose a bill of economic rights,[29] so that all Americans could have this basic freedom.

Homelessness is an important example of both the interdependence of human rights and the reliance of human rights on the actual possession of a basic level of economic resources. Canada is one of the original signatories to the UN's Universal Declaration of Human Rights, in which Article 12 asserts a right to privacy and Article 25 specifies that housing is a basic human right. Having privacy requires having control over a definable personal space, which, in a market economy, requires the ownership of property or the income with which to rent property. Hence, the right to housing and the right to privacy are interdependent. Similarly, a constitutional right to protection against unreasonable search and seizure (Article 8 of Canada's Constitution Act of 1982) is meaningless unless an individual has a definable personal space. The lack of income to buy or rent housing (or the absence of public housing for those who have insufficient income) means people have no choice but to live on the street. Since Canada has not actually instituted right-to-housing policies to deliver on its treaty commitments under the Universal Declaration of Human Rights, privacy rights are nothing but hollow words for Canada's homeless. The lack of sufficient income to obtain housing and the absence of compensating public housing is therefore a human rights issue. However, the tent encampments of the homeless throughout Canadian cities are continuing evidence that maintaining the basic human rights of all citizens has not in fact been a priority of Canadian governments.

Additionally, Article 22 of the Universal Declaration of Human Rights states, "Everyone, as a member of society, has a right to social security." Article 25 also declares:

Everyone has the right to a standard of living adequate for the health and well-being of himself and of his family, including food, clothing, housing and medical care and necessary social services, and the right to security in the event of unemployment, sickness, disability, widowhood, old age or other lack of livelihood in circumstances beyond his control.[30]

A human rights perspective does not say that everyone should have equal income, but it does say that everyone should have equal rights, and for that to happen, all citizens must have at least a minimum command over economic resources.

In practice, as long as they stay affluent, rich people have no need to worry about homelessness and are unlikely to ever have to avail themselves of a right to housing. People with wealth can also buy private schooling for their children, private health care for themselves and private security guards to protect their property. Wealthy people also do not need social insurance benefits. If they lose a job or get injured or get old, they have money in the bank to rely on. They do not need the Universal Declaration of Human Rights to specify these basic human rights (Articles 26, 25 and 17, respectively) or governments to provide them. It is the less affluent and the more insecure who benefit from the actual delivery of social and economic rights. There is no getting around the fact that a Canada which actually delivered on its human rights commitments would be a substantially more equal place than the Canada we live in today.

Chapter 9
WHAT TO DO?

What could be/should be done to reduce economic inequality in Canada? This chapter sketches five specific policy proposals: (1) inheritance taxation, (2) full employment macroeconomic policy, (3) a participation income, (4) fair taxes for top incomes and (5) a high wage strategy. These brief sketches should be read with the warning that "the devil is in the details." Detailed micro-simulation analyses have been done in some cases for similar proposals in other countries,[1] but the Canadian context is unique and always changing. Adding up the numbers to a financially feasible overall package depends on the specific details of the tax and expenditure changes proposed, and on the economic context at the time of implementation. These are rough initial sketches, not detailed architectural blueprints.

There are many other things that could be, and should be, done.[2] Economic inequalities have many dimensions and, conversely, just about all policy issues have implications for economic inequality. The policies discussed here are moderate changes that could make a difference, but they would certainly not eliminate inequality. When it comes to economic inequality, very few people are purists: less than 1 per cent of survey respondents in advanced countries say they want absolute equality of wages.[3] But when asked, the vast majority of the citizens of affluent countries do say clearly that economic inequality is "too high." For example, when asked specifically how much the chairman of a large national company should make compared to an unskilled factory worker, on average across countries,[4] a clear majority (over 70 per cent) think that a CEO should earn no more than 8.8 times what an unskilled factory worker makes.[5] This is certainly not absolute equality, but in Canada in 2023 that ratio would have implied a maximum CEO salary in the $400,000 to $450,000 range,[6] which is very much less than the $14.9 million average of Canada's top one hundred CEOs in 2022. The relevant issue is how best to reduce economic inequalities, not how to eliminate all inequalities.

The suggestions of this chapter are also made with the recognition that some big trends affecting economic inequality are likely to continue. Technological change is, for example, not going to stop. Indeed, the Age of Robots, additive manufacturing (also known as 3D printing) and artificial intelligence is accelerating. The crucial issue is whether the gains from technological change will be broadly shared or concentrated at the top. In Canada, population aging is also inescapable, although its impacts are reduced a bit by the increased labour force participation of older Canadians. Personally, I think globalization is also here to stay — even if there is little point in pushing it ever-further (Canada's average tariff rate has been less than 2 per cent for decades, so there is just not much more to be gained from further cuts).[7]

Inheritance Taxation

> *Death duties, in general, are a very good type of tax, second only to income tax in their essential fairness and the possibilities of adjusting them progressively to ability to pay. They are even better than income tax in so far as they do not have as much tendency to reduce an individual's incentive to hard work and initiative. It is reasonable and just that one should be able to provide*

> *something for his wife and children, and others, after his death. It is also reasonable and just, however, that the state should share in what one leaves, at a rate dependent upon the amount of wealth being transferred. Indeed, I find this view so generally held in this country that it is not necessary to do more than call it to mind.*
>
> — *James Lorimer Ilsley (Hansard, April 29, 1941)*[8]

When Canada's Minister of Finance rose in the House of Commons to announce the new "Dominion Succession Duties Tax" as part of the Federal Budget for 1941, Canada was mobilizing for World War II. As a nation, our big collective problem then was how to win the war and defeat Nazi Germany. A recurring theme of his speech therefore was the importance for the war effort and public morale of a fair sharing of the tax burden. The budget announced increases in top rates of personal income tax as well as the new tax on inheritances. In Canada, both provincial and federal governments have jurisdiction in this area and all the provinces had established estate taxes much earlier, between 1892 and 1905.[9] The new federal tax was on top of existing provincial statutes but was similar in rate and structure.[10]

Compared to the 77 per cent estate tax rate then charged on large estates in the US,[11] Canada's 1941 tax on inherited wealth was pretty puny — the initial tax rate was only 3 per cent and the top rate was a 20 per cent tax on estate values in excess of $5,000,000 (equal to about $88.9 million in 2022 dollars). Since the average annual salary in manufacturing in Canada then was $1,801, the basic exemption of $50,000 of the new tax corresponded to just under twenty-eight years of average earnings — a corresponding basic exemption in 2022 would have been about $1.8 million.[12]

While they existed, Canada's succession duties were a useful, but not huge, revenue source. Estate and inheritance tax revenues of the federal and provincial governments were $216 million in 1965, which was then about 6.4 per cent of the total taxes on income and profits paid by individuals.[13] If estate and inheritance taxes had been a similar fraction in 2021 of individual income taxes, they would have raised $19.48

billion. To put that amount of revenue in context, it would be well more than enough to pay all Canada Student Loans as grants ($3.97 billion in 2021), fund the full annual cost ($7.7 billion) of the federal government's Early Learning and Child Care Plan when fully phased in 2025–26[14] and also increase disability benefits by $3,000 each ($2.9 billion).[15]

However, Canada's federal succession duties were abolished in 1971, and all the provinces followed suit shortly thereafter.[16] So why is it that most OECD nations have inheritance or estate taxation but Canada now does not? What explains why in 1941 Canada's Minister of Finance could describe inheritance taxation as a "reasonable and just" tax supported by a "view so generally held in this country that it is not necessary to do more than call it to mind," but thirty years later they were abolished?

In Canada, inheritance taxes disappeared after 1971 because fixing one taxation problem (non-taxation of capital gains) produced another taxation problem (non-taxation of inheritances). In the 1950s and 1960s, capital gains were not taxed in Canada, but income tax had to be paid on wages and salaries. Because top tax rates were then quite high[17] the large differential in tax treatment of different income types created an enormous incentive for upper-income taxpayers to invent transactions that reclassified income as capital gains. Since increasing tax avoidance was eroding the tax base and the equity and efficiency of the tax system, a Royal Commission on Taxation (the Carter Commission) was appointed. Its 1968 report is probably best remembered for its mantra that "a buck is a buck is a buck," expressing the core idea that the same tax should be paid on income however it is labelled — wages, salaries, royalties, dividends, rents, capital gains, fees, whatever. If that mantra had been fully adopted, 100 per cent of capital gains would have been included in taxable income but that was too radical a shift for the Liberal government of the day. In the end, only 50 per cent of capital gains were included in taxable income, starting in 1972[18] — which implied that the rewards to tax avoidance were not eliminated, just halved.

The inclusion of 50 per cent of capital gains in taxable income was a major improvement in the equity and efficiency of the Canadian tax system but it came at a considerable cost. An increase in the market value of an asset that one owns implies an increase in potential consumption whether the item is actually sold (i.e., realized) or not.[19] (Even if the owner does not sell the asset, the capital gains from its increase in value can be used as security for increased borrowing which can enable increased consumption.) However, in order to tax unrealized capital gains it is administratively necessary to estimate the change in market value of assets that do not change ownership. The new tax on capital gains was therefore assessed only when things were sold (i.e., when capital gains were realized). "Deemed realization at death" meant that transfer of the title to an asset through bequest at death was treated as being equivalent to transferring the title by sale, so capital gains tax became payable on any increase in market value of the assets owned by the decedent[20] (other than owner-occupied housing).[21] Taxes on the unrealized capital gains that are part of an estate are payments of the deferred capital gains tax that would have been paid earlier if the asset had been sold earlier. Hence when an estate is settled, the capital gains taxes owed, along with any other debts owing, are one of the liabilities of the estate which have to be paid from the assets of the estate before its net value can be known.

However, since the new tax on unrealized capital gains was paid at the same time (probate of the estate) and by the same entity (the estate) as the old estate tax, affluent taxpayers raised the cry of "double taxation" and the federal government retreated from the taxation of estates, followed over the next few years by each of the provinces. Surveying the history of inheritance taxation in Canada ten years later, economist Richard Bird commented:

> The abolition of the federal estate tax in 1971 was the most important reform of tax legislation in Canada since the Second World War — important in terms not of revenue but of what it symbolized: a retreat from decades of attempts to alter wealth distribution through taxation . . . Canada has gained few, if any, benefits from its move away from death taxes and has paid a significant price in terms of reduced equality of opportunity, probably increased inequality of wealth, and certainly increased fossilization of the structure of wealth.[22]

As Chapter 6 discusses, the inequality of wealth in Canada is significantly greater than the inequality of income — an inequality that is passed on, from one generation to the next, by the untaxed inheritance of property. In improving the fairness of taxation of wealth, there are basic choices to be made among taxes on capital income, wealth and inheritances.[23] Capital income is the return each year on the stock of wealth which an individual owns, so the same tax revenue can be raised either by taxing the annual income from wealth or by taxing the wealth from which that capital income came. If the rates of return on wealth differ, there are substantial efficiency gains from taxing the stock (wealth) rather than the flow (capital income).[24] If wealth is taxed, that can be done either once a year or once a lifetime (i.e., at death) — the same tax revenue can be raised by charging a higher tax rate on lifetime wealth assessments or a lower rate on annual wealth assessments.

An annual wealth tax is a more administratively complex way to tax wealth because it requires an annual recording of all assets owned and an annual estimation of their fair market prices, including assets that did not change ownership. This is clearly feasible — annual wealth taxes in Swiss cantons have meant, since the 1870s, that annual accountings of both income and wealth are normal aspects of tax collection there.[25] However, in Canada, a new set of tax administration procedures would be required and taxing wealth once every lifetime, at death, would be simpler because there already is a well-established legal process in place. The probate court process to settle an estate is a necessary step (which long predates inheritance taxation) in legally transferring the ownership of assets to the heirs of an estate. That process already requires the listing and valuation of the assets and liabilities of the estate. In my view, the simplest way to tax wealth is to implement an effective inheritance tax which builds on the probate process.[26]

If this is not done and if large inheritances continue to escape taxation, there are at least three sorts of social costs. First and most obvious is the foregone tax revenue, which could have gone either to financing public services or to reducing other taxes. As inherited wealth increases in importance ever more of the potential tax base escapes taxation so the cost of foregoing inheritance tax revenues increases over time.[27] A second type of cost is the impact of not taxing large inheritances on long-run political stability. When an aristocracy of wealth can pass its elite position from generation to generation unimpeded but the middle class face austerity in public services combined with market incomes that are uncertain, insecure and on average stagnant, a perception of fundamental unfairness can become entrenched, with deeply unpredictable implications for Canada's political economy.

A third cost of leaving large inheritances untouched by taxation is that it exposes all the wealth created by the founding generation of a family fortune to the continued hazard that their future descendants may try to run things themselves. Entrepreneurs often argue that they perform a valuable social function because they "create wealth and jobs" and society as a whole is indeed better off with a larger capital stock, more jobs and more tax revenue. That also implies that society as a whole has an interest in wealth and jobs not being destroyed by bad management. Arguably the person who first founded the family firm and built it up initially must have had the ability (and the good luck) to make a series of good business decisions — but that is no guarantee that their children or grandchildren will have similar abilities. Since paid employees can be selected and promoted for their competence, a large inherited fortune which is administered by hired help can be expected to earn a "normal" rate of return on its capital, and not be dissipated. However, when large inherited fortunes are actually managed by the descendants, corporate decision makers are being selected by genetic lottery. On average that genetic lottery will produce people of average ability, who will make business decisions of average acuity, and occasionally they will be worse than average. Using the genetic lottery to select the CEO of major corporations is a bit like betting the pot on every spin of the roulette wheel. The more times that the decision makers for large pools of capital are selected by yet another draw from the family genetic pool of abilities, the higher is the cumulative probability of incompetence — that eventually somebody with disastrously lower than average ability will become CEO. Inherited pools of capital that are owner-operated are repeatedly exposed to the likelihood, each generation, of being destroyed by below-average business talent.

The old cliché — "shirtsleeves to shirtsleeves in three generations" — about intergenerational wealth mobility expresses the idea that great wealth amassed by a fortune's founder may be partly spent by their children and completely dissipated by their grandchildren. It is often presented as a story of social mobility but it is actually a narrative of social waste. Some very well-known Canadian family dynasties have ended abruptly (e.g., Conrad Black, the Eatons), with collateral damage to employees and suppliers, when successor generations have tried to demonstrate their business acumen. Although middle-class family lineages who would like to pass the family home from one generation to the next also bear the risk that any one generation in the family line can mess up, the consequences of that are limited to that particular family lineage. Dissipating the small inheritance of an ordinary family does not destroy jobs, but the crash of large family firms affects many people outside the owner's family. As an American study of family CEOs concluded: "Firms that promote family CEOs significantly underperform after successions relative to firms that hire unrelated CEOs . . . finding a competent heir among the offspring of a retiring head is often disastrous."[28] Although it is true that inequalities of opportunity among future generations are reduced when the heirs to a large fortune burn it all up by trying to manage it, that process also wastes any wealth and job creation involved in the initial creation of the fortune.

As the OECD has argued: "If promoting equality of opportunity is a major objective of inheritance taxation, there is a strong case for a recipient-based inheritance tax rather than an estate tax levied on donors. It is the amount of wealth received by each recipient that should matter for equality of opportunity rather than the overall amount bequeathed by the donor."[29] For example, an inheritance tax might specify that if a taxpayer inherits more than a certain amount (e.g., $2.5 million) over the course of their lifetime from any combination of donors, they would have to include any inheritances above this threshold as ordinary income on their income tax.[30]

In order to be politically feasible in Canada, in my opinion inheritance taxation has to leave a path for parents to provide housing for their children. Maintaining the capital gains exemption for owner-occupied housing and setting a sizeable exemption level for inheritance taxation would enable that because a lifetime exemption of, for example, $2.5 million in inheritances for each individual recipient would imply an effective inheritance rate of tax of zero for almost all inheritances. If, for example, an individual with three children wanted to split their estate equally, the inheritance tax rate for their heirs (assuming they had no inheritances from any other source) would be zero if the estate was $7.5 million or less (which would enable tax-free intergenerational transfer of housing). As Table 6.1 in Chapter 6 indicates, 99 per cent of Canadian families in 2019 had net worth of $6.1 million or less and 99.5 per cent had net worth of $9.7 million or less, so the overwhelming majority of families would entirely, or almost entirely, be unaffected.

Taxing the inheritance income of individuals together with their other income at income tax time would separate the taxation of the inheritance incomes of individuals from the payment of deferred capital gains tax liability by estates. The payer of the tax, the timing of tax payments and the tax base and tax rate on which tax is based would all be different, thereby helping avoid the confusion of "double death taxation" arguments. The amount of revenue to be raised would depend crucially on the lifetime exemption level chosen and, to a lesser degree, on the annual value of gifts disregarded entirely and the time span allowed for averaging of inheritance income.

With a tax exemption of $2,500,000, taxing inheritances as individual income would thus have no impact at all on roughly 99 per cent of Canadians. Large estates would be taxed more heavily, at rates closer to the top marginal income tax rate. If inheritance taxation is repeated over multiple generations, it would slowly whittle down the encrusted advantages of Canada's financial aristocracy. However, it has to be recognized that even at an effective tax rate of 50 per cent inheritance taxation is a slow road to more equal opportunities for wealth.[31] It takes a long while for inheritance taxation, even at 50 per cent, to reduce the inherited advantages of a large fortune. However, that never happens without inheritance taxation.

Talk of inheritance taxation is likely to produce bleats of protests from the very wealthy — including threats of emigration if such a tax were implemented. Fear of billionaire flight may then paralyze reform — but US evidence is informative. In the US, a different state tax jurisdiction is often just across the river and in 2021, roughly a third of US states imposed either estate taxes (twelve states and the District of Columbia) or inheritance taxes (six states). The state-level taxes varied in rates and exemption levels, with Hawaii and Washington State having the highest estate tax top rates at 20 percent, but most others being 16 per cent to 18 per cent.

Until 2001, differences in estate tax rates between states did not affect the total tax burden of an estate because the United States also has a federal estate tax with a top rate of 40 percent,[32] and taxes paid to the states could be offset against federal taxes. However, in 2001 the US federal credit was phased out and suddenly the ultra-wealthy found their estate tax liability was highly dependent on their domicile state, which did affect location decisions, with a sensitivity that increased significantly with age.[33] However, estate taxes still raised money for the US states that kept them. In estimating the revenue costs and benefits for each state of having an estate tax, the benefit/cost conclusion was: "The benefit is the tax revenue gain when a wealthy resident dies, while the cost is the foregone income tax revenues over the remaining lifetime of those who relocate. Surprisingly, despite the high estimated tax mobility, we find that the benefit exceeds the cost for the vast majority of states. Of the states that currently do not have estate taxes, all but California would experience revenue gains if they adopted estate taxes."[34]

Succession duties and inheritance taxes were imposed by individual Canadian provinces long before the federal government's 1941 introduction of Dominion Succession Duties. If a Canadian province were to apply provincial income tax rates in taxing inheritances as income they would be applying tax rates[35] that are quite comparable to the inheritance tax rates applied in the eighteen US states that had estate or inheritance taxation in 2021. The same cost-benefit analysis of tax-induced mobility could therefore be expected to apply, so for Canadian provinces as for US states "the benefit exceeds the cost" of taxing inheritances as income. In Canada, the provinces do not have to wait for the federal government to act on inheritance taxation.

Full Employment

Article 23 of the Universal Declaration of Human Rights states:

- *Everyone has the right to work, to free choice of employment, to just and favourable conditions of work and to protection against unemployment.*
- *Everyone, without any discrimination, has the right to equal pay for equal work.*
- *Everyone who works has the right to just and favourable remuneration ensuring for himself and his family an existence worthy of human dignity, and supplemented, if necessary, by other means of social protection.*
- *Everyone has the right to form and to join trade unions for the protection of his interests.*

The UN General Assembly adopted the Universal Declaration of Human Rights in 1948 and until the late 1970s, keeping unemployment low was a major objective of Canadian macroeconomic policy. However, since the early 1980s, unemployment has largely dropped off Ottawa's radar.[36]

When you live in a high unemployment economy for a long time, you get used to the many implications of not enough jobs. You think it is normal that people will always be competing for each job rather than choosing between job offers. You see it as reasonable that new graduates should try to get unpaid internships and then have to work second jobs to pay their bills. You grow accustomed to the fact that firms can advertise positions and say "experience required," knowing they will be able to choose from a queue of qualified applicants, without themselves investing in training workers.

My own "Aha!" moment, when I realized just how differently things work when jobs are available, came while interviewing a government economist on a consulting trip to Norway. He remarked, in a matter-of-fact tone, that their current policy priority was to close the few remaining textile mills in the country. I was shocked. Coming from Nova Scotia where every job, no matter how badly paid, is a precious possession, it seemed to me inconceivable that a public official would want to see a factory close. He explained to me that labour hoarding by low-productivity firms was slowing down Norway's productivity growth. At the time, Norway's national unemployment rate was 2.1 per cent. High-productivity firms could not get the labour they needed to expand because workers were not quitting their jobs in textile mills fast enough, despite lower wages and the availability of retraining and mobility programs. Hence, the mills had to actually close to enable high-productivity firms to expand.

In a low-unemployment labour market, everything works differently. Employers have to give new workers a chance. Youth are big winners, as are disadvantaged minorities, new immigrants and poorly credentialed people. In a high unemployment economy, firms do not have to take a chance on such people because there are so many applicants for every available position. But when unemployment is low, firms face a different kind of risk — the risk that sales and profits might be lost because a vacancy remains unfilled. Firms then have incentives to compete for workers. It becomes in their interest to make their jobs attractive and to provide the training that workers need. Adequate daycare for potential workers suddenly becomes, for example, an employer priority, and if more convenient and predictable shift schedules can attract workers, better scheduling becomes an employer initiative, not an employee grievance. And in general, when labour is scarce, firms also have much stronger incentives to use labour more efficiently — faster growth of labour productivity is an important implication, which enables faster growth of real wages.

Economists tend to emphasize the monetary implications of low unemployment — the decrease in poverty and the increase in the earnings of lower middle-class households that occurs when labour shortages mean that the unemployed can get jobs, new workers can enter the labour force and part-time workers can find full-time work. But this is only part of the story. Harder to measure, but often equally important to well-being, is the shift in the balance of power at the workplace that happens when employers start to worry about possibly losing their workers instead of workers always worrying about possibly losing their jobs.

That shift in power can be deeply disconcerting to those who were previously on top. Since for many years there have been many job-seekers for every vacancy,[37] employers in Canada have gotten used to a labour market in which they have the power. However, as the Canadian economy recovered from the Covid-19 recession in 2021–22, the job vacancy rate surged suddenly and briefly came close to the unemployment rate. By underpinning the ability to bargain for better wages and working conditions labour market shortages are a worker's best friend, but labour shortages also make employers work harder for their profits. The business press was filled with their complaints — the federal government listened, and drastically expanded immigration under the Temporary Foreign Worker Program.

Chapter 2 presents statistics on the stagnation in middle-class real hourly wages during Canada's two decades of over 8 per cent unemployment, but these numbers only captured the financial implications for Canadian families. Low unemployment increases the prevalence of long-term jobs and changes the security equation on short-term contracts and "precarious employment." In a high unemployment labour market, short-term contracts mean economic insecurity, but in a labour market with enough vacancies, there is always a replacement job available. There is strong evidence[38] that the stress created by the economic insecurity prevalent in a high unemployment economy causes both physical and mental health problems, which directly affect the quality of life of Canadians (and also increase the costs of the healthcare system).

Economic policy decisions on interest rates, public spending and taxes affect the national unemployment rate by influencing the level of investment, net exports and consumer spending. These changes added together, imply changes in total spending and total employment. However, as Chapter 2 discusses, the single-minded focus of the Bank of Canada on "price stability" produced two decades (1981 to 2001) of high unemployment and middle-class wage stagnation, during which inequality increased strongly. With its control over interest rates, the Bank of Canada could in the future have a positive impact on equality. For decades, the framework for interest rate policy in the United States has assigned equal priority to low unemployment and low inflation. The Bank of Canada could adopt a similar balance of policy objectives — and it should.

In my opinion, although population aging and slowing productivity growth mean that the possibilities for robust middle-class earnings growth are now less than they have been in the past, it is still worthwhile to get as much economic growth as possible. However, that will only happen if the demand for labour is kept strong and the Bank of Canada does not choke off growth by raising interest rates every time it gets paranoid about inflation possibilities. Because technological change is continually altering the distribution of jobs in profound ways, and developments in artificial intelligence are likely to produce layoffs in many sectors, low unemployment is essential if individuals are to find personally satisfying matches between their own aspirations and available labour market options. It is therefore crucial for the Bank of Canada to return to its legislated mandate[39] and place the same weight on maintaining low unemployment[40] as it does on preventing excessive inflation.

A Participation Income?

In small ways, Canada's GST/HST credit and Canada Carbon Rebate payments can be seen as an introduction[41] to the larger agenda of a Guaranteed Annual Income (GAI) — sometimes also called a Negative Income Tax (NIT), or a Basic Income Guarantee (BIG).[42] The basic idea is that all citizens should be guaranteed by the government enough basic income to keep them out of poverty and if people have income from labour earnings or dividends or interest payments, their payments from the government are reduced by some fraction of that market income. Together, the size of the basic income guarantee and the rate at which benefits are reduced with other income determine the "break-even" income, defined as the income level at which payments from government have been reduced to zero, and above which people start to pay net taxes.[43]

Many Canadians already have a guaranteed annual income. Canadians over sixty-five years of age are eligible for Old Age Security

(OAS), which in 2024 provided a universal payment of $9,420 annually. The Guaranteed Income Supplement (GIS) for people over sixty-five who have little or no other income provides an additional $12,792 annually to a fully eligible[44] single person with no other income. Together, the OAS/GIS system effectively provides a guaranteed annual income for Canadians over sixty-five, with a minimum guarantee in 2024 of roughly $22,212 for a single person.[45]

The Canada Child Benefit can also be seen as a guaranteed annual income system for families of working age with children, although it is a system whose payments are too small to live on. At $7,437 per child under six for families with income under $30,000 (reduced to $6,275 per child between the ages of six and seventeen), the Canada Child Benefit in 2024 was an important assistance to low-income families.[46]

The concept of a guaranteed annual income has been around for a long time as an anti-poverty proposal. Today, there is a new level of interest in the idea, because there is a new level of worry that in a future world in which robots can make the robots which will make the stuff that we consume, paying jobs may be scarce. In a capitalist system in which robots have replaced all the repetitive tasks which now exist, it is easy to see how the owners of those robots will get paid for the robot's services. In the future, there will also undoubtedly be some jobs for robot designers (although perhaps not for long — artificial intelligence is vastly economizing on the programming hours necessary for machine design). For a while, robot maintenance technicians will also be needed — at least until repair robots are perfected. Presumably, robot designers and AI systems owners will want to employ maids for their houses, nannies for their children and gardeners for their estates. But how will the rest of us get paid? Where will the consumer demand come from to absorb the output from the automated factories of the future?

People have been worrying about the job losses caused by mechanization and automation ever since the start of the Industrial Revolution, in the late 1700s. So far, jobs in the service sector have replaced the jobs which have disappeared in agriculture, manufacturing and the resource sector.

Today's worries about job loss are fed by the fact that new sensors, "big data" computer technology and artificial intelligence machine learning algorithms have the potential to take labour replacement to an entirely new level. As Chapter 8 discusses, early estimates of possible job loss varied between 9 and 47 per cent of the workforce but in 2024, the IMF estimated that 60 per cent of jobs in advanced economies were exposed.[47]

Whatever the actual number turns out to be, there will be a major impact on the labour market and on economic inequalities. Chapter 8 talks about the potential for robotics to usher in an "Age of Green Abundance," in which humans are freed from repetitive tasks. However, if no adjustments to social policy are made, this will become the Age of Increasing Inequalities with increasing insecurity and poverty for the people who lose their jobs and "winner-take-all" super-profits for the designers and owners of the robots and artificial intelligence systems. It will be more important than ever for Canada to have a financially adequate income guarantee for all humans.

But how should that income floor be designed? The Guaranteed Annual Income idea is not new, but until now it has only actually been implemented for people who are not of working age, like children and the elderly. In the early 1970s, economists of all political ideologies were interested in the Guaranteed Annual Income design because of its absence of bureaucracy (everyone receives the basic benefit) and its incentives to work effort (recipients always keep part of what they earn). Both the American and Canadian governments funded the best economists and sociologists of the day to do groundbreaking empirical research to examine the implications of Guaranteed Annual Income program details for labour supply, family formation, health and well-being.[48] And in the primaries for the 1972 presidential election in the United States, the eventual Democratic candidate, George McGovern, was unwise enough to mention the GAI idea — which turned out to be one of the two things thing Republicans most wanted to remind voters of on election day. One of my mementos from the days when I was in graduate school in New Haven, Connecticut, is an obviously fake $1,000 bill which the Republicans distributed outside polling stations. It proclaimed, "Here is the $1,000 which McGovern promised you."[49] Nixon won in a landslide; McGovern took only Massachusetts and the District of Columbia.

The "something for nothing" aspect of a guaranteed annual income for working-aged people was not popular in 1972 and is still problematic today. Most adults do not want to get "handouts," even if they are in need. A norm of reciprocity underlies many people's ideas of self-respect. It is okay for small children to be dependent on their parents, and perhaps the elderly should be supported because they worked all their lives, but a self-respecting adult of working age should "give" as well as "get." Work in a paying job is respected as a source of income, because the individual is contributing their labour time in return for income.

However, a major problem with using market wages as a criterion of social value is that many of the ways in which people actually now contribute to society — as volunteers or as the carers of children or the elderly — are not paying jobs. These roles require human-to-human interactions and Canada will need more of this labour in future years, even as humans are replaced by robots in the making of things and the manipulation of data. If we were to organize our society to meet human needs, we would set it up so that, as the development of robotics and AI marches on, more and more of our human time is spent in doing the tasks which only humans can do, such as caring labour. But the way our society is currently organized, much of that caring work is unpaid, even though people need cash income.

In Canada, there is a general social expectation (which I agree with) that adults should work if they possibly can — but too often the definition of "work" now excludes unpaid caring labour. Furthermore, the low-wage/long-hours equilibrium that the market mechanism has produced for many people is a long way from the life they would like to live — and even that is under threat from AI and automation. Unmet caring needs are accumulating because of the imbalance between an increasing need for caring labour in an aging society and the time pressures on families created by long working hours at low wages (which people have to take because of the decreasing availability of secure, well-paid positions).

The "Participation Income"[50] idea tries to remedy these imbalances by combining a Guaranteed Annual Income with a substantial increase in the minimum wage and the requirement that receiving the basic income guarantee of the Guaranteed Annual Income would be contingent on some form of participation in society. Having a paid job would be one form of participation but going to school or doing unpaid labour (such as volunteer work or caring for relatives, friends or neighbours) would also qualify. The intention is to recognize the many ways in which individuals can contribute outside of paid employment, at the level at which it is possible for them to do so. Since historically there has long been an important gender dimension to caring labour,[51] one of the implications of a Participation Income is monetary recognition of the type of social contributions which have often in the past been labelled "women's work" — and a Participation Income would contribute to the evolution of gender roles as the option of contributing through unpaid caring labour becomes financially feasible for men, as well as for women.

One of the claims often made for a Guaranteed Annual Income or Basic Income Guarantee is that it can replace other social programs and thereby generate offsetting financial savings for governments. These claims are only partly true. The administrative costs of regular social assistance benefits are not that large as a percentage of total program costs, so although there is a savings in eliminating those costs, it is not a huge amount. A basic income guarantee set at the poverty line would mean regular social assistance benefits would not be necessary, but some social assistance clients have greater needs than others — wheelchairs, medications and special diets can be expensive — so the programs that now provide for special needs would remain necessary.

As well, more money is often a "necessary but not sufficient" part of solving social problems. Some social assistance clients need more than money: counselling, labour market information and social support can be crucial to getting people back into employment. Sometimes it is also employers who can use some help in, for example, making the workplace more accessible for people with disabilities. Middle-class families will also still need the security from income volatility that unemployment insurance and worker's compensation now provide. Adding it all together, a Guaranteed Annual Income or Participation Income cannot replace the full range of social programs that now exists.[52]

Furthermore, the design of a Guaranteed Annual Income or a Participation Income system should not be seen in isolation. To the extent that all citizens can depend on a reasonable "social wage" of public services, cash income needs are less and economic insecurity is reduced. People who can live in public housing with rent scaled to income, travel on cheap and efficient mass transit, send their children to good public daycares and schools and depend on high quality public healthcare when they are ill do not have to buy these essentials in the cash market. Making them available to all citizens also means Canada's "new precariat," who depend on short-term jobs, would face much less stress in their lives. They and their children would be far better off for it. Knowing, for example that public daycare services are available would mean parents would not have to worry about how to cover the daycare fees if there is a gap between their "gigs" — and their three-year-olds would not be repeatedly getting anxious about changing daycare arrangements yet again.

In summary, if the Canada Child Benefit and OAS/GIS systems were expanded and a "Participation Income" introduced for working-age adults, there would be strong gains in income equality and security. These gains would primarily affect, in the first instance, lower middle-class and working-class families in the middle and at the bottom of Canada's income distribution.[53] But there would be gains in economic security for everyone. By putting a floor to real incomes, the "worst-case scenario" outcome would shift upward for all Canadians, which is a contribution to everyone's well-being. Since we do not now know exactly how many of today's jobs will be eliminated in future years by technical change, it makes sense to expand the Participation Income gradually.

The success of a micro-economic policy like the Guaranteed Annual Income or a Participation Income depends on the macroeconomic context — the "work incentives" of a Guaranteed Annual Income system for individuals to accept jobs are irrelevant if not enough jobs are available. If there is no commitment to full employment macroeconomic policy, high unemployment will mean the unemployed will have to depend entirely on transfer payments and the costs of a Guaranteed Annual Income scheme will escalate. Change in macroeconomic priorities therefore also has to be part of the policy mix. Fundamentally, however, it does not make sense to pretend that the problems of income maintenance and technological unemployment do not exist, and therefore do nothing at all.

Fairer Taxes at the Top

As Chapters 2 and 3 document, over the last forty years market incomes at the top of Canada's income distribution have soared while middle-class wages have stagnated. Simultaneously, top-income tax rates declined significantly. An increasing fraction of Canada's total potential tax base became concentrated at the top but taxed at a lower rate. At the same time, cuts to social programs and public services have undermined the well-being of less-affluent Canadians — cuts that could have been less severe or even avoided if Canadians with the greatest ability to pay taxes had not received tax rate reductions. As the income share of the top 1 per cent increases, top tax rates become increasingly important for both government budgets and the fairness of the distribution of disposable income. For many years, Canada's top-income tax rate has been well below the tax rate that would maximize revenue.[54] Furthermore, because Canadian tax law now allows income of different types to be taxed at different rates and enables multiple "tax planning opportunities" for the affluent, the average income tax rate actually paid by top-income earners is considerably lower than the published tax rate. For the top 1 per cent, the top tax rate actually paid has been only about 30 per cent.[55]

In Canada's tax history, the period after 1982 stands out as a time of exceptionally low income tax rates at the top. By contrast, the 1940 to 1980 period, when real incomes for the bottom 90 per cent of the Canadian population were increasing significantly, was a period when the top marginal income tax rate was well over 70 per cent.[56] Trends in the US and the UK have been similar. As a consequence, a chorus of public finance economists now recommend the top income tax rate be raised substantially.[57]

A key word in discussing tax rates is the "effective" part of "effective tax rates" because tax policy is always only partly about published tax rates. Actual tax yield also depends heavily on the definitions of taxable income built into tax law (what some people call "loopholes") and on government enforcement efforts. A low actual rate of income taxation can in practice be achieved by building in tax avoidance mechanisms that are easily accessed or by tolerating low levels of compliance with tax law. Tax avoidance and tax evasion are largely invisible to the general public, because the complexity of tax law precludes much public discussion of the accounting and tax law provisions that enable tax avoidance, while tax evasion is, by its nature, concealed.[58] Since the beneficiaries of the quiet public policy decisions that enable tax avoidance or tolerate tax evasion have no reason to complain and few other people know what is going on, there is little impetus for reform. One example of tax avoidance in Canada, already discussed in Chapter 3, is the tax treatment of Canadian Controlled Private Corporations (CCPCs). Another example is the tax break in Canada for receiving income in the form of capital gains. A third example is the tax advantages accorded to family trust funds.

These tax avoidance mechanisms have interacting advantages. Some of the biggest Canadian family fortunes (e.g., Desmarais, Rogers, Richardson, Shaw) do not appear in "Rich Lists" of individual billionaires because the wealth is held by family trusts, which legally own the assets and are administered by trustees for the benefit of family members using a complex web of family trusts, holding companies, operating companies and CCPCs, all structured to minimize tax liabilities.

As a recent legal article has noted: "A defining feature of Anglo-Canadian tax law is that transactions are characterized according to their legal, rather than economic, substance . . . Sophisticated taxpayers can manipulate the legal form of a transaction to avoid or minimize tax liability. When presented in the right legal form, a payment that functions in practice as salary, a dividend or the receipt of a capital gain becomes an event that escapes taxation."[59] Top law firms which assist, at their usual hourly rate, in this process not only advertise their own in-house expertise in creative tax avoidance, they also advertise their access to the expertise of the recently retired top civil servants[60] who played major roles in designing and implementing economic policy before making their lucrative transition to the private sector.

Since the federal government, through the Canada Revenue Agency, administers the definition of the taxable income base and the collection of income taxes, the federal government makes, on a daily basis, administrative decisions that can lighten the tax load of affluent taxpayers. The federal government also defines the tax code and the regulations that can either impede or facilitate tax avoidance — including the banking regulations that either do or do not effectively monitor the offshore transfer of funds. However, a straightforward way for the federal government to reduce the amount of tax cheating that now goes on would be to copy the Americans and pay "whistle-blower" rewards.

Whistle-blower rewards are effective because hiding serious money from taxation necessarily leaves a paper trail. Carpenters and electricians who work off the books can hide their undeclared cash in the garage and spend it on groceries, because the sums of money involved are trivially small compared to tax evasion at the top. But hiding very large sums of cash under the mattress is not really an option for the very rich. No interest is being earned, burglary is always a possibility and adverse attention will be attracted when you later try to make large cash purchases. The only alternative to holding cash is to acquire financial assets or real property, but some sort of paper trail is always essential if the tax evader is to be sure of being able to eventually get their hidden money back again. As a result, hiding serious money requires the cooperation of lawyers, accountants and bankers (and their secretaries and assistants, who sometimes may feel underpaid and unappreciated).

In the United States, rewards to tax whistle-blowers are a legal entitlement if the amounts in dispute exceed $2 million US. Because the IRS is legally obliged to pay whistle-blowers 15 to 30 per cent of the amount collected, the payout can be substantial. To date, the maximum whistle-blower reward has been $104 million.[61]

Whenever the possibility of higher taxes for the top 1 per cent is mentioned, there is a chorus of dire warnings in the business press that tax rates in Canada are already too high and if they are raised any further, top income earners will leave for the United States. However, although some American states have no state income tax, most states (and some municipalities) do. Adding state and federal taxes together, the two highest top-tax rate jurisdictions in North America in 2024[62] (as in earlier years) were New York City and California — states which included two of the most dynamic and high-income areas in the United States, Wall Street and Silicon Valley. On average, Canadian provinces have for years been relatively low-tax jurisdictions for the affluent; in 2013, for example, the average American top marginal income tax rate on labour income (47.9 per cent) was higher than the average top Canadian rate (45.7 per cent).[63]

Furthermore, the fact that American states vary widely in their income tax legislation has provided strong evidence that high-income people hardly ever move when top tax rates are raised. Complaining is cheap but migration is costly: in addition to the cost of job changes that may accompany changes of residence, there is the cost of separation from family, friends and neighbourhood. But even where these mobility costs are very low, as in US metropolitan areas that bridge state lines (like New York or Chicago), actual tax-induced mobility is tiny.[64] The definitive study of the issue tracked all million-dollar plus income-earners in the United States over thirteen years using forty-five million tax records. It examined both state-to-state migration of millionaires over the long term, and whether the millionaire population living along state borders moved across the state line in response to income tax rate changes. Millionaire tax flight was not found to be exactly zero, but it is very small: "At the margins of statistical and socioeconomic significance."[65] Top income-earners are not in fact "transitory millionaires," always searching for lower-tax places to live, but instead are better seen as "embedded elites" — people who can afford to live where they want to and are reluctant to migrate away from places where they have been highly successful.

Moving to a lower tax jurisdiction means leaving both the networks and the positions that generated the high income and giving up the public services which taxes pay for. Taxes and expenditures are the flipsides of government — lower taxes mean fewer public services are possible. Even for those of the very wealthy who might be comparing the pleasures of life in different places, the thing that matters for their decision is the net advantage, counting both the cost of taxes paid and the benefits of public expenditures received.

In many ways, choosing a place to live is like choosing a restaurant to eat in. Relatively few people decide on price alone and always choose the cheapest item on the menu at the very cheapest restaurant they can find. Most people prefer to look for good value for money. Rich people can afford to pay more for good value, and when it comes to choosing a place to live, they like the things that tax dollars enable, such as pothole-free roads, nice parks and crime-free public spaces. The sky-high real estate prices of rich areas of Toronto and Vancouver (and of Paris, London and Manhattan) are concrete evidence that the affluent can afford to live where they want to and are willing to pay more in order to live in nicer neighbourhoods.

In fact, the expensive furniture, high-end sound systems and fine art which wealthy people have inside their homes can be delivered anywhere in the world. Rich people can consume much the same items within their homes wherever they might choose to live. The real differences in their quality of life emerge when they consider what they can do when they go out in public. So although one can get much more acreage for the dollar in Mogadishu than in Manhattan, rich people are not lining up to move to Somalia, despite the gulf in top tax rates (0 per cent in Mogadishu vs. 51.7 per cent in New York City). This is not due to differences in personal security within the home, since armed guards can be easily and cheaply hired in Somalia. The problem with very low-tax places like Somalia is that personal security outside the home is problematic and high-quality public spaces and elite cultural services are just not available.

Some of the desirable amenities which the affluent like to enjoy, like walking in public without fear of mugging, are in part the joint product of the many agencies of the welfare state. Tax revenue is essential to their provision. Tax revenues also help subsidize some elite activities like symphony orchestras, live theatre and the opera. Even if these activities are primarily of interest to the affluent, public subsidies are essential to their survival. Their costs are typically beyond the capability of a single patron to finance, and arguably going to the opera is a social occasion for the display of wealth. The availability of such cultural activities is an important aspect of the attractiveness for the economic elite of particular places to live, and public spending on cultural activities can be seen as a partial return for the economic elite on their payment of taxes.

The bottom line is that partly because higher top-end taxes help enable jurisdictions to be more attractive places to live, rich people very often complain about taxes, but very rarely leave. And in a world where, as Chapter 3 discusses, top executive compensation is determined by compensation norms of "pay compared to peers," increases in top tax rates also have little impact on work effort. If everyone at the same market income level pays the same tax rate, the pecking order of after-tax incomes is unaffected by a general increase in top tax rates. Tax rate changes that apply to everyone leave status rankings unchanged, so "getting ahead" and being "top dog" remain motivators just as powerful as they ever were at the top of the income distribution. Although there are large differences across countries in the tax rates that people at the top end of the income distribution pay, top executives work about the same hours everywhere[66] — which implies that there are very small costs in decreased work effort when top income tax rates are uniformly raised.

How much more income tax could the top 1 per cent pay? A true 65 per cent top tax rate would involve two things: increasing the published top tax rate and limiting opportunities for tax avoidance and evasion so that 65 per cent was the actual effective top tax rate. Available data record only the income now reported for income tax purposes given current Canadian enforcement procedures, so working with those data arguably underestimates the increase in tax revenue by combining higher tax rates with fewer loopholes and stiffer enforcement. Nevertheless, if in 2023 Canada had implemented an effective top marginal 65 per cent tax rate for a new income tax bracket for the top 1 per cent, it could have been expected to produce roughly 12.3 to 14.7 per cent additional income tax revenue for federal and provincial governments, which in 2023 would amount to between $46.6 billion and $55.7 billion.[67]

The Economy of Higher Wages

Minimum wages have been changing in North America. As a 2017 American study noted, "Minimum wage policy in the US has entered a new wave of state and local activity, in response to over a decade of inaction at the federal level."[68] As of January 2024, fifteen states[69] had hourly minimum wages of $14 US or more (i.e., over $19 Canadian, at 2024 exchange rates). Dozens of smaller cities and counties have also enacted wage standards in this range, covering well over 20 percent of the US workforce. Remembering that the American federal minimum wage has been stuck at $7.25 since 2009 and that thirteen states have remained at that level,[70] this is a pretty remarkable change — and the lack of adverse impacts in the US states that have raised minimum wages is remarkable evidence. Raising the minimum wage in Canada has thus been part of a much wider movement, one which is undoubtedly a response to the growing economic inequalities of North American life. Nevertheless, decisions to join this trend have elicited predictable criticisms arguing that higher minimum wages will result in job losses, raise consumer prices and do little to help low-wage workers.

In the 1980s, most economists would probably have joined in this criticism, based on the then-common belief that the labour market behaves like a classic competitive market, in which individual employers have no control over wages because the forces of demand and supply determine a unique equilibrium wage. In the 1980s it was widely believed that higher minimum wages would do little to reduce inequality and improve the lot of low-wage workers, in part because the benefits to those workers who kept their jobs would be offset by the costs imposed on workers who lost their jobs, and also because many minimum-wage workers were assumed to be teenagers in well-to-do families.

But evidence does matter, and this simple-minded picture has been abandoned by professional economists for quite some time. The prevailing judgement in economics has changed because better data and better research methodology have shown, for well over thirty years now, that when similar jurisdictions with and without an increase in the minimum wage increase are compared, the job loss effects of higher minimum wages have been very close to zero and that higher minimum wages succeed in lifting incomes for low-paid workers and reducing wage inequality.[71]

Among economists, the prevailing view of how labour markets function has also changed. Most research economists now think of labour markets as having imperfect information and frictional unemployment when workers are between jobs. Such markets are quite unlike the simple competitive model (with its strong assumptions, like perfect information and costless mobility). In such an environment, employers typically have some market power in wage setting. "High-wage" and "low-wage" firms can coexist in the same sector. Walmart and Costco, for example, compete directly. Pay and employee benefits are higher at Costco, but so are sales and labour productivity, so both firms can remain competitive in product markets. Since high-wage employers have lower recruitment costs, reduced turnover, more motivated employees and higher productivity, both high-wage/higher-productivity firms and low-wage/lower-productivity firms can be profitable and remain in business.[72]

Although both high-wage and low-wage firms may continue to survive if the market is left to its own equilibrium, Canadian workers would be better off if all firms paid higher wages. One of the desired implications of a higher minimum wage is that it takes wage rates out of the competitive struggle between firms because a higher minimum wage prevents firms from using a low-wage strategy to lower their costs. Instead, firms have to compete by looking for productivity and quality improvements. A higher minimum wage is thus a key ingredient in a national economic strategy that emphasizes productivity growth. Higher labour productivity is in the national interest, in combination with a macroeconomic policy that maintains adequate demand so that enough jobs are created.

Other Policies

These five policy changes would work together to decrease inequality by changing the distribution of market income, the distribution of the tax burden and the distribution of transfer income. Many other policies that would reduce inequality of outcome and inequality of opportunity could also be mentioned — indeed just about all public policies affect the distribution of income, wealth and security in some respect.

All the policy proposals suggested here can be said to be "reformist." Each alters some specific aspect of Canadian public policy, but even if they were all adopted the fundamental nature of Canada's market economy and political framework would not be changed. My hope is that such reforms can maintain the flexibility, productivity and freedoms of a market-based economy by helping to increase the fairness of income distribution which underpins widespread public acceptance of that economic and social system. My worry is that many of the people now securely at the top of Canada's income distribution, who have done very well for themselves financially over the last few decades, may still buy into the policy agenda that produced their personal prosperity — and that they cannot quite see the anger and anxieties of other Canadians.

As this book went to press in 2024, a key question for Canada was whether or not post-Covid-19 public policies would snap back to the same Neo-Liberal agenda that fueled the increasing inequality of the previous forty years. The Covid-19 pandemic highlighted some of the limitations of that market faith. Having so many incomes evaporate overnight, in a way that so obviously was not due to personal failings, was a strong advertisement for the insurance value of social safety nets. Global value chains failed, just when medical supplies were urgently needed. Fundamentally, the market mechanism inherently cannot cope with a pandemic because each individual's chances of remaining healthy depend directly on the health and behaviour of their fellow citizens in a process that market prices cannot assist.

Like the ongoing climate crisis or the long-ago challenge of defeating Nazi Germany, a pandemic creates a collective action problem. In dealing with a common threat to all citizens, government plays an unavoidably essential role, but government policy decisions cannot be effectively implemented without a basic level of social cohesion and buy-in. The Covid-19 pandemic and the climate crisis have tested, and are testing, how much social cohesion Canada actually has. Both issues have been greatly complicated by the shimmering allure of denialism and the multiplicity of rabbit holes to be found "doing your own research" on the web. Public trust in emerging scientific information and public cooperation in behavioural change is essential to the effective solution of both problems. But also central to the cooperation and trust necessary in solving collective action problems is a widespread belief that costs and benefits to individuals are being fairly shared. When the gains from growth have gone to the top for decades and when most of the 99 per cent struggle with affordability in an increasingly insecure and unequal economy, one cannot expect the social cohesion, public trust and cooperation needed to deal with big collective action problems. Increasing economic inequality thus matters both in itself and because of the other big problems whose solution it prevents.

It is quite possible that mild reforms, such as those advocated here, will not happen. It is possible that Canada's elites will just double down on the failed economic policies of the past forty years, that inequality and insecurity will continue to increase and that scapegoats and manufactured culture wars will for a while divert public resentments. There are plenty of international examples of that dismal scenario. I hope that does not happen. I hope that the tolerant and inclusive political and social framework which is so uniquely (and wonderfully) Canadian does not continue to be undermined by increasing inequality and insecurity. Personally, I continue to believe that Canada in the early twenty-first century is still one of the best possible places to live that the world has ever seen — and that reducing Canadian economic inequalities is essential to keeping it that way.

ENDNOTES

Introduction

1. Between February and April of 2020, 5.5 million Canadian workers, amounting to 28.5 per cent of the workforce, lost their job or most of their work hours. The official unemployment rate increased from 5.9 per cent in February to 13.8 per cent by May, but that massively understated the job market crash because it did not count the increase in jobless people who had not looked for work, believing none was available. If they had also been counted as unemployed, the May 2020 unemployment rate would have been 18.2 per cent (see Statistics Canada. Table 14-10-0077-01 Supplementary unemployment rates, monthly, unadjusted for seasonality). Canada's GDP dropped at an annualized rate of 38.7 per cent between April and June before bouncing back somewhat with reopening in the third quarter and then stalling again with the onset of the second wave, new variants and new lockdowns in late 2020.
2. See https://www.canada.ca/en/department-finance/services/publications/economic-fiscal-snapshot/overview-economic-response-plan.html.
3. See Canadian Wildland Fire Information System Weekly graphs, cwfis.cfs.nrcan.gc.ca/home.
4. As well, gasoline is a standardized commodity that drivers have to buy repeatedly at a very visibly advertised price, so changes in its cost are much more salient to consumers than an objective analysis would predict. In 2011, for example, when the price of gasoline rose between January and May in the United States by roughly $0.25 per litre, the increase in average annual household spending on gasoline was about $500, which was approximately 1 per cent of median US annual household income. But Gallup (2011) found that 67 per cent of Americans reported this had caused them financial hardship (21 per cent reported "severe hardship"). Although this is surely massively overstating the objective impacts of the gasoline price increase, the key political fact is that two-thirds of Americans thought they were experiencing hardship because of higher gasoline prices.
5. See Osberg (2016). I was one of the over 240 economists who signed "An Open Letter from Economists on Canadian Carbon Pricing"; https://ecofiscal.ca/2024/03/26/open-letter-carbon-pricing.
6. The "Neo-Liberal" label is commonly affixed to a package of policies: monetary policy that aims only at low inflation, fiscal policy targeting balanced government budgets and structural policies emphasizing privatization, deregulation, reduction of social spending and taxation and expansion of "free trade" agreements. That agenda has dominated public policy in Canada since the early 1980s. However, since zero-deficit government budgets were at the heart of the Neo-Liberal agenda until discarded during and after the Financial Crisis and Great Recession of 2008 to 2010, in my opinion, 1981 to 2008 can be called "Triumphant Neo-Liberalism" while the 2011 to 2019 period is best described as "Zombie Neo-Liberal." For a trenchant critique see Sullivan (2023).
7. Osberg (1981:205). Both my Honours B.A. thesis at Queen's (1968) and my PhD thesis at Yale (1975) were on earnings inequalities. My first book was *Economic Inequality in Canada* (1981), which was followed by *Economic Inequality in the United States* (1984; reprinted by Routledge Revivals in 2015).
8. Aaron (1978).
9. Osberg (1981:1).
10. Mathematically, the Gini index (G) is calculated as the average of the absolute value of the relative mean difference in incomes between all possible pairs of individuals, as in Equation (1.1): $G = \frac{1}{2\overline{v} \cdot n \cdot (n-1)} \cdot \sum_{i \neq j}^{n} \sum_{j}^{n} |v_i - v_j|$

where y_i and y_j = income of individuals i and j, n = total population size, y = average income of all individuals.

Since most people, and most possible pairs of people, are in the middle of the income distribution, the Gini is most sensitive to income changes in the middle ranges of the income distribution. See Chapter 2 of Osberg (1981) or (1984).

11. See Osberg (2017) for formal proof and numeric examples.
12. Coldwell (1948:2) and Apostolic Exhortation (2013).
13. Unless specifically noted otherwise, all income numbers reported in this book are adjusted for inflation and expressed in 2022 dollars using the All-Items Consumer Price Index from Statistics Canada, Table 18-10-0005-01, *Consumer Price Index, annual average*, https://www150.statcan.gc.ca/t1/tbl1/en/tv.action?pid=1810000501. Tax return data on tax filer incomes are taken from Statistics Canada, Table 11-10-0055-01, *High income tax filers in Canada*, https://www150.statcan.gc.ca/t1/tbl1/en/tv.action?pid=1110005501. The minimum total income, including capital gains, necessary to be in the top 1 per cent nationally in 2021 was $327,700 in current 2021 dollars, which is equivalent to $349,917 when adjusted to $2022 using the All Items CPI. CEO salaries are taken from MacDonald (2024).
14. For comparison, 95 per cent of Canadian taxpayers declared total incomes of $159,422 or less in 2021, and 75 per cent had total incomes under $76,775.
15. The wealth of the Thomson family increased from $54.3 billion to $57.9 billion. Strictly speaking, since income is equal to consumption plus savings their $3.6 billion increase in wealth is only the savings from their income; see https://www.forbes.com/profile/david-thomson/?sh=7de69ad45628.
16. Chapter 6 will discuss the role capital gains on housing plays in middle-class wealth formation.
17. Osberg (1981).
18. See, for example, Osberg and Xu (2008) or Osberg and Sharpe (2014).
19. See Anderson (1983).
20. Differences in life experience and spiritual framework can create a huge gulf in mutual comprehension between Indigenous and non-Indigenous people. My own story can perhaps be illustrative. I now live in Nova Scotia but I was born and raised in Ontario. My parents were both born and raised in Alberta, but none of my grandparents were. Three immigrated, from Norway and England, and one came from Nova Scotia, all following economic opportunity to homestead in Alberta during the early 1900s Wheat Boom. When boom turned to bust and Alberta became a "have-not" province, my parents followed the jobs east in the 1940s. In all these moves, land has been something that is bought and sold. In this respect, I think the Osberg clan is quite similar to most non-Indigenous Canadians. Very, very few non-Indigenous Canadians (almost entirely in Quebec and Atlantic Canada) now live where their ancestors lived, and even for them, religious traditions like Christianity or Islam place no particular importance on living in a particular place. This is a sharp contrast to Indigenous belief systems, in which connection to ancestral lands forms a central part of spiritual identity.
21. As a non-Indigenous person, I would feel uncomfortable writing such a book on my own.
22. Looking back on things, I do wonder if I might not have been encouraged in this attitude by my mother, who was a remarkable woman.
23. See the program's site at http://www.dairygoodness.ca/milk-in-school/ontario/school/run-a-milk-program/set-up-a-payment-system.
24. See, for example, Kahneman (2011).
25. This finding is often referred to as the "Easterlin Paradox." Originally advanced in the 1970s, Easterlin has ably defended it ever since. See Easterlin (2013).
26. See Phipps, Osberg and Burton (2001).
27. See Frey and Stutzer (2001) and Helliwell and Huang (2014).

28. Tanzania Food and Nutrition Centre (2014:10). In the 2012 Tanzania census, 39.7 per cent of households reported owning a bicycle and 2.5 per cent of all households owned a motor vehicle.
29. Environmental costs are particularly important to consider if there are "tipping points" in the natural environment (such as the melting of polar glaciers), above which costs may escalate rapidly.
30. See Osberg and Sharpe (2002) for an early exposition and http://www.csls.ca/iwb.asp for up-to-date estimates.
31. Including civil liberties within an index that also includes, for example, average income makes the implicit assumption that a few dollars more of income could compensate Canadians for a few less civil liberties — a perspective which I reject.

Chapter 1

1. Using current exchange rates — see GDP per capita (current US$) — India | Data (worldbank.org), https://data.worldbank.org/indicator/NY.GDP.PCAP.CD?locations=IN&.
2. Because transfer payments, like the HST tax credit, have been increasingly delivered through the income tax system, low-income Canadians have an incentive to file. Coverage of the adult population by the income tax system has been nearly complete since 1992.
3. See Milligan and Smart (2014) and https://realtimeinequality.org.
4. Income funnelled through Canadian Controlled Private Corporations (CCPCs) is not recorded in the individual income tax data. This has become an increasingly used method of tax avoidance — CCPC revenues more than doubled as a percentage of GDP between 2002 and 2014, increasing from 3.1 per cent of GDP in 2002 to 6.9 per cent in 2014 — see Finance Canada (2017:11 Chart 4). A trend to greater tax avoidance at the top means data based on income tax records will increasingly understate actual top incomes. Nevertheless, Figure 1.2 still does illustrate how changes in Canada's tax system can affect reported top-end incomes. In the 2015 federal election, a campaign promise of the winning Liberals was to increase the top marginal tax rate for federal income tax. Middle class people typically have little control over when to report their income but tax planning (e.g., in the timing of when to take capital gains) is very common at the top of the income distribution. Since top income earners could expect, in late 2015, that income reported in 2016 would face a higher tax rate, it was clearly advantageous for them to shift 2016 income into the 2015 tax year — so the income tax data show a spike in the reported 2015 incomes and a crash in the reported 2016 incomes of top income recipients.
5. A single employable person on social assistance got significantly less in 2022: $9,493 per year. See All-Canada overview — Maytree, https://maytree.com/changing-systems/data-measuring/welfare-in-canada/all-canada/.
6. In the fairy tale, Cinderella marries the wealthy prince, and if rich people frequently married poor people, that marriage pattern would tend to equalize family income even if individual incomes were unequal. However, in the real world, the opposite is true — people of similar income, education and backgrounds tend to marry each other. An increase in that tendency further increases family income inequality (e.g., in bygone days, when doctors were almost exclusively men and lower-income nurses were almost always female, doctors marrying nurses equalized family incomes a bit compared to today, when doctors often marry doctors). While some of that is going on, it has only a small impact on trends in family income inequality. See Hou and Myles (2007) and Lu, Morissette and Schirle, (2011).
7. Total household income determines the potential consumption by all household members, but the available data is rarely able to detect inequality in the sharing of household income — see Osberg (2015c).
8. The average per person cost of living is lower in larger households because, for example, a two-bedroom apartment rents for less than twice the cost of a one-bedroom apartment of similar quality (since both apartments only need one kitchen and bath-

room). To account for the economies of scale in consumption of larger households, total after-tax income is transformed by dividing the household's total income by the square root of household size to calculate the disposable income per adult equivalent. Statistics Canada then assumes all household members share equally in household consumption, and all persons are ranked from lowest to highest by the value of their adjusted equivalent household after-tax income. There are several equivalence scales in use in the international literature, and the methodology of calculation of "equivalent income" has a specialist literature of its own; see, for example, "Equivalence Scales over Time and Space," Session 2B: at IARIW 33rd Conference, Rotterdam, the Netherlands, August 24–30, 2014. Papers can be downloaded at http://www.iariw.org/c2014netherlands.php.

9. Statistics Canada, Income Distribution by Size in Canada (1998), Catalogue No. 13-207, CANSIM Table 202-0701 V1546461 to V1546465, CANSIM Table 206-0031 and Podoluk (1968). The income concepts in Table 1.2 and Figure 1.4 do not align exactly. In the 1950s and 1960s, statistics were presented on the shares in the distribution of total income before tax of families and unattached individuals, without adjustment for household size. Table 1.2 presents more recent data using the same concepts, in order to keep comparability over time. As discussed in the text, it is now normal practice in comparisons over time and internationally to deduct income taxes paid and report "equivalent disposable income" after adjusting total after-tax household income to reflect economies of scale in household size. That data is available at Table: 11-10-0193-01 since 1976 and Figure 1.4 uses this concept, but it is not possible to go back to the historic data from before 1976 and make these adjustments.
10. Osberg (1981:205).
11. See Osberg (1981, 2017) or Jenkins (1991) for more complete discussions.
12. See https://data.oecd.org/inequality/income-inequality.htm.
13. Since governments also raise revenue from other sources (e.g., HST, corporate taxes) and provide in-kind benefits (e.g., health care, police services), Figure 1.5 presents only part of the impacts of government on inequality.
14. Atkinson (1970) remains the classic article. Writing at a time when different researchers often used different indices of inequality (e.g., the Gini index, Theil index or coefficient of variation), he showed how the mathematical construction of these different indices of inequality emphasized more or less heavily income changes at the top, middle or bottom of the income distribution, which meant that they often disagreed in their inequality rankings of countries. He therefore argued that a researcher's empirical choice of inequality index to use was implicitly also an ethical choice about which aspect of inequality was most important to them. His work set the technical agenda for inequality research for decades, but the Atkinson index of inequality required an explicit statement of ethical priorities and never really caught on. Written for a general audience as he was dying of cancer, his last book — *Inequality: What can be done?* Atkinson (2015) — only presented data on the Gini index. Osberg (2017) discusses some of the limitations of the Gini index.
15. Researchers on income inequality are well aware that assigning average equivalent income to all individuals within households assumes inequality within the household (e.g., between men and women or between adults and children) to be zero. That assumption implicitly denies the importance of gendered inequalities of power in allocating resources within households, an assumption which is highly unlikely to be accurate — but data constraints mean there is usually no option. Osberg (2015c) is an exception.
16. The Gini index of market income inequality increased from 0.369 to 0.403 between 1981 and 1983 (i.e., by 0.034 Gini points), but there was a much smaller increase (from 0.285 to 0.296, or 0.011 Gini points) in the Gini index of disposable personal income. Frenette, Green and Milligan (2009) have documented how policy shifts in both taxes and transfers increased income redistribution in Canada during the 1980s and early 1990s.

17. Osberg (2017) showed how the Gini index could stay at exactly 0.317, even if the top 1 per cent income share increased from 1.8 per cent to 32.7 per cent.
18. See Statistics Canada, Table: 11-10-0192-01 (formerly CANSIM 206-0031); If one ignores unattached individuals, in 2022 the 20th to 80th percentile of economic families spanned the substantially higher total income range $64,200 to $159,700, due to multiple earners in most families.
19. Other index numbers which summarize income or wealth inequality include the coefficient of variation, the Atkinson index, the Theil or other Generalized Entropy indices. For a fuller discussion, see Osberg (1981, Chapter 1) or Jenkins (1991).

Chapter 2

1. See CANSIM, Table 383-0027.
2. Canadian pessimism is not at all unique. In sixteen of the nineteen countries surveyed, a majority of respondents thought that children would be worse off financially than their parents. See https://www.pewresearch.org/short-reads/2022/08/11/large-shares-in-many-countries-are-pessimistic-about-the-next-generations-financial-future.
3. The question asked was "Comparing your current annual income to what your father earned at the same age as you are now, would you say that, using inflation-adjusted dollars, you earn more, less, or about the same as your father?"
4. The other available self-identification categories of "poor" (11 per cent) and "upper class" (4 per cent) were stable in size. In addition, some respondents either did not answer or said, "don't know." See Graves (2017). In 2023, 6 per cent of respondents to an Angus Reid poll self-identified as "lower/poverty class," 17 per cent as "working class," 17 per cent as "lower middle class," 42 per cent as "middle class," 17 per cent as "upper middle class" and 1 per cent as "upper class." See Korzinski (2023).
5. See Middle-Class-Identity-Release-Dec-2023-1.pdf (pollara.com), https://www.pollara.com/wp-content/uploads/2023/12/Middle-Class-Identity-Release-Dec-2023-1.pdf. The Pollara data have been repeated most years since 2014. The percentage who self-identify as "middle class" is always sharply higher if no other options are presented than if other options, such as "working class," are also presented.
6. Pollara did not allow the fence-sitting response category "about the same." The data split 51/49 per cent depending on which alternative is mentioned first.
7. The question asked was, "How important are each of the following factors in causing the stagnation or decline of Canada's middle class?" (Graves 2014:26, 27).
8. Figure 2.1 splices together two data series (for 1914 to 1961 and for 1961 to 2000). It shows "real average hourly labour compensation" defined as total labour compensation (taken from the National Income accounts, and therefore including the employer cost of CEO stock options, as well as social insurance contributions and fringe benefits such as employer-paid pension and health plans), adjusted for changes in the consumer price index and divided by total hours worked in the economy in the same year. Hourly labour compensation is therefore greater than survey respondents' reports of their money wages directly received, which is the wage concept recorded in the Census data underpinning Table 1.1 or the survey data of Figure 2.2.
9. Alvaredo, et al. (2013:13).
10. See Duclos and Pellerin (2016), Table 4.
11. Examples of privatization at the provincial level include Ontario Hydro, Nova Scotia Power and the Potash Corporation of Saskatchewan.
12. Duclos and Pellerin (2016:261).
13. The year to year volatility of top end incomes in the past means projection of trends can be quite sensitive to the years chosen for forecasting top end income trends. If income changes are, for example, assessed relative to a base year of 2000, rather than relative to the initial year of 1982, income gains will appear to be concentrated in the 1982 to 2000 period — but income tax data on top income percentiles after 2000 was

heavily influenced by greater tax avoidance through CCPC usage. In a volatile time series, assessment of trends can be quite sensitive to selection of the starting and ending points.

14. Since the annual income of the 25th percentile in 2021 was especially affected by transfer payments (like CERB benefits) implemented during the Covid-19 pandemic, but since rescinded, the calculation of a simple 1982 to 2021 trend for the 25th percentile is likely to be misleading.
15. The federal government's jurisdiction includes roughly 10 per cent of employment.
16. Catalogue no. 14280001, *Collective bargaining coverage rate, 1997 to 2021.* Release date: May 30, 2022, http://www.statcan.gc.ca/pub/11-630-x/11-630-x2015005-eng.htm.
17. Canada's Labour Force Survey has collected the data necessary to calculate the unemployment rate using essentially the same conceptual methodology since 1945 (quarterly) and 1952 (monthly). Since 1976 an enlarged sample size has enabled the examination of cities and labour market regions within provinces and the data since 1976 has been easily available on the CANSIM computer database. (Chart 9 of the 2024 federal budget documents plotted annual unemployment since 1976.) That easy availability of recent unemployment data may be part of the reason why earlier years, and the possibility of low unemployment, have largely been forgotten by many federal government economists. The federal government's 2024 budget stated, for example: "The unemployment rate, at 6.1 per cent, is low by historical standards (Chart 9) [Finance Canada, 2024:7]" — which ignored the fact that in the twenty-eight years from 1946 to 1974, Canada's unemployment rate averaged 4.6 per cent. See History of the Canadian Labour Force Survey, 1945 to 2016 (statcan.gc.ca), https://www150.statcan.gc.ca/n1/pub/75-005-m/75-005-m2016001-eng.htm.
18. In the last quarter of 1974, consumer price inflation averaged 12.2 per cent, compared to 8.8 per cent in the last quarter of 1978. See CANSIM Table 326-0020.
19. CANSIM v122497.
20. Crow (1988).
21. As of January 2024, the ten-year average of the monthly real rate of interest (i.e., the nominal interest rate minus the rate of inflation) on five-year mortgages in Canada was 1.68 per cent. Twelve Month change in Monthly Consumer Price Index from Table 18-10-0004-1; Average Residential Mortgage Lending Rate: 5 Year from Table 34-10-0145-01.
22. CANSIM v122497. See McCracken (1996) and other chapters in Osberg and Fortin (1996).
23. Regular beneficiaries as a percentage of the unemployed averaged 37.9 per cent in 2023/2024. See Statistics Canada, Table 14-10-0017-01 and Table 14-10-0009-01, https://www150.statcan.gc.ca/t1/tbl1/en/tv.action?pid=1410001701 and https://www150.statcan.gc.ca/t1/tbl1/en/tv.action?pid=1410000901.
24. See Chapter 4 — especially Figure 4.1.
25. Kneebone (1996:57) and Chapter 3 in Osberg and Fortin (1996).
26. Unless there is a surplus of tax revenue over program expenditure, that is, a positive "primary balance."
27. The "debt stability" equation has been most often used in the context of public sector finances, but its logic is equally applicable to households and the private sector. It starts from the accounting identity that the stock of debt at any particular time is equal to the previous period's debt plus interest accruing on past debt minus whatever amount was paid back on the debt (for governments, the pay-back amount is often called the "primary balance" and is the surplus of current revenue over current spending). The Debt Stability Equation can be expressed as Equation (2.1):

    (2.1) $D_t = (1 + r_t)^* D_{t-1} - PB_t$
    D_t = debt in period t;

r_t = average rate of interest of debt in period t;
PB_t = primary balance in period t
D_{t-1} = revenue - program expenditure in period.

The burden of debt depends on its size relative to income and the interest rate. When income grows faster than debt, the debt-to-income ratio declines and debt becomes easier to handle, year after year. If debt and income grow at the same rate, their ratio is constant. In either event, debt is on a sustainable path. However, if the debt/income ratio is increasing over time, an ever-larger fraction of expenditure must go to servicing the debt rather than financing current spending, a process which is eventually unsustainable. Equation (2.2) derives directly from (2.1); just take the difference between 2.1 and 2.1 in the previous year and divide by income.

(2.2) $\Delta\,(D/Y)_t = (r_t - g_t)*(D_{t-1}/Y_t) - (PB_t / Y_t)$

Y_t = income;
g_t = growth rate of income;
$\Delta\,(D/Y)_t$ = change in debt/income ratio.

In Equation (2.2) the first term makes clear how much debt stability depends on the interaction between the overhang of debt from the past (D_{t-1}/Y_t) and the interest rate/growth rate differential ($r_t - g_t$). Whenever the interest rate exceeds the income growth rate (i.e., when $r_t - g_t > 0$), past debt is compounding faster than income is growing. When the stock of past debt starts to feed on itself in this way, primary balance surpluses must be continual and increasing just to stabilize the debt/income ratio. (Note that it does not matter in this discussion whether we talk about real or nominal interest and growth rates, since inflation cancels out.)

28. A useful website with up-to-date data on the Debt and Debt/GDP ratio is Government Finances — Finances of the Nation, https://financesofthenation.ca/federal-debt/.
29. See Gillespie (1996) and Chapter 1 in Osberg and Fortin (1996). In 1980, as Finance Minister, Allen MacEachen tabled a budget which attempted to end a large number of "tax expenditures" (a.k.a. loopholes). After a hugely negative reaction by the financial community, most of its proposals were withdrawn — thereby ensuring continuing deficits.
30. This increase in interest rates cannot be explained by international trends. The comparable American interest rate (the Federal Reserve Bank discount rate) was 6.0 per cent in March 1988 and 7.0 per cent in March 1990, which meant that the US/Canada interest rate differential widened to an unprecedented level. Nor can increased interest rates be explained by trends in core inflation (4.7 per cent in the second quarter of 1988, 4.4 per cent in the second quarter of 1990). Real short-term interest rates were raised to dramatic levels.As the contributors to Osberg and Fortin (1996) note, there is disagreement about whether or not Canadian governments should have taken action to control their expenditures earlier. However, there is no disagreement about the implications for the national debt in the decision to raise interest rates in 1988. As the debt stability equation implies, when the federal debt-to-GDP ratio is at the level (0.539), as it was in 1988–89, any increase in interest rates has a huge impact on the national debt — much larger than the impact of social programs. Since the increase in interest rates was large, and the consequent recession was severe, a substantial increase in the national debt and the debt-to-GDP ratio was the result. McCracken (1996) estimates the impact on the federal debt at $696 billion, or an increase of nine percentage points in the debt/GDP ratio (over and above the implications of the international recession of the early 1990s). All this occurred despite the fact that during the 1980s elected Canadian governments had adjusted their taxation and expenditure decisions

so as to generate, by 1989, a surplus on their primary balances. The impact of a rise in interest rates on the deficit depends, in part, on the term structure of the federal debt and the percentage of that federal debt that has to be refinanced during the period when interest rates are kept high (quite a while, in this case). The importance of a five-percentage point hike in interest rates can be partly gauged from the fact that, if applied to the entire debt, when the debt/GDP ratio is 0.539, it would amount to an increase in the deficit equal to 2.84 per cent of GDP (which in 1988 would have been over $13.9 billion). This increase in interest costs is over twice the total expenditure of the federal government on social assistance under the Canada Assistance Plan ($5.108 billion in 1988–89). The increase in federal debt in the early 1990s meant deficit reduction became the overriding objective of all Canadian governments, forcing a substantial retreat of the federal government from social policy areas it had influenced since the Second World War. This was all foreseeable — the debt stability equation was well known and the experience of the 1981 to 1983 recession had already shown that a run-up in interest rates would produce a substantial increase in the debt-to-GDP ratio. In the end, tight monetary policy imposed substantial social policy changes on Canadian society.

32. See Ferris and Winer (2007).
33. The Bank of Canada Act (1934) mandated a balancing of objectives: "To regulate credit and currency in the best interest of the economic life of the nation, to control and protect the external value of the national monetary unit and to mitigate by its influence fluctuations in the general level of production, trade, prices and employment." This legislation has never been formally amended but by agreement with successive governments the Bank of Canada has limited its objectives to "keeping inflation low, stable, and predictable," specifically interpreted as a target consumer price index inflation rate of 2 per cent, plus or minus 1 per cent.
34. The Bank of Canada has estimated potential output (above which inflation is presumed to accelerate) using past data on output and inflation and a modified Hodrick-Prescott filtering technique (see Pichette et al., 2015). Because this is essentially a weighted moving average of past events, higher unemployment and lower output growth in the past generate lower estimates of future potential output that can be used to justify restraining growth in aggregate demand, and in turn generate lower actual output, creating path-dependence by policy.
35. Mark Carney (2008–2013) and David Dodge (2001–2008) were exceptions.
36. The terms of trade of Norway and Australia also vary with resource prices. Within Canada, the terms of trade of Alberta, Saskatchewan and Newfoundland are sensitive to commodity prices, but those of the other provinces, home to 85 per cent of the population, are not. See Osberg et al. (2016a, 2016b).
37. All oil prices reported in US dollars.
38. Quoted in Hester (2007).
39. Benes et al. (2012:31).
40. The actual unfolding of events has been that during the last half of 2014, the real price of oil fell from just over $100 USD per barrel (July 2014) to under $50 per barrel (January 2015), before falling even lower over the next year to $28 per barrel in January 2016 and then recovering somewhat to $45.83 in March 2017. The International Monetary Fund's (IMF) 2012 forecast came with estimates of its uncertainty. Confidence intervals (i.e., ranges of values with a specified probability) that the price of oil would be within particular bounds were calculated — e.g., the IMF estimate for 2016 had a 90 per cent confidence interval with an upper bound of $170 per barrel and a lower bound of $100 per barrel. The actual price of oil was thus, in 2016, less than half the lower bound of the 90 per cent confidence interval of the 2012 IMF prediction of world oil prices. The 2014 price drop, and the absence of a full recovery to date, were definitely not expected.
41. See http://www.energy.alberta.ca/OilSands/791.asp. In current dollars, Canada's GDP at market prices at the end of 2013 was $1,904 billion CAD, so oil sands investment was of the order of 1 per cent of GDP on a per-year basis.

42. Hays (2014) estimated average annual salaries in Canada's oil and gas industry at \$123,000 USD in 2013, which is higher than the CANSIM (Table 281-0063) broader aggregate measure for "Mining, Quarrying, and Oil and Gas Extraction" of average weekly earnings of \$1,878 CA in 2013. Both are more than twice as high as the Industrial Aggregate average of \$911 weekly for Canada in that year.
43. Even if a tax cut produces an increase in labour supply (and the micro-econometric evidence consistently indicates this effect is at best very small), a labour supply increase produces a one-time increase in the level of money income, not a change in its growth rate — at the cost of a decrease in leisure time.
44. Similarly, for real individual market income from income tax data 1982 to 2014, the 25th percentile declined at 1.34 per cent while the 75th percentile rose at 0.14 per cent.
45. For example, Cross and Sheikh (2015).
46. For example, Beach (2014, 2016a, 2016b) defines "middle class" in terms of individual earnings, as those individuals within 50 and 150 per cent of the gender-specific median.
47. For example, from 2000 to 2015 the average real equivalent disposable income of the lower-middle class in the fourth decile (the 30th to 39th percentiles) grew at 1.41 per cent annually, which is only slightly less than the 1.47 per cent yearly growth of the upper-middle class in the eighth decile (70th to 79th percentile).
48. Because the Gini index is most sensitive to middle-income differences (see Osberg, 2016), this similarity of household income growth rates in the middle of the income distribution is what implies the Gini index of inequality in disposable household income is almost flat after 2000, at approximately 0.317, for the population as a whole (as Figure 1.3 shows).
49. Time and space constraints have prevented this book from discussing the inequalities of leisure and "time available for self," that hide in the background of inequalities of money income. See Phipps, Osberg and Burton (2001).

Chapter 3

1. Pareto's "law" can be expressed by the equation:

   $$\text{Log } N = \log K - \alpha \log x,$$

   In this equation, x is any particular level of income, N is the number of people with incomes equal to or greater than x and K and α are parameters. The Pareto distribution has long been found to provide a good fit to the upper tail of the income distribution and, as Atkinson et al. (2011:13) noted, it implies the average income of people with income greater than x is always equal to a constant multiple of x, which is α/α-1. Hence, the inverse of the coefficient α in a Pareto distribution is a measure of the steepness of the income pyramid, and World Top Incomes Database data indicate it increased by about half between 1984 and 2012 in the United States (from 2.012 to 2.934). Lydall (1959) showed how α depends on the span of control in wage hierarchies and norms of relative wages. Pareto (1896) himself believed α to be an immutable constant, a conclusion Creedy (1977) showed to be unwarranted, even with Pareto's own data.

   Nevertheless, Pareto himself drew very strong implications from his "law": that the people who are at the top of the social pyramid are those who are "aptes à la lute vitale" ("fit for the vital struggle") and if any attempt is made to redistribute income "la société tout entire tomberait en decadence" ("all society will fall unto decadence") (Pareto 1907:391). Later in life Pareto was a prominent supporter of Mussolini and the Fascist regime in Italy.
2. See Frenette, Green and Milligan (2007).
3. In the United States, income tax records are used to create an over-sample of households likely to be high-income, which only partially solves the problem.
4. Economic historians have worked with historical records to estimate national income back to the early 1800s; see, for example, Maddison (1991).

5. Wolfson, Veall and Brooks (2014) note that for high-income individuals in Canada, there can be major tax advantages in flowing income through a Canadian Controlled Private Corporation (CCPC) in deferral of taxation, the potential to income split with family members in lower tax brackets and the potential to restructure income as capital gains, for advantageous tax treatment. Although not usually an option for most salaried employees, it is relatively cheap to incorporate and receive professional or business income through a CCPC — income that does not appear in the statistics on top-end incomes (such as those reported in Chapter 1).

   Wolfson et al. also note (2014:9) that sophisticated tax planning may often involve multiple layers of CCPCs. In total, there were about 1.95 million CCPCs in 2010, of which 1.7 million were traceable and they emphasize the complexity of CCPC structures and ownership; fewer than 5 per cent of tax filers in the bottom half of the income distribution owned shares in a CCPC (and these could be other family members who are income splitting with top earners). However, roughly 70 per cent of tax filers at the very top 0.01 per cent own one or more CCPCs. There is a similar tax option for Americans in their income tax code, but in the United States, all such income is attributed back to the taxpayer. (Wolfson, Veall and Brooks (2014:12,13).)

   CCPC income is more important the further up one goes in the income distribution; it adds more than $600,000 for the top 0.1 per cent, and from $2.7 to $3.5 million to measured annual income for the top 0.01 per cent. CCPC income in 2010 (the latest year available for research) was estimated to be at least $48 billion, which was about 44 per cent of the total declared income of the top 1 per cent of tax filers. Adding CCPC income would increase average top 1 per cent income by over $100,000 per year and would increase their income share by at least 3.3 percentage points. See Wolfson, M., Brooks, N., Murphy, B. & Veall, M. R. (2016).

   Trusts are another device to spread income among beneficiaries, shift income to lower tax offshore jurisdictions and defer or avoid taxation. The Desmarais, Rogers and Shaw family trusts are Canadian examples.
6. Xuereb, Fisher, Delorme and Lajoie (2023: 10,11).
7. Alvaredo, Atkinson, Piketty and Saez (2013: 13). See also Atkinson and Piketty (2007); Atkinson, Piketty and Saez (2011); Burkhauser et al. (2009); or Morelli, Smeeding and Thompson (2014: 79), who noted, "the rise in the top end has driven much of the distribution in the United States." Murphy et al. (2007, 2008), Yalnizyan (2010), Veall (2012) and Osberg (2008a, 2013) had earlier come to a similar conclusion for Canada.
8. In Osberg (2018) Figure 3.1 shows the top 1 per cent share up to 2010 in the US, Australia and Canada. That data shows a lower Canadian top 1 per cent share, albeit with a similar long run trend. However, high-income Canadians can save on taxes by incorporating themselves as a Canadian Controlled Private Corporation (CCPC) and the income they funnel through a CCPC does not appear on income tax forms and therefore does not show up in the Statistics Canada data on top income earners (unlike the situation in the US where such income is attributed back to taxpayers). Increasing tax avoidance through CCPCs meant CCPC revenue more than doubled as a percentage of GDP between 2002 and 2014, increasing from 3.1 per cent of GDP in 2002 to 6.9 per cent in 2014 — see Finance Canada (2017: 11, Chart 4).

   (Data for later years probably exists within government, but it is not available to outside researchers.)

   Chapter 1 used data derived from income tax records to make the point that income growth in Canada has been considerably faster at the very top of the income distribution. That conclusion is only strengthened by noting that the income tax data are, year by year, missing an increasingly large fraction of the actual incomes of the top 0.1 per cent. However, that increasing omission also means that since the US data includes income from private corporations attributed back to the taxpayer, the US and Canadian data are becoming increasingly non-comparable over time. In this book they are therefore not graphed together in the same figure.
9. See Statistics Canada, (1998) and J. R. Podoluk (1968).

10. See The Demographic Statistical Atlas of the United States — Statistical Atlas, https://statisticalatlas.com/United-States/Household-Income.
11. Balanced growth and stability of the income distribution is a necessary condition for the "representative agent" methodology of macroeconomic theorizing, which became popular among some academic economists in the late 1970s.
12. However, even if more inequality might be guilty of causing these problems, proving it rigorously is difficult. Wilkinson and Pickett (2010) use correlations and scatter plots that cannot establish causation, and they depend heavily on data from only twenty-five affluent countries, and sometimes the US, which exposes their work to the critique that this or that "outlier" might be dominating their results. As Leigh, Jencks and Smeeding (2009: 399) put it, in discussing the relationship between inequality and health, "a fundamental problem is the fact that this is a field with too many theories for the number of available data points."
13. Milligan and Smart (2014) estimated a regression model of the relationship between Canadian top 1 per cent income share and top marginal tax rates, with and without a control for the top 1 per cent share in the United States. Their test of whether top-end pay rates in Canada in the post-Free Trade Agreement era are driven by comparisons with peers in the US found the American share variables to be highly significant, tightly determined (about 1:1), providing a much improved statistical fit and rendering local tax rates statistically inconsequential at the standard 5 per cent significance level. Hence, my reading of their results is that pay norms within the broader North American business community primarily drive pre-tax top-end incomes in Canada.
14. In a "segmented" labour market, pay and working conditions are determined by very different processes in different parts (segments) of the labour market and there is limited mobility between segments. The market for CEOs in Canada nicely satisfies both aspects of this definition of segmentation.
15. See D. MacDonald (2024) *Canada's new Gilded Age — CEO pay in 2022.* https://policyalternatives.ca/sites/default/files/uploads/publications/National%20Office/2024/01/canadas-new-gilded-age.pdf/.
16. See Magnan, St-Onge and Thorne (1995), and Salazar and Raggiunti (2014).
17. See https://albertaworker.ca/news/canadas-100-highest-paid-ceos-were-paid-1-5b-in-2022/.
18. See D. Milstead, "Telus CEO yields title of best-paid telecom chief to new Rogers head," *The Globe and Mail,* April 1, 2023.
19. In 2021, holdings of the Rogers Control Trust and other Rogers Family members in Rogers Communication were 151.4 million shares — which at the August 16, 2022 stock price of $59.34 CAD would be worth $8.984 billion. Shaw Family Trust Shares of Shaw Communications totaled 56.7 million (11.4 per cent ownership) which at a stock price of $35.32 implies wealth of $2.002 billion. Both families obviously have many other assets, so Rogers Communications shareholding of $9 billion and Shaw Communications shareholding of $2 billion are only part of their wealth picture. See Osberg (2022).
20. See https://www.cppinvestments.com/public-media/headlines/2023/cpp-investments-net-assets-total-536-billion-at-third-quarter-fiscal-2023/#:~:text=The%20base%20CPP%20account%20achieved,end%20of%20the%20previous%20quarter.

    Bédard-Pagé, Demers, Tuer and Tremblay (2016:37) examined the performance of the "Big Eight" public pension funds In Canada concluding that: "Over the past 10 years, the Big Eight have . . . an average return of about 8 per cent. This target was achieved despite the sharp losses during the financial crisis." If that lower 8 per cent return is imputed to the $9 billion of the Rogers family and the $2 billion of the Shaws, it implies annual incomes of $720 million and $160 million respectively.
21. Statistics Canada. Table 11-10-0055-01, *High-income tax filers in Canada.*
22. https://www.cbc.ca/news/business/grocery-executive-compensation-1.6802091.
23. Bakija, Cole and Heim (2012). Celebrities in entertainment and sports are widely known, but the visibility of their pay is way out of proportion with their frequency

within the top 1 per cent. Nevertheless, for those at the top of show business who can now reach global audiences, total pay also depends on audience size.

24. In 2021, 39.9 per cent of market income came from wages and salaries for the top 1 per cent and 30.3 per cent for the top 1 per cent of the top 1 per cent — see Statistics Canada Table: 11-10-0055-01 (formerly CANSIM 204-0001).
25. http://www.institutionalinvestorsalpha.com/Article/3716778/The-2017-Rich-List-of-the-Worlds-Top-Earning-Hedge-Fund-Managers.html.
26. See https://www.institutionalinvestor.com/article/2bstpd4t08pc8xwj4we80/corner-office/the-rich-list-the-22nd-annual-ranking-of-the-highest-earning-hedge-fund-manage. Since hedge funds are financial intermediaries, the income derived from their trading is classified as capital income in the System of National Accounts but since they are limited partnerships, not corporations, that capital income is counted as the income of the household sector, not the corporate sector.
27. Lemieux and Riddell (2016:128) discuss the occupational composition and pay levels of Canada's top 1 per cent, which varies substantially by urban area.
28. The 2024 federal budget proposed an increase, for capital gains in excess of $250,000 annually, to 66 per cent of normal income tax rate. The incentive to relabel income as capital gains was reduced but not eliminated. Although the new inclusion rate was less than the 75 per cent inclusion rate instituted by the Conservative government of Brian Mulroney in the 1980s, the business press was filled for weeks with the complaints of aggrieved taxpayers.
29. See Keller and Olney (2017).
30. Canadian Pacific Railway Limited (2015).
31. Keller and Olney (2017:30).
32. See Doeringer and Piore (1971).
33. Western and Rosenfeld (2011).
34. ILO, 2015:3.
35. Statistics Canada. Table 36-10-0103-01, *Gross domestic product, income-based,* https://www150.statcan.gc.ca/t1/tbl1/en/tv.action?pid=3610010301. (The "labour share" of national income is greater than 50.8 per cent because the self-employed receive an income that is partly a return to their capital investments and partly a return to their labour supplied and to calculate labour's share one should add the labour component of self-employment income to the compensation of employees. Unpacking the components of self-employment income can be problematic — but it makes little difference to the trend.)
36. See Lemieux and Riddell (2016:113).
37. When Galen Weston Jr. became CEO of Loblaws at age thirty-four he was two years older than his father had been when he became CEO of Loblaws. https://en.wikipedia.org/wiki/Galen_Weston.
38. When, as in Canada, there is no inheritance taxation, the wealth created by the founder of a family fortune and bequeathed to their descendants is exposed to the continued hazard that future generations of their descendants may try to run things themselves. As an American study of family CEOs concluded: "Firms that promote family CEOs significantly underperform after successions relative to firms that hire unrelated CEOs . . . finding a competent heir among the offspring of a retiring head is often disastrous." Pérez-González, F. (2006:1585).
39. As Saez (2016) notes, the capital component of top 1 per cent income in the United States has been increasing.
40. See Milanovic, Lindert and Williamson (2011) for evidence on economic inequality over the ages.
41. In England, the acquiescence of the lower classes to the social status quo was also greatly assisted by the fact that landed gentry had the right to nominate the local Church of England pastor and often served as the local justice of the peace. A social egalitarian who rejected the established order could expect to suffer both the sanction of the penal code in this life and eternal damnation in the hereafter. These reinforcements to deferential behaviour are no longer available to today's economic elite.

42. https://www.forbes.com/sites/aliciaadamczyk/2015/04/08/how-much-does-a- superyacht-really-cost/#1d3bc4db36bc.
43. Bertrand and Morse (2016).
44. Financial Times (2012:3).
45. In a less materialistic society, there might be a number of status rankings. Some people might get respect because they can tell jokes well, while others might be appreciated for their singing and still others might have reputations as excellent carpenters. Although we are bombarded by messages stressing the pleasures of competitive consumption, nobody pays for advertisements which emphasize the respect and status that can come from non-materialist capabilities.
46. See, for example, Page, Bartels and Seawright (2013).
47. Eighty-five per cent in the Pollara poll and 77 per cent in the EKOS data.

Chapter 4

1. Bottles of 500 ml or less get five cents while larger bottles are worth ten cents. https://novascotia.ca/nse/waste/beverage.container.deposit.refund.program.asp.
2. See http://homelesshub.ca/about-homelessness/homelessness-101/how-many-people-are-homeless-canada.
3. Oxford (1998, 1135).
4. See "Low income measure (LIM) thresholds by income source and household size" Table: 11-10-0232-01 (formerly CANSIM 206-0091), https://www150.statcan.gc.ca/t1/tbl1/en/tv.action?pid=1110023201.
5. See Fellegi (1997).
6. See https://www.statcan.gc.ca/en/topics-start/poverty.
7. See Statistics Canada, *Towards a Poverty Reduction Strategy — A backgrounder on poverty in Canada*, https://www.canada.ca/en/employment-social development/programs/poverty-reduction/backgrounder.html. The consultation process is described in detail in Heisz (2019), and at https://www.statcan.gc.ca/en/consultation/2018/mbm.
8. See Mendelson (2005:34): Rowntree, (1922).
9. Maddison (2003; 59) estimated (using 1990 Purchasing Power Parity USD) that in 1820, UK GDP per capita was $1,706, and for the rest of Europe was $1,245. For comparison, India's GDP per capita was $1,208, rising by 2007 to $2,756 (World Development Indicators — Current PPP International $).
10. Adam Smith (1776) Book 5, Chapter 2, Article 4.
11. Podoluk (1968:184). In 1941, half of Canadian households did not have installed showers or baths and 45 per cent did not have inside toilets.
12. CMHC (1987:Table 1, page 6).
13. In bygone days, management would post next week's shift assignments on a bulletin board at the workplace. Today, it is much more convenient to send everyone a text or to email an Excel file — on the assumption that everyone is online.
14. World Bank (2016:2).
15. Changing food recipes (e.g., for hummus, chili or baked beans) provide an illustration of the socially-defined nature of necessities — and of how many middle-class Canadian students have lost the capability to feed themselves cheaply. In poorer countries today, as in Canada decades ago, beans are the major protein source. The recipes in Canadian cookbooks printed decades ago specify that to make hummus, chili or baked beans, dried chickpeas or beans should be soaked overnight and then cooked before being used. Since buying dried beans is much cheaper than buying cans of beans, that is still how things are done in most of the world — even if it does require some forethought. However, Canadians now get their recipes online and those recipes almost always specify canned beans or chickpeas. Canadian supermarket shelves are therefore dominated by cans and many younger Canadians have no idea that beans or chickpeas can come any other way.
16. When the median real income is rising, as it was during the 1970s, the distinction between an "absolute" and a "relative" poverty line is important and was duly emphasized in Osberg (1981). But when the median real income is stagnant, as it has often

been in Canada since 1980, updating for price inflation and updating for growth in median incomes amounts to much the same thing.

17. Opportunity for All — Canada's First Poverty Reduction Strategy, https://www.canada.ca/content/dam/canada/employment-social-development/programs/poverty-reduction/reports/poverty-reduction-strategy-report-EN.pdf.
18. Djidel et al (2019).
19. For example, based on the assumption of a reference household of two adults and two children, it obtains data on local apartment rents in fifty different geographic areas across Canada and calculates the median cost of rental accommodation for a three bedroom apartment in each local market area.
20. In Canada, because public housing in which rent is geared to income is a much smaller fraction of the housing stock than in most other OECD countries, increased rents in the private rental market have a much bigger impact on poor people than in most other OECD countries.
21. In the European literature, 60 per cent of the median is usually the measure chosen.
22. For example, a community that contained ninety-nine people making $50,000 and one person making $5,000,000 would have an average income of $99,500. If that top 1 per cent person doubled their income to $10,000,000 and everyone else stayed the same, the average income would increase to $149,500 — but 99% of people would still be living on $50,000. Because the median income is not sensitive to large changes at the very top, it is better indicator of the prevailing level of living standards.
23. CANSIM Table 206-0091 reports the LIM.
24. The Fraser Institute has also published a much lower poverty line, based on a costing of the minimum expenses to meet a "basic needs" living standard; in 2021 it was $30,000 for a four-person family, which really should be called "extreme poverty" in the Canadian context. See https://www.fraserinstitute.org/sites/default/files/files-2023/thinking-about-poverty2-counting-the-poor-empirical-evidence.pdf.
25. For international comparisons of the poverty rates of children (0–17), elderly (65+), working age (18–65) and overall using the half median income criterion, see "Inequality — Poverty rate — OECD Data" at https://data.oecd.org/inequality/poverty-rate.htm.
26. Because median income falls in a recession, the LIM poverty line also decreases in a recession, so the impact of higher unemployment on poverty does not show up — as Figure 4.2 shows. Osberg (1981:63) suggested this defect could easily be fixed by drawing the poverty line at half the five-year moving average of median income, not just this year's median income — but that idea has never caught on.
27. See Osberg and Xu (2008,) and references therein.
28. Economists will recognize this as the principle of the diminishing marginal utility of consumption.
29. Matthew (2016) and Rawls (1982:162).
30. Calculated as the average MBM poverty gap (0.361) in Canada in 2021 times the simple average of MBM poverty lines across non-Northern localities in Canada in 2021 divided by the number of people (four) in the reference households. This calculation significantly overstates the cash required to eliminate poverty since economies of scale in consumption are not accounted for (e.g., for a four-person family, and an equivalence scale parameter of 0.5, an additional $1,000 in cash income produces a total increase of $2,000 in equivalent income for all household members — $500 for each of four persons).
31. Until 2011, Statistics Canada published every year its estimate of the "aggregate low-income gap," the percentage of the total income of all Canadians that would eliminate poverty, by bringing the income of all poor Canadians up to the poverty line (see CANSIM Table 202-0804 and Table 206-0041). In 2011, this calculation showed how if the MBM were used to draw the poverty line, it would take 1.3 per cent of total household income to fill the poverty gap, but only 0.9 per cent of total household income would be needed if the LICO-AT were used to draw the poverty line. If the in-

ternational criterion of one half the median after-tax household income (i.e., the LIM) were used to define poverty, a transfer to the poor of 1.4 per cent of the total income of Canadian households would suffice to eliminate poverty entirely. Although such transfers are unlikely to actually happen, these calculations are useful reminders that poverty is a social problem that Canada could actually afford to solve, if there were the political will to do so.

32. Similar tables are available for other years; see Tweddle, Battle and Torjman (2017), Table 3, and https://maytree.com/changing-systems/data-measuring.
33. See Tweddle, Battle and Torjman (2017). The exception to the general Canadian rule of cuts for the least well-off was Newfoundland and Labrador where a serious provincial anti-poverty initiative, fuelled at least partly by oil revenues, raised social assistance rates significantly. See http://www.cwp-csp.ca/wp-content/uploads/2012/05/Newfoundland-Poverty-Progress-Profile-FINAL-.pdf.
34. OECD (2024), Adequacy of minimum income benefits (indicator). doi:10.1787/dcb819cd-en. (Accessed on 18 April 2024.)
35. This increase was mostly concentrated at the top, since (as Figure 2.1 shows) incomes rose very little in the bottom 80 per cent of the population. See CANSIM Table 384-5000, *Data on Long-run Provincial and Territorial Economic Performance, Annual.*
36. See https://maytree.com/wp-content/uploads/Social_Assistance_Summaries_All_Canada.pdf. The provinces do not all report their social assistance caseload data on a consistent basis, either over time or across provinces. Social Assistance beneficiaries in Ontario are down by almost 20 per cent in absolute numbers and since the population has grown by over a third, social assistance beneficiaries have fallen from 9.4 per cent to 5.6 per cent as a fraction of the population. The data for Alberta and B.C. are clearly consistent with the Ontario data cited in the text but data for other provinces are sometimes missing and sometimes inconsistently categorized.
37. See Chen, Osberg and Phipps (2019).
38. See http://www.oecd.org/publications/sickness-disability-and-work-breaking-the-barriers-9789264088856-en.htm and http://www.oecd.org/els/emp/ transformingdisabilityintoability.htm.
39. Jahoda (1979:423).
40. Statistics Canada. Table 14-10-0226-01, *Job vacancies, unemployed and unemployment-to-job vacancies ratio, three-month moving average, unadjusted for seasonality, inactive,* https://www150.statcan.gc.ca/t1/tbl1/en/tv.action?pid=1410022601.
41. It has been known for a long time that labour supply by individual workers does not in fact change much when their after-tax wage rate changes. In economic jargon, the compensated and uncompensated wage elasticities of individual labour supply are both small (typically estimated to be 0.1 or less). See, for example, Killingsworth (1983), Heckman (1993) and Jäntti, Pirttilä and Selin (2014) and the references therein.

Chapter 5

1. See https://www.pollara.com/wp-content/uploads/2023/12/Middle-Class-Identity-Release-Dec-2023-1.pdf and Pollara (2014).
2. See https://www.cashmoney.ca/rates-and-terms/nova-scotia.
3. See Ruggles (1991).
4. See Brooks-Gunn and Duncan (1997).
5. As older workers with higher wages reach retirement age each year and leave the workforce, they are replaced by lower-wage younger workers who are entering the workforce. If wages typically increase with seniority income mobility for individuals as they age is quite compatible with the average wage staying constant. Like people on an escalator which is always running between the same two floors, individuals can experience upward mobility, even when the average remains constant (as Figure 1.1 shows was the case after 1980). The social issue is that before 1980 workers typically experienced both age progression increases and the increase in the average real wages of workers of all ages. After 1980, the rate of material progress for individuals slowed dramatically.

6. See *An ABC of closed Canadian pulp and paper mills — Paper Advance*, https://www.paperadvance.com/blogs/martin-fairbank/an-abc-of-closed-canadian-pulp-and-paper-mills.html.
7. See Beaudry and Green (2000).
8. Boudarbat, Lemieux and Riddell (2010).
9. See Beaudry, Green and Sand (2016).
10. See https://www.oecd.org/future-of-work/reports-and-data/AI-Employment-brief-2021.pdf.
11. See *Gen-AI: Artificial Intelligence and the Future of Work*, (imf.org), https://www.imf.org/en/Publications/Staff-Discussion-Notes/Issues/2024/01/14/Gen-AI-Artificial-Intelligence-and-the-Future-of-Work-542379.
12. Household pre-tax income, after adjustment for inflation.
13. Chetty et al. (2016).
14. Ostrovsky (2017:3). Although there has been no decline in the Canadian intergenerational mobility rate, unlike the American decline, the Canadian intergenerational mobility rate ends up roughly the same as the "coin toss" in the United States. Using the same income concept as used in the American study, absolute income mobility rates varied between 48 and 55 per cent for different birth cohorts, which means it was basically a coin toss whether thirty-year-old Canadians made more or less income than their parents had made at the same age. Similar results were obtained when forty was the comparison age.
15. Guvenen, Kaplan, Song and Weidner (2017).
16. Bowlus and Robin (2012).
17. When incomes vary over a lifetime, researchers who want to summarize the entire earnings stream by calculating the present value of lifetime income have to assume income received at different points of time during a person's life can be made comparable by discounting at a particular rate of interest. That "perfect capital market" assumption that everyone can always borrow or lend at a single constant interest rate is highly problematic, since there is a huge range of interest rates between the rates banks and payday loan companies are now actually charging borrowers, compared to the interest rates they are paying to depositors.
18. See, for example, Barr (2001).
19. Historically, the private sector insurance market could insure against fire hazard because housefires were independent risks and probabilities could be estimated based on long periods of stable risk. Climate change is altering this market reality because the increased prevalence of large wildfires now implies correlated risk, whose future probability cannot be predicted from past historic data.
20. Social assistance in Canada can also be seen as providing insurance against life events for which private insurance is unavailable, as the example of Betty in Chapter 4 illustrates. As well, because low-income people are more exposed to some important risks (like workplace injury or layoff) than high-income people, social insurance programs like EI or workers' compensation are also pro-poor redistributive in an expected lifetime income sense.
21. See Chetty (2008).
22. See Himmelstein et al. (2019).
23. In any given year, the elderly consume more healthcare services than younger cohorts. As well, some people are born with congenital conditions that require more health care all their lives. However, seen from a lifetime perspective at the moment of birth, the expected benefits of the healthcare system are per capita.
24. The benefits of police services are, for example, partly the protection of property (which arguably should be allocated to individuals in proportion to the wealth that they own) and partly the protection of individuals (which should be allocated on an equal per-person basis). Deciding the proportion of each is a bit arbitrary, but in any event the cost of police services is small compared to the cost of healthcare and education.
25. See OECD (2015).

26. For example, Norris and Pendakur (2015), Attanasio, Hurst and Pistaferri (2012), and Krueger and Perri (2006).
27. Simons (1938:58).
28. Hicks (1946:75).
29. Aficionados of fine detail can consult http://www.lisdatacenter.org/wp-content/ uploads/canberra_report.pdf.
30. If some millionaires are miserly and spend very little of their income in a given year, they have consumed relatively little of society's scarce resources for that year. An ethical argument for a focus on income inequality is that millionaires have the choice of how much to consume.
31. In the academic economics literature, advocates of measuring consumption inequality often assume individuals know their "permanent income," but annual income in any given year fluctuates because of transitory shocks. If one also assumes individuals can smooth consumption over time by borrowing and lending on perfect capital markets (i.e., at the same interest rate), then lifetime utility maximizing agents will adjust their consumption in any given year to their permanent incomes, and consumption inequality is a good measure of inequality in permanent income. It is perhaps already obvious from my emphasis on imperfect access to capital and uncertainty in individual earnings that I think these assumptions are very far from empirical reality.
32. See *The Daily — To buy or to rent*, https://www150.statcan.gc.ca/n1/daily-quotidien/220921/dq220921b-eng.htm.
33. In 2024, the federal budget announced that for individuals, 50 per cent of capital gains less than $250,000 per year would, as previously, be included in taxable income while 66 per cent of capital gains in excess of $250,000 annually would be included in taxable income. (Capital gains on owner-occupied housing remain untaxed.)
34. Table: 11-10-0055-01 (formerly CANSIM 204-0001). The argument for including unrealized capital gains in measured income is that even if an asset was not actually sold at an increased price, it could have been sold and can be used as collateral. Indeed, tax specialists sometimes advise clients to retain ownership of assets which have increased in value and finance increased consumption by borrowing, using those assets as collateral. Since loans received are not taxable income, the increase in the value of the asset can be consumed without any tax being payable at all.

Chapter 6

1. I owe this metaphor to my cousin, Martin Spencer.
2. $10 million is the round number — $9.7 million is the exact figure in Table 6.1 (but there has been significant wealth growth since 2019).
3. Gellatly and Richards (2019).
4. Osberg (1981:27) noted the longstanding importance of minority control for concentration of economic power in Canada. An example was the Beaudoin family's control of the Bombardier empire through a limited class of shares with preferential voting rights. See https://www.theglobeandmail.com/report-on-business/bombardiers-founding-family-holds-tight-as-companys-fortunes-shift/article26874902/.
5. Newman (1975:57), quoted in Osberg (1981:33).
6. See Bossart and d'Ambrosio (2013) and Osberg (2015b).
7. The Gini index of Net Worth in 2015 was 0.732, compared to 0.317 for equivalent disposable income — see *Credit Suisse Global Wealth Databook* (2016:106); and Table 3-1, Morissette and Zhang (2006) show there has been an unambiguous increase in wealth inequality in Canada. The Gini index of inequality in wealth increased from 0.691 in 1984 to 0.727 in 1999 and reached 0.746 in 2005. The poorest 40 per cent of Canadian families had very little wealth in 1984, and this did not change by 2005. Meanwhile, the wealth of the top 40 per cent rose substantially, with the largest increases at the very top. In constant 2022 dollars, the net worth of the family at the 95th percentile was $755,971 in 1984, $1,022,493 in 1999 and $1,688,222 in 2005, which represents an increase of 65 per cent in 2005 over 1999, and an increase of 35 per cent in 1999 over 1984. There was no gain in wealth at all in the bottom half of the distribution. Earlier,

Osberg and Siddiq (1988) used probate records in Nova Scotia to compare wealth distribution in the 1870s and the 1970s. Their best estimate of the Gini coefficient of wealth for Nova Scotia in 1871 was 0.89, significantly greater than Davies' estimate of 0.75 of the wealth Gini for Canada in 1970.

8. Both wealth and income thus have a time dimension, but wealth is measured at a point in time (e.g., my net worth as of December 31, 2024) while income is measured over a period of time (e.g., the income I received between January 1 and December 31, 2024).
9. An accounting identity is a statement that is true by definition of terms. Net savings are positive when income exceeds consumption but negative when households dissave, that is, when consumption exceeds income.
10. MacDonald (2024:4).
11. Up-to-date numbers are available at Statistics Canada. Table 36-10-0103-01, *Gross domestic product, income-based, quarterly*, https://www150.statcan.gc.ca/t1/tbl1/en/tv.action?pid=3610010301, and at Federal Reserve Economic Data (FRED) — variable LABSHPCAA156NRUG (Share of Labour Compensation in GDP at Current National Prices for Canada, Ratio, Annual, Not Seasonally Adjusted), https://fred.stlouisfed.org/tags/series?t=canada%3Blabor.
12. See https://fredblog.stlouisfed.org/2019/08/capitals-gain-is-lately-labours-loss/.
13. National income statistics understate the trend to a shrinking labour share because capital's share of national income only counts the income (i.e., rent, interest and dividends) received from the ownership of capital. The salaries, stock options and bonuses of corporate CEOs and other top executives are counted as part of labour's share of national income, even though executive compensation is highly correlated with firm size and arguably derives from control over the firm's capital stock, if not from its formal ownership. As noted earlier, Lemieux and Riddell (2016:113) calculated that if the incomes of the top 1 per cent are excluded from labour's share of GDP, the annual rate of decline in labour's share from 1982 to 2008 in Canada nearly doubled (increasing from 0.17 to 0.30 percentage points annually).
14. Parliamentary Budget Office. (2021). "Estimating the top tail of the family wealth distribution in Canada," Parliamentary Budget Office (2021-Table 4.2 https://www.pbo-dpb.gc.ca/web/default/files/Documents/Reports/RP-2021-007-S/RP-2021-007-S_en.pdf.
15. Although the world's billionaires typically do not respond to sample surveys, they are few enough in number that the business press can keep track of their changing fortunes. It is now common practice to merge journalists' "rich lists" on the very wealthy with survey data on the general population using a Pareto-function interpolation (see Atkinson and Piketty, 2017), as the PBO did, using the Canadian Business "rich list." *Forbes* magazine also maintains a "rich list" of billionaires (see https://www.forbes.com/billionaires), which includes Canadians. Although these lists differ somewhat, and often miss large fortunes held through family trusts and foundations, they are the best available data on the very top end of the wealth distribution.
16. The PBO estimates in Table 6.1, like all the Statistics Canada survey data cited elsewhere in this book, refer to the distribution of wealth among nuclear families (i.e., people related by blood, marriage or adoption sharing a common residence), which will in general differ from estimates of the distribution of wealth among individuals. Estimates of the distribution of wealth among individuals face the formidable problem of attributing wealth within households — e.g., assigning to spouses the value of jointly owned assets like family homes. Hence for most Canadians wealth inequality among nuclear families is the appropriate concept. However, for many reasons — e.g., tax minimization, maintenance of corporate control, intra-family dynamics — ownership of wealth at the very top is often a complex affair of family trusts and a maze of private companies. (For example, in 2023 the $20 billion-plus Rogers/Shaw merger of cellphone networks was a deal between companies controlled by the Rogers Control Trust and Shaw Family Living Trust.) Since the family trusts of the very wealthy link the fortunes of individual family members between generations and across households, the wealth of the extended family is for them the relevant concept.

17. During the first nineteen months of the pandemic (i.e., March 18, 2020 to October 15, 2021), American billionaires increased their wealth by a total 70.3 per cent — a little over two trillion dollars ($2,071,900,000,000). American billionaires sit at the top of a country with a population in 2021 of 332 million and GDP of $23 trillion which dominates world trade and finance. Canada's population in 2021 was thirty-eight million with GDP of $1.6 trillion (US$) — smaller than California. Since Canada is a region within the continental economy, which is only part of the global economy, the top tier of Canadian billionaires have substantially smaller fortunes than the top tier of US billionaires. However, the average rate of growth of billionaire wealth in Canada and the US during the pandemic was fairly similar, at least until late 2021. https://americansfortaxfairness.org/issue/u-s-billionaires-wealth-surged-70-2-1-trillion-pandemic-now-worth-combined-5-trillion, https://docs.google.com/spreadsheets/d/1tJwAN-HA0ZEj39OZz2bnfslxCf4YewjSv8eJH71T-X4/edit#gid=1259834744.
18. Since the financial fortunes of individual members of the second and subsequent generations of the super-wealthy are often linked by family trusts, joint ownership of holding companies and other legal mechanisms unknown to the middle classes, the rankings of ultra-rich families depend on whether wealth held in trusts is attributed back to the beneficiaries of those trusts and whether assets of individuals are aggregated to family totals.
19. Osberg (1981: 27).
20. https://www.nytimes.com/2013/10/10/business/paul-desmarais-canadian-magnate-dies-at-86.html.
21. See Silcoff, S. (2017); Ward, T. (1994).
22. See Osberg (2022).
23. Fix and Cochrane (2023) have used Statistics Canada's database on Intercorporate Ownership (see Intercorporate Ownership, https://www150.statcan.gc.ca/n1/en/catalogue/61-517-X) to trace the linkages of corporate control of ten billionaire families, including the Richardsons, in Canada. Their interactive website provides more detail than is possible in printed figures. (See "Mapping the Ownership Network of Canada's Billionaire Families — Economics from the Top Down" at https://economicsfromthetopdown.com/2023/06/23/mapping-the-ownership-network-of-canadas-billionaire-families/.)
24. The history of the Richardson fortune can be found at https://www.jrsl.ca/history/.
25. https://www.forbes.com/profile/david-thomson/?sh=7de69ad45628.
26. https://www.forbes.com/billionaires/.
27. Using the Canadian Business list of wealthiest Canadian residents, MacDonald (2018) compared Canada's top eighty-seven families in 1997 and 2016 and found that over half (53 per cent) in 2016 had inherited their fortunes.
28. Fix and Cochrane (2023).
29. https://livinghistoryfarm.org/farminginthe50s/machines_05.html.
30. For a fascinating history of why Silicon Valley in California is where it is, see Penn (2022).
31. See "How Irving's Bermuda insurance company piled up millions in offshore tax-free profits," CBC News at https://www.cbc.ca/news/canada/new-brunswick/irving-paradise-papers-1.6628921. In 2022, New Brunswick Premier Blain Higgs, a former Irving employee, defended the practice: see https://www.cbc.ca/news/canada/new-brunswick/irving-offshore-revelations-higgs-no-policy-change-1.6639598.
32. Fix and Cochrane (2023)
33. Newman's 1975 estimates of Canada's wealthiest, included, for example, the Eaton and Molson families. The Eaton family fortune started in Toronto in 1869 and Eaton's department stores dominated retailing across Canada for decades. Their position at the top lasted 130 years — until Eaton's bankruptcy in 1999. John Molson, who emigrated to Canada in 1782, started the Molson family fortune, but they have slipped out of Canada's top twenty fortunes although, with an estimated $1.75 billion, the family was still in the top one hundred in the 2020s.

34. https://maytree.com/wp-content/uploads/Appendix_1.pdf.
35. In some American states, the standard mortgage contract is that the lender cannot seize other assets of the debtor to make up a deficiency in mortgage repayment (this is commonly called a "no recourse" mortgage). Canadian homebuyers do not have this option. See Wolff (2016).
36. Wolff (2011:39, 125).
37. Remortgaging or taking out a home equity line of credit can enable homeowners to monetize their capital gain while remaining in their house. To date, this appears to have been less common in Canada than it has been in the United States, partly because in the US mortgage interest is deductible for income tax purposes, which provides a tax incentive to remortgaging.
38. Part (about 20 per cent) of the increase in my parents' house value just reflects the general increase in consumer prices over this period of time.
39. CANSIM Table 205-0002.
40. Realized capital gains on owner-occupied housing are not taxable, so are not included in income tax data (and are not asked for in survey data). Unrealized capital gains are not included in either survey or tax data.
41. See Marx, *Capital, Volume 1*, Chapter 1.
42. Quoted in Folbre, N. (2011). "Field Guide to the U.S. Economy," p. 15. Source: https://quotepark.com/quotes/1775639-edgar-bronfman-sr-to-turn-100-into-110-is-work-to-turn-100-milli/.
43. Kaissar (2016) notes, "Cambridge Associates' U.S. Private Equity Index returned 13.4 percent annually net of fees from April 1986 to December 2015, with a standard deviation of 9.4 percent (the longest period for which data is available), while the Russell 3000 Index returned 9.9 percent annually over the same period, with a standard deviation of 16.7 percent (including dividends)."
44. See Piketty (2014:440) for examples.
45. Although Dynan et al. (2004) conclude, as theory would suggest, that the marginal propensity to save increases with income, the argument here only requires the marginal propensity to save of the top 1 per cent is positive and some of that increase in saving is in financial assets. Increased savings by the affluent is quite consistent with the likelihood that greater consumption, and net dissaving, by the poorer 99 per cent, might imply a declining average national savings rate. Cynamon and Fazzari (2014) have documented the accumulation of liabilities by the bottom 95 per cent in the US that preceded the financial crisis of 2008. See also Bordo and Meissner (2012) and Kumhof, Rancière and Winant (2013).
46. The statisticians who calculate GDP and other measures of national income always report both "expenditure-based" and "income-based" estimates, which in principle should always add up to the same total.
47. For example, Summers (2013, 2014) and Milanovic (2009).
48. See Finance Canada (2016) or King and Low (2014).
49. The key issue for debt fragility is the differential in growth rates. If top 1 per cent incomes grow at r_1 and bottom 99 per cent incomes grow at r_{99} and $r_1 > r_{99}$, then when net financial claims of the top 1 per cent on the rest of society [A_1] are a non-decreasing fraction of income, $\partial A_1/\partial t \geq r_1$. But financial assets are the liabilities of their issuers, either other households [D_{99}] or governments [D_G] — so $A_1 = [D_{99} + D_G]$. Because the total liabilities of other agents grow at r_1 and $r_1 > r_{99}$, the growth of liabilities is faster than the private income growth rate of the 99 per cent or the total tax base (which is an income share weighted average of r_1 and r_{99}), hence debt/income ratios rise over time.
50. This key idea — that ever-growing gaps between incomes at the top and the middle produce an ever-increasing flow of loanable funds, which eventually produces either a crisis in financial markets and a recession in the real economy or a period of secular stagnation — has a long history. In the nineteenth century, Marx argued strongly that cyclical instability was inherent to capitalism, and in the late 1800s "under-con-

sumptionists" like Hobson ascribed the growth of British imperialism and overseas investment to inadequate domestic absorption of the potential output of capitalism. See Marx (1894), Volume 3, Chapter 15 and Hobson (1900, 1905). Amdekar (2012) provides a modern reinterpretation.

51. Leamer (2007:1).
52. Selected treasury bill yields — Bank of Canada. https://www.bankofcanada.ca/rates/interest-rates/t-bill-yields/. Note that between 2020 and 2022, Canada's national debt increased dramatically but the interest cost of that debt as a percentage of government revenue fell to sixty-year lows because the interest rate on new debt issued was close to zero. See Government Revenue and Expenditure — Finances of the Nation, https://financesofthenation.ca/real-fedprov/.
53. When interest rates on issued debt are zero, or when the central bank creates the money necessary to purchase debt issue (which amounts to the same thing), the public sector deficit can be insulated from a rising debt/GDP ratio — but these options have severe disadvantages and are unavailable to the household sector.
54. This point is developed by Piketty (2014).
55. IMF (2024:18).

Chapter 7

1. Justice Bertha Wilson was the first female Supreme Court justice, appointed in 1982.
2. Constitution Act (1982), Section 15.
3. Burton and Wong (2004), see http://www.catalyst.org/knowledge/women-law-canada-and-us.
4. See https://www.cma.ca/En/Pages/canadian-physician-statistics.aspx and https://www.cma.ca/Assets/assets-library/document/en/advocacy/05-age-sex-prv.pdf.
5. Zawilski (2010).
6. Behavioural psychologists like Kahneman (2011) have long told economists that although it is logically exactly the same to describe a glass as "half full" or "half empty," these descriptors frame the issue differently and that matters. In practice, humans are greatly influenced by framing, which is why it is so central for politics. In both sociology and economics, discussions of equal opportunity and social mobility almost always use examples which illustrate equal opportunity as upward mobility, a framing of mobility that ignores what is happening at the bottom. One never hears "an equal chance of homelessness" advocated as a criterion for "social equity."
7. See Statistics Canada. Table 36-10-0103-01, *Gross domestic product, income-based, quarterly*, https://www150.statcan.gc.ca/t1/tbl1/en/tv.action?pid=3610010301.
8. Since the purpose of this example is to examine the relationship between inequality of outcome and opportunity for individuals, we ignore for present purposes the possibility that the men and the women are married to each other, which would imply family income is equally distributed if secretaries always married executives but would accentuate inequality of family income if executives married executives and secretaries married secretaries. (Note the key issue in family income inequality is the occupations of spouses.) The example would also become a bit more complicated if non-binary gender identities were considered explicitly. These complications illustrate the complexity of measurement of inequality trends, but they do not affect the key point that inequalities of opportunity in access to unequal positions in society are a different issue from the inequalities of outcome associated with those positions.
9. Osberg (2017) shows that in a two-class society with a Gini index equal to G, the population share (N_1) and income share (Y_1) of the poorer group are bound by the relationship that $G = N_1 - Y_1$. In this example, $N_1 = 0.5$ and $Y_1 = 0.166$, so $G = 0.334$.
10. In an accounting sense, some indices of total inequality (like the coefficient of variation or the Theil index) can be additively decomposed, that is, one can say that x per cent of total inequality is associated with "within group" inequality and y per cent is due to "between group" inequality, and x and y will add up to 100 per cent. When that calculation has been made in Canada, as in other countries, within-group inequality by age, gender, region, ethnicity and country of birth typically dominates the calculation of

aggregate inequality, usually by a very large margin. For example, although the average pay of older workers is greater than the average pay of younger workers, this gap is small compared to the inequality among people of the same age, so the percentage of total income inequality associated with between-group inequality by age is rather small. Unfortunately, the Gini index cannot be additively decomposed into the sum of within-group and between-group components except in the unusual case in which groups do not overlap in income. Because the more usual case in the real world is for the income distributions of different groups in society to overlap somewhat (for example, although on average men have higher incomes than women, some women have higher incomes than some men), the Gini index cannot help in answering the question of the size of "within-" and "between-" group inequality. See Osberg (2003) and Chapter 1 of Osberg (1981, 1984) or Jenkins (1991) for exact definition of these indices and fuller discussion

11. In this new situation of a 2:1 gender wage ratio, the "simple" solution to gender inequality of doubling all female wages would equalize the gender wage ratio but would increase inequality of incomes among all people.
12. The academic literature on inequality of opportunity distinguishes between the circumstances (i.e., constraints) and the efforts (i.e., choices) of individuals, within a one-generation framework and without much discussion of the ambiguity of "choice" in the intergenerational inheritance process (e.g., children's inheritance of education). Ramos and Van de Gaer (2017) surveys the wide range of empirical estimates of inequality of opportunity coming out of that literature, which are sometimes very poorly correlated.
13. Note that if everyone gets an A, marks no longer are informative for employers. Grade inflation reduces the information content of academic transcripts and enhances the relative importance of reference letters (which can be less visible vectors for discrimination).
14. My own view is that education both signals underlying ability and adds to individual productivity; the crucial issue is the proportion of private and social returns ascribable to each. Fortin et al. (2012:138) note, "caution is required in thinking about education as an inequality reducing policy," since under some circumstances it may not improve equality of pay. Within a neo-classical perspective, Beaudry and Green (2003, 2005) argue that when skilled labour is more plentiful, one of the implications of endogenous technology choice by firms may be a decline in the labour demand facing low-skill workers.
15. My own experience is that both my parents very much valued education, and their expectations were always made very clear — I went with the flow. At the age of twenty-three, I did make a conscious decision to go to graduate school and get a PhD, but the availability of that choice depended on my previous educational history. Personally, I count myself as one of the lucky ones in the parental influence process.
16. Brunori, Ferreira and Peragine (2013:17). See also Corak (2004, 2013), Bjorklund and Jantti (2009), and many others.
17. Marshall (1913:562).
18. See also Hurd (2017:14–19).
19. Becker and Tomes (1979).
20. Parents who follow an optimal bequest policy only switch to leaving a financial bequest when the marginal return on human capital falls below the rate of return available on financial assets.
21. Becker and Tomes (1979).
22. Note that since some students need more resources to achieve the same education (e.g., children with poor eyesight need glasses if they are to be able to read), providing "an equal education" does not mean "equal dollar expenditure per student." It means providing educational resources adequate to individual needs.
23. Corak (2013).
24. See Wolfe and Haveman (2001) or Osberg (2003).
25. See *Education at a Glance, 2023 : OECD Indicators*, OECD iLibrary (oecd-ilibrary.org), https://read.oecd-ilibrary.org/education/education-at-a-glance-2023_e13bef63-en#page1.

26. See "To have kids or not to have kids: That is the question!" (statcan.gc.ca), https://www150.statcan.gc.ca/n1/pub/11-627-m/11-627-m2023006-eng.htm.
27. https://iariw.org/wp-content/uploads/2021/08/wu_et_al_paper.pdf, https://www.sciencedirect.com/science/article/abs/pii/S0927537121001196.
28. The tour guide may have exaggerated — see Christianson J. R. (1981) — but he got me thinking.
29. For example, Andreoli and Fusco (2019); Brunori, 2016; Brunori, Ferreira and Peragine, 2013; Fleurbaey, Peragine and Ramos (2017); Hufe, Kanbur and Peichl (2018); Van de Gaer, Martinez and Schokkaert (2019). Motiram (2018) does mention "wealth" three times very tangentially but otherwise has zero hits.
30. See Piketty (2014; Chapter 11), OECD (2021).
31. Adermon, A., Lindahl, M. and Waldenström, D. (2018) emphasize that inheritance is particularly important at the top. See also Björklund, A., Roine, J. and Waldenström, D. (2012).
32. France (1894), Chapter 7.

Chapter 8

1. Förster, Llena-Nozal and Nafilyan (2014: Table 1) compare twelve OECD nations from 1975 to 2007 and show how in Canada, the lowest income 99 per cent had the slowest growth rate of incomes (0.7 per cent annually) and the second-highest (after the United States) percentage of total growth captured by the top 1 per cent (37.3 per cent).
2. All population numbers taken from Table: 17-10-0009-01 (formerly CANSIM 051-0005).
3. When I was writing *The Age of Increasing Inequality* in 2018, Canadian house prices had risen dramatically compared to household incomes, but population growth had not yet accelerated. I thought then that the growing unaffordability of housing in Canada implied a price bubble that had to, at some point, burst. I did not then foresee the change in federal immigration policy to a high population growth setting.

   By 2024, the size and speed of the actual acceleration of population growth in Canada and its associated increase in housing demand had massively affected house prices, apartment vacancy rates, rents and homelessness. Rapid population growth also fueled growth in healthcare demand, with implications for family physician adequacy and emergency healthcare congestion — a "health care crisis" on top of the "housing crisis."

   One lesson to be learned from my forecast error about house prices is the importance of background assumptions. Economic forecasts are always conditional on social context and actual outcomes can always be influenced by major public policy shifts (e.g., in immigration policy). A second possible lesson to draw is that it might be wise to have open democratic debates on major policy shifts before such shifts occur, since open debates about population growth could have drawn out implications (such as the inadequacy of capacity for new housing construction or healthcare) that might not otherwise be adequately considered.
4. Statistics Canada. Table 36-10-0434-02, *Gross domestic product (GDP) at basic prices*; Table 17-10-0009-01 *Population estimates, quarterly*; here, as elsewhere, income estimates are converted to 2022 dollars using Table 18-10-0005-01 *Consumer Price Index, annual average*.
5. See Table A1.9 *Budget 2024, Finance Canada* and Finance Canada (2023 — Tables A1.10 and A1.11, pages 93-94) F*M1 scenario* from Statistics Canada's official population projections, http://www. statcan.gc.ca/pub/91-520-x/91-520-x2014001-eng.pdf.
6. See Summers (2016). Gordon (2012, 2016).
7. Gordon (2012) suggests that future growth in consumption per capita for the bottom 99 per cent of the American income distribution could fall below 0.5 per cent per year for an extended period of decades.
8. Forecasts of long-term future economic growth always depend on assumptions about future short-term economic policy decisions. The long-run may be years in the future but we can only get to it a day at a time. At each point in the future time, short-term

macroeconomic policy decisions will be made, and monetary policy decisions about inflation control are especially important. The realism of a long term forecast of approximately 0.7 or 0.8 per cent annual growth in real per capita GDP in Canada depends crucially on the sequence of monetary policy decisions at each point of future time and in recent years the Bank of Canada has quite often been willing to sacrifice growth whenever it has become anxious about future inflation. Unless there is some change in that tendency, long term growth prospects will remain hostage to inflation anxieties. If there were a change in monetary policy in Canada to emphasize full employment, there might be new jobs available for displaced workers. However, when (as now) low unemployment is a secondary consideration and employment insurance benefits are low and reach less than 40 per cent of the unemployed, those who lost their jobs are the people who pay the costs of structural adjustment.

9. With similar percentage changes the absolute gap in dollars between median income and the top 1 per cent would of course grow continuously.
10. Frey and Osborne (2013:23).
11. Frey and Osborne (2013) argue that 47 per cent of all persons employed in the United States are now working in jobs that could be performed by computers and algorithms within the next ten to twenty years. Arntz, Gregory and Zierahn (2016:4) suggest that "on average across the 21 OECD countries, 9% of jobs are automatable."
12. IMF (2024:2).
13. IMF (2024:17).
14. Knight (1933:3).
15. Maddison (2003:89) and CANSIM Tables 051-0005 and 380-0084.
16. Keynes (1930:365).
17. Although Keynes recognized that avarice was a functional trait when capital was scarce, he was quite scathing about its inherent worth. He argued, "when the accumulation of wealth is no longer of high social importance there will be great changes in the code of morals. We shall be able to afford to dare to assess the money-motive at its true value. The love of money as a possession — as distinguished from the love of money as a means to the enjoyment and realities of life — will be recognized for what it is, a somewhat disgusting morbidity" (1930:369).
18. Korpi and Shalev (1979).
19. See Lapuente and Rothstein (2010:8).
20. The higher figure of over eighty million includes deaths from war-related disease and famine.
21. Many of the parents of the 1920s would have personally known relatives and friends who died in the trenches of World War I — and some would also have observed the profiteering of wartime munitions suppliers on the home front. Their reminiscences would often have been overheard by their children.
22. Samuelson (1948:3).
23. Until quite recently, a shared conception of facts also did not have to compete with the "alternative truths" of conspiracy theorists and the denialist rabbit holes now available to people who "do their own research" on the web.
24. Canada has also signed numerous other human rights covenants, for example, the United Nations Convention on the Rights of the Child.
25. Rawls (1982:162) is also quite clear that his "maxi-min" social welfare criterion is the second criterion of "social justice," that is, subject to the prior attainment of the first principle of "equal basic liberties for all."
26. Graves (2017).
27. Roosevelt's January 11, 1944, message to the US Congress on the State of the Union; see http://www.presidency.ucsb.edu/ws/?pid=16518. See also Roosevelt (1936) or Sen (1999).
28. This judgement is a landmark of property law in applying the criterion of free and informed contracting, but it is one of those ironies of history that the property in question was a sugar plantation in Jamaica in the mid-1700s, which means that most of its market value would have been the slaves who belonged to the property.

29. Roosevelt's second Bill of Rights included:
    - The right to a useful and remunerative job in the industries or shops or farms or mines of the Nation;
    - The right to earn enough to provide adequate food and clothing and recreation;
    - The right of every farmer to raise and sell his products at a return which will give him and his family a decent living;
    - The right of every businessman, large and small, to trade in an atmosphere of freedom from unfair competition and domination by monopolies at home or abroad;
    - The right of every family to a decent home;
    - The right to adequate medical care and the opportunity to achieve and enjoy good health;
    - The right to adequate protection from the economic fears of old age, sickness, accident, and unemployment; and
    - The right to a good education.

    See https://billofrightsinstitute.org/activities/franklin-roosevelt-second-bill-of-rights-1944.
30. The use of gendered terms such as "his" in Article 25 reflects the language conventions of 1948. Article 2 asserts that all rights are to be guaranteed equally to male and female persons. Van Langendonck and contributors (2007) survey the human rights covenants that assert a right to "social security." As he notes (2007:3), even before the UN Declaration, the Anglo-American "Atlantic Charter" of 1941 had asserted the goal of "securing for all improved labor standards, economic advancement and social security," an affirmation he attributes to a necessity of counteracting Nazi propaganda about worker security in Germany. Van Langendonck also conjectures that the US (then a social policy leader, having instituted Social Security in 1935) wanted access to free international trade to be restricted to nations with comparable social protection costs.

Chapter 9

1. See, for example, Atkinson, Leventi, Nolan, Sutherland and Tasseva (2017).
2. Tony Atkinson's book *Inequality: What Can Be Done?* (2015) has an excellent list.
3. Specifically, 0.59 per cent of respondents to the International Social Survey Project; see Osberg and Smeeding (2006:457) and Osberg and Bechert (2017).
4. Bechert and Osberg (2023:428).
5. Osberg and Bechert (2017), Table 3.
6. Statistics Canada Table: 14-10-0417-01 reported that full-time "machine operators, assemblers and inspectors in processing, manufacturing and printing" in manufacturing in Canada averaged $998 in weekly pay in 2023 or about $52,000 annually while "labourers in processing, manufacturing and utilities" (which is closer to the "unskilled factory worker" concept used in the ISSP data) averaged $875 weekly, or $45,500 annually. A pay ratio of 8.8 (or less) thus implies a CEO salary of $400,000 to $450,000.
7. Canadian tariffs (weighted mean, all products) averaged 7.02 per cent in 1989, dropping to under 2 per cent since 1997–98 and 1.49 per cent in 2020. See http://databank.worldbank.org/data/reports.aspx?source=2&series=TM. TAX.MRCH.WM.AR.ZS&country=. See also CA_E.pdf (wto.org) Increasingly, the text of "free trade" agreements actually concerns the details of policies, such as health and safety regulations, that might or might not advantage local producers. One of the hidden costs of these international agreements therefore is a shrinkage of the space for democratic local politics. When trade treaties remove the possibility of local policy changes by the democratic process, citizens lose the sense that voting matters. The winning slogan in the Brexit referendum of 2016 in the UK was "Take Back Control."
8. Ilsley, (Hansard, April 29, 1941). Parliamentary Debates Canada: House of Commons.
9. Taxes payable on the transfer of wealth from a deceased to a living person can have several names — succession duties, wealth transfer taxes, probate fees, death duties, inheritance or estate taxes. An important distinction is the difference between an estate tax, levelled on the total value of the wealth bequeathed, and an inheritance tax,

payable by the recipient and assessed on the amount each heir acquires. Both within Canada and internationally there has been great variation in the design of such taxes — a useful survey is Chapter 3 in *Inheritance Taxation in OECD Countries*, OECD 2021, https://www.oecd-ilibrary.org/taxation/inheritance-taxation-in-oecd-countries_e2879a7d-en.

10. Perry (1989; Table 16.12 page 403). Through a series of federal-provincial agreements, the provinces repealed their own provincial taxes and estate taxation in Canada became a federal tax, with first 50 per cent and later 75 per cent of the revenue raised in a province remitted to that province.
11. The top US tax rate on large estates went from 50 per cent to 70 per cent in 1935 and then to 77 per cent from 1940 to 1977; see Luscombe (2022).
12. https://www65.statcan.gc.ca/acyb02/1947/acyb02_19470552021-eng.htm. In 2022, when average weekly manufacturing earnings for full-time workers were $1,259, 27.7 years of earnings would be about $1.81 million. Statistics Canada. Table 14-10-0064-01, *Employee wages by industry, annual.* DOI: https://doi.org/10.25318/1410006401-eng.
13. https://stats.oecd.org/Index.aspx?DataSetCode=REVCAN. Estate and inheritance taxes trended up in dollar amounts but down as a percentage of tax revenue over the late 1960s; see also https://www.canada.ca/en/department-finance/services/publications/annual-financial-report/2022/report.html and https://stats.oecd.org/img/transparent.gif.
14. Student loan numbers from Table 2B, *Canada Student Loans Program annual report.* https://www.canada.ca/en/employment-social-development/programs/canada-student-loans-grants/reports/cslp-annual-2020-2021.html#table2. Childcare cost numbers from https://www.canada.ca/en/department-finance/news/2021/12/a-canada-wide-early-learning-and-child-care-plan.html; "the Canada-wide early learning and child care transfer payments from the federal government to the provinces and territories will increase from $3.0 billion in 2021–22 to $7.7 billion in 2025–26."
15. Ontario, with 38.7 per cent of Canada's population had 371,462 social assistance cases receiving disability support in 2021–22. If other provinces classified eligibility for disability benefits similarly, that would imply 958,800 cases nationally. See https://maytree.com/wp-content/uploads/Social_Assistance_Summaries_2023.pdf.
16. Perry (1989:396-402) provides a brief history.
17. See Osberg (2015, Figure 2 Page 11).
18. The 50 per cent inclusion rate for capital gains can equivalently be seen as a 50 per cent tax rate cut for capital gains income. The Conservative government of Brian Mulroney increased the inclusion rate to 66.66 per cent in 1988 and further to 75 per cent in 1990. It was cut in 1999 to 50 per cent by the Chretien Liberals and then in 2024 was increased again to 66.66 per cent (for capital gains in excess of $250,000) by the Justin Trudeau Liberals.
19. Vaillancourt and Kerkhoff (2019).
20. The US does not have deemed realization at death. When the price of an inherited asset on the date of the decedent's death is above its original purchase price, the US tax code allows for the raising of the cost basis to the higher price, minimizing the capital gains taxes owed if the asset is sold later. Indeed, no tax need ever be paid if an asset is never sold and just increases in value as it passes from generation to generation by inheritance. If each generation borrows on the collateral of increased asset value for their own consumption, repay the loans from capital gains at the time of each inheritance and then the heirs "step-up" the asset valuation on inheritance, no generation of descendants need ever pay tax, since loans are not income.
21. Capital gains tax for assets inherited by one spouse on the death of the other is deferred until the death of the surviving spouse.
22. Bird (1978:134.144).
23. See Boadway and Pestieau (2022).
24. See Guvenen et al. (2024).

25. Switzerland also provides some evidence on the implications of wealth taxation. Some cantons do not have an annual wealth tax, and the wealth tax rate varies substantially among the cantons that do tax wealth, so one can test whether changes in wealth tax rates influence the inequality of wealth, which appears to be the case, or the prosperity of the different cantons, which does not appear to be affected. Marti, Martínez and Scheuer (2023) examine the impact of reducing wealth tax rates on increasing the concentration of wealth within cantons. Since income is taxed at the federal, cantonal and municipal levels (with tax rates set separately at each level) there is also very substantial variation in income tax rates by municipality and canton. See https://www.credit-suisse.com/ch/en/articles/private-banking/steuerranking-der-kantone-und-gemeinden-so-viel-zahlen-natuerliche-personen-202307.html.
26. Since gift-giving just before death could be an easy way to avoid a tax at death, 23 of the 24 OECD countries that levy an estate or inheritance tax also levy a gift tax on inter vivos transfers — see OECD (2021).
27. The theoretical literature in economics on optimal inheritance taxation takes into account the responsiveness of bequests to the tax rate on them, the well-being of both donors and recipients, inequality in the concentration of bequests and the value that society puts on the consumption by bequest receivers and bequest leavers. Considering all these issues and calibrating their model of optimal inheritance taxation using micro-data for France and the United States, Piketty and Saez (2013:1851) find that, "for realistic parameters, the optimal inheritance tax rate might be as large as 50%–60%—or even higher for top bequests, in line with historical experience."
28. Pérez-González, F. (2006:1585).
29. OECD (2021: Chapter 3).
30. Batchelder (2020:56) estimates that only the top 0.02 percent of US inheritances would be affected by such a tax. To smooth out income spikes, she suggests that taxable inheritances could be averaged with other income over the previous five years. Taxpayers would also disregard entirely up to $15,000 in gifts and inheritances each year, so there would be no need to keep track of the vast majority of gifts and inheritances but to prevent tax avoidance by breaking inheritances into many small payments, all receipts of gifts from all sources in excess of $15,000 each year would count against the total $2.5 million lifetime exemption of each taxpayer, whether received as gifts from individuals or as disbursements from trusts.
31. If inheritances are taxed at 50 per cent each generation and if capital gets a real rate of return of 5 per cent, a $100 million fortune produces a $50 million inheritance which yields an annual income of $2.5 million. If only the interest is consumed then a $100 million fortune becomes inheritances of $50 million (children) then $25 million (grandchildren), then $12.5 million (great-grandchildren) and the great-great-grandchildren still get $6.125 million, which is more than the 2019 wealth of 99 per cent of Canadian families. On the other hand, zero taxation of inheritances, as at present in Canada, implies a legacy of affluence of potentially infinite length for descendants.
32. https://taxfoundation.org/tax-basics/estate-tax/.
33. Moretti and Wilson (2020).
34. Moretti and Wilson (2020:1). Each US state that does not now have an estate tax but decides to implement one thereby reduces the number of tax-free jurisdictions available within the US for potential tax-migrants, which would reduce the probability of tax-induced migration and thereby reduce the revenue costs for other states associated with implementing an estate tax. Hence the cost/benefit revenue calculation would predict a "race to the top" in estate taxation by jurisdictions, not a race to the bottom. However, billionaires have the incentive and the opportunity to contribute to public relations campaigns which affect public opinion and they can fund political campaigns to elect cooperative politicians to shape taxation policy in billionaire-friendly ways.
35. In Canada, the top federal income tax rate for 2023 was 33 per cent (on taxable income over $235,675) while the top provincial marginal income rate varied from 13.16

per cent in Ontario to 25.75 per cent in Quebec. Top marginal provincial income tax rates kicked in at varying taxable incomes from $63,969 in PEI and $79,625 in Manitoba to $341,502 in Alberta. See https://www.canada.ca/en/revenue-agency/services/tax/individuals/frequently-asked-questions-individuals/canadian-income-tax-rates-individuals-current-previous-years.html#federal.

36. For many years, the mere mention of unemployment almost entirely disappeared from official Ottawa documents, as Osberg (2011, 136-139) showed, using the word search function in Acrobat (since budget documents and the Monetary Policy Report are available in PDF format). When in 2024 I looked again for mention of unemployment in the federal government budget documents, I found statements such as: "The unemployment rate is expected to rise to 6.5 per cent in the fourth quarter of 2024, remaining historically low" (Finance Canada 2024:356). Since over the twenty-eight years 1946 to 1974 Canada's unemployment rate averaged 4.6 per cent, this wildly false statement raises the question of whether it is better for federal government economists to ignore unemployment or to believe egregious falsehoods about unemployment.
37. Between 2011 and 2019 in Canada there were an average of 5.3 unemployed people for every vacancy. See Statistics Canada. Table 14-10-0226-01, *Job vacancies, unemployed and unemployment-to-job vacancies ratio*, https://www150.statcan.gc.ca/t1/tbl1/en/tv.action?pid=1410022601.
38. See Watson and Osberg (2017); Rohde, Osberg, Rao and Tang (2017); Rohde, Osberg and Tang (2016); and Watson, Osberg and Phipps (2016).
39. The Bank of Canada Act (1934) states that the Bank of Canada is to "mitigate by its influence fluctuations in the general level of production, trade, prices and employment." These legislated objectives have never been formally amended.
40. Osberg (2019) discusses why 4.5 per cent is a plausible estimate of "full employment" in Canada in the early 2020s. See https://www.researchgate.net/publication/324983832_Full_Employment_in_Canada_in_the_early_21_st_Century_1_Lars_Osberg.
41. However, since the environmental objective of a carbon tax is to raise the tax high enough to reduce carbon emissions to zero, which necessarily would also mean reducing carbon tax revenues and rebates to zero, a Carbon Tax Rebate can only be a temporary introduction to a GAI.
42. See Boadway, Cuff and Koebel (2016).
43. If G = the basic guarantee level, Y = income from other sources, t = the rate at which benefits are reduced when other income increases and net income = Y_N, then net income is given by the calculation $Y_N = G + (1-t)*Y$. This implies that "break-even" income is $Y^* = G/t$ (i.e., taxes paid are equal to the guarantee level so the net payment is zero). The core design problem for a GAI scheme is that a lower tax rate (to preserve work incentives for those who can work) and a higher guarantee of basic income (to prevent poverty for those who cannot work) together imply a higher break-even income and higher total program costs. Hence, keeping program costs low implies trade-offs between work incentives (1-t) and income adequacy (G).
44. For immigrant families and for Canadians who have lived abroad, an important detail is that full benefits are only received by people who have been resident in Canada for forty years after the age of eighteen. Otherwise, partial payment are made based on the number of years in Canada divided by forty.
45. OAS benefits are taxed back at an accelerated rate for individuals with income greater than $73,000. Because GIS benefits are cut by $0.50 for each dollar of income from other sources, in 2024 net GIS payments were reduced to zero if the other income of a single person exceeded $21,624.
46. All adults are also eligible for the HST/GST tax credit (in 2024, $496 for single people). It is similar in structure to a GAI, but at a very small level.
47. Frey and Osborne (2013); Arntz, Gregory and Zierahn (2016:4); IMF (2024).
48. The big worry at the time was that people would stop working if they were able to collect a GAI, but very few labour supply effects were found (in the jargon of economics,

both the income and substitution elasticities of labour supply are quite small). In the Canadian Mincome experiment, the GAI produced substantial health benefits; see Forget (2011).

49. The other side of the fake bill featured a picture of Thomas Eagleton, who was briefly the vice presidential candidate until news reports surfaced that he had received electroshock therapy for clinical depression during the 1960s.
50. For the original proposal, see Atkinson (1996). Atkinson, Leventi, Nolan, Sutherland and Tasseva (2017) provide a detailed costing in the UK context.
51. During the 1950s and 1960s, much of the architecture of the welfare state was premised on the "male breadwinner" model of the family, in which men were expected to do paid work outside the home and women did care labour and home production. Those days are long gone, but their replacement for women has been in many instances the "double work day" of paid jobs plus unpaid labour in the home, which creates stresses of its own. See Phipps, Osberg and Burton (2001).
52. In 2018, the government of British Columbia appointed an Expert Panel to study the implementation of a basic income in B.C. The multiplicity and diversity of needs and of existing social programs to address those needs, were key considerations in the panel's negative recommendation. See *Basic income report* — Province of British Columbia (gov.bc.ca).
53. Boadway, Cuff and Koebel (2016) have demonstrated that a basic income guarantee of $20,000 per adult is fiscally feasible in Canada. (They combined a basic guarantee of $20,000 with a 30 per cent tax-back rate and reforms to the income tax system to produce a revenue-neutral program which would substantially equalize the distribution of after-tax income.)
54. See the International Monetary Fund (2013) and Osberg (2015a), Tables 1, 3.
55. See Osberg (2015a), Table 4.
56. Here and elsewhere in the text, the term "top tax rate" refers to the "marginal" top tax rate (i.e., the rate of income tax paid on an additional dollar of income in the top income tax bracket).
57. Diamond and Saez (2011) and Saez, Slemrod and Giertz (2012) argued for a 73 per cent top marginal tax rate. Piketty, Saez and Stantcheva (2011) advocated 83 per cent and Kindermann and Krueger (2014) suggested the top tax rate should be 90 per cent. Atkinson's (2014) suggestion was 65 per cent.
58. Some data on tax evasion is becoming available, partly from occasional data leaks (such as the Panama Papers) from the international accounting and law firms that now facilitate tax avoidance. Even for high tax compliance countries, accounting for tax evasion significantly increases measured incomes at the very top; see Alstadsæter, Johannesen and Zucman (2017).
59. Gillis (2022:1) — who also comments, "The Anglo-Canadian approach is in contrast to American tax law, which generally characterizes transactions according to their economic substance. Since it is costly and often impossible for taxpayers to change the economic substance of a transaction, the American approach to characterization is less conducive to creative tax avoidance."
60. For example, in April 2023, the Bennet Jones law firm in Toronto advertised its expertise in tax avoidance (https://www.bennettjones.com/TaxDisputeResolution) and its access to the expertise of, among others, David Dodge (past Deputy Minister of Finance and past Governor of the Bank of Canada — https://www.bennettjones.com/DodgeDavid), Michael Horgan (Past Deputy Minister of Finance — https://www.bennettjones.com/HorganMichael), Serge Dupont (past Deputy Clerk of the Privy Council and past Deputy Minister of Intergovernmental Affairs — https://www.bennettjones.com/DupontSerge) and Jonathan Fried (past Senior Assistant Deputy Minister for the Department of Finance and Canada's past G7 and G20 Finance Deputy — https://www.bennettjones.com/FriedJonathan).
61. Although Bradley Birkenfeld had to serve two-and-a-half years' jail time for his roles in the tax fraud he revealed, his award amounted to more than $4,600 for every hour

he spent in prison. See Kocieniewski (2012), Canada Revenue Agency (2015) and Internal Revenue Service (2016).

62. See https://taxfoundation.org/data/all/state/state-income-tax-rates-2024/.
63. Osberg (2015), Table 3.
64. Young and Varner (2011:258, 260) examined the 2004 New Jersey "millionaire's tax." As they point out, "Few other places in the country make it easier to move to a different state without leaving one's city or completely separating from the social ties of friends and family." But in fact, there was hardly any change in the millionaire migration rate into or out of New Jersey. Their summary of the research literature is that "the consensus emerging from the migration literature — and from a range of research designs — is that people do not generally migrate in response to tax increases."
65. See Young, Varner, Lurie and Prisinzano (2016).
66. See Osberg (2003a).
67. For the calculations underlying the 12.3 per cent and 14.7 per cent estimates see Osberg (2015a, Table 5), updated to reflect that General Government Income Tax revenues in Q4 2023 were $378,620 million. See also Statistics Canada. Table 36-10-0477-01, *Revenue, expenditure and budgetary balance — General governments (x 1,000,000).* DOI: https://doi.org/10.25318/3610047701-eng.
68. See Reich, Allegretto and Godoey (2017:3).
69. See *Consolidated Minimum Wage Table*, U.S. Department of Labor, https://www.dol.gov/agencies/whd/mw-consolidated.
70. Iowa, Idaho, Indiana, Kentucky, North Carolina, North Dakota, New Hampshire, Oklahoma, Pennsylvania, Texas, Utah, Virginia and Wisconsin.
71. See in particular the comprehensive reviews of Belman and Wolfson (2014a, 2014b).
72. Ton (2012) discusses the many positive implications for productivity of a high-wage strategy in retailing.

BIBLIOGRAPHY

Aaron, H. J. (1978). *Politics and the professors.* Washington, DC: Brookings Institution.

Alstadsæter, A., Johannesen, N., & Zucman, G. (2017). *Tax evasion and inequality.* NBER Working Paper No. w23772. Retrieved from https://ssrn.com/abstract=3035109.

Alvaredo, F., Atkinson, A. B., Piketty, T., & Saez, E. (2013). *The top 1 percent in international and historical perspective.* Journal of Economic Perspectives, 27(3), 3–20. Retrieved July 4, 2017, from http://pubs.aeaweb.org/doi/pdfplus/10.1257/jep.27.3.3.

Amdekar, S. D. (2012). *Inequality surplus capital and under-consumption: A contemporary analysis of J. A. Hobson's economic theory of new imperialism.* Working paper, University College, University of Durham.

Anderson, B. (1983). *Imagined communities: Reflections on the origin and spread of nationalism.* London, UK: Verso.

Apostolic Exhortation. (2013). Evangelii Gaudium of the Holy Father Francis.

Arntz, M., Gregory, T., & Zierahn, U. (2016). *The risk of automation for jobs in OECD countries: A comparative analysis.* OECD Social, Employment and Migration Working Papers 189. Paris: OECD Publishing. http://dx.doi.org/10.1787/5jlz9h56dvq7-en.

Atkinson, A. B. (1970). *The measurement of inequality.* Journal of Economic Theory, 2, 244–263.

Atkinson, A. B. (1996). *The case for a Participation Income.* The Political Quarterly, 67(1), 67–70. http://dx.doi.org/10.1111/j.1467-923X.1996.tb01568.x.

Atkinson, A. B. (2015). *Inequality: What can be done?* Cambridge, MA: Harvard University Press.

Atkinson, A. B., & Brandolini, A. (2011). *On the identification of the "middle class."* Society for the Study of Economic Inequality Working Paper 2011-271. Retrieved July 4, 2017, from https://www.ecineq.org/milano/WP/ECINEQ2011-217.pdf.

Atkinson, A. B., Leventi, C., Nolan, B., Sutherland, H., & Tasseva, I. (2017). *Reducing poverty and inequality through tax-benefit reform and the minimum wage: The UK as a case-study.* INET Oxford Working Paper No. 2017-04. Employment, Equity & Growth.

Atkinson, A. B., & Piketty, T. (2007). *Top incomes over the 20th century: A contrast between continental European and English-speaking countries.* Oxford, UK: Oxford University Press.

Atkinson, A. B., Piketty, T., & Saez, E. (2011). *Top incomes in the long run of history.* Journal of Economic Literature, 49(1), 3–71.

Attanasio, O., Hurst, E., & Pistaferri, L. (2012). *The evolution of income, consumption and leisure inequality in the US 1980–2010.* NBER Working Paper No. 17982.

Autor, D., Dorn, D., Katz, L. F., Patterson, C., & Van Reenen, J. (2017). *The fall of the labor share and the rise of superstar firms.* CEP Discussion Paper 1482. Retrieved July 4, 2017, from http://cep.lse.ac.uk/pubs/download/dp1482.pdf.

Bakija, J., Cole, A., & Heim, B. T. (2012). *Jobs and income growth of top earners and the causes of changing income inequality: Evidence from U.S. tax return data.* Retrieved from https://web.williams.edu/Economics/wp/BakijaColeHeimJobsIncomeGrowthTopEarners.pdf.

Barr, N. (2001). *The welfare state as piggy bank: Information, risk, uncertainty and the role of the state.* Oxford, UK: Oxford University Press.

Beach, C. M. (2014). *What has happened to middle-class earnings? Distributional shifts in earnings in Canada 1970–2005.* Canadian Labour Market and Skills Researcher Network, Working Paper 13.

Beach, C. M. (2016a). *What has happened to middle-class earnings in Canada?* In D. A. Green, W. C. Riddell, & F. St-Hilaire (Eds.), Income inequality: The Canadian story. Montreal, QC: Institute for Research on Public Policy.

Beach, C. M. (2016b). *Changing income inequality: A distributional paradigm for Canada.* Canadian Journal of Economics, 49(4), 1229–1292.

Beaudry, P., & Green, D. A. (2000). *Cohort patterns in Canadian earnings: Assessing the role of skill premia in inequality trends.* Canadian Journal of Economics, 33(4), 907–936.

Beaudry, P., & Green, D. A. (2003). *Wages and employment in the United States and Germany: What explains the differences?* American Economic Review, 93, 573–602.

Beaudry, P., & Green, D. A. (2005). *Changes in US wages 1976–2000: Ongoing skill bias or major technological change?* Journal of Labor Economics, 23, 609–648.

Beaudry, P., Green, D. A., & Sand, B. M. (2016). *The great reversal in the demand for skill and cognitive tasks.* Journal of Labor Economics, 34(1).

Bechert, I., & Osberg, L. (2023). "A Few People Make all the Difference — an International Comparison of "Fair" Pay Differentials" *International Journal of Sociology.* https://doi.org/10.1080/00207659.2023.2274713.

Becker, G., & Tomes, N. (1979). *An equilibrium theory of the distribution of income and intergenerational mobility.* Journal of Political Economy, 87, 1153–1189.

Bédard-Pagé, Guillaume, Annick Demers, Eric Tuer and Miville Tremblay (2016) *Large Canadian Public Pension Funds: A Financial System Perspective.* Bank of Canada, Financial System Review, June 2016, https://www.bankofcanada.ca/wp-content/uploads/2016/06/fsr-june2016-bedard-page.pdf.

Belman, D., & Wolfson, P. J. (2014a). *The new minimum wage research.* Employment Research, 21(2), 4–5.

Belman, D., & Wolfson, P. J. (2014b). *What does the minimum wage do?* Kalamazoo, MI: W. E. Upjohn Institute for Employment Research.

Benes, J., Chauvet, M., Kamenik, O., Kumhof, M., Laxton, D., Mursula, S., & Selody, J. (2012) *The future of oil: Geology versus technology.* IMF Working Paper WP/12/109.

Bertrand, M., & Morse, A. (2016). *Trickle-down consumption.* Review of Economics and Statistics, 98(5), 863–879.

Bird, Richard M. (1978) "*Canada's Vanishing Death Taxes.*" Osgoode Hall Law Journal 16.1 (1978): 133–145. http://digitalcommons.osgoode.yorku.ca/ohlj/vol16/iss1/5.

Bjorklund, A., & Jantti, M. (2009). *Intergenerational income mobility and the role of family background.* In W. Salverda, B. Nolan, & T. Smeeding (Eds.), The Oxford handbook of economic inequality (pp. 491–517). Oxford, UK: Oxford University Press.

Boadway, R., Cuff, K., & Koebel, K. (2016). *Designing a basic income guarantee for Canada.* Queen's Economics Department Working Paper No. 1371, 12-2016. Retrieved from http://qed.econ.queensu.ca/working_papers/papers/qed_wp_1371.pdf.

Boadway, Robin and Pierre Pestieau (2022) "*The Wealth Tax and the Tax Mix*", Canadian Tax Journal / revue fiscale canadienne 70 (supp.), 185–208, https://doi.org/10.32721/ctj.2022.70.supp.boadway.

Bordo, M. D., & Meissner, C. M. (2012). *Does inequality lead to a financial crisis?* NBER Working Paper No. 17896. Retrieved from http://www.nber.org/papers/w17896.

Bossert, W., & d'Ambrosio, C. (2013). *Measuring economic insecurity.* International Economic Review, 54(3), 1017–1030.

Boudarbat, B., Lemieux, T., & Riddell, W. C. (2010). *The evolution of the returns to human capital in Canada, 1980–2005.* Canadian Public Policy, 36.

Bowles, S., & Gintis, H. (1976). *Schooling in capitalist America: Educational reform and the contradictions of economic life.* New York, NY: Basic Books.

Bowlus, A. J., & Robin, J. M. (2012). *An international comparison of lifetime inequality: How continental Europe resembles North America.* Journal of the European Economic Association, 10, 1236–1262.

Brunori, P., Ferreira, F. H. G., & Peragine, V. (2013). *Inequality of opportunity income inequality and economic mobility: Some international comparisons.* World Bank Policy Research Working Paper 6304 and IZA DP No. 7155. Retrieved July 4, 2017, from http://ftp.iza.org/dp7155.pdf.

Brunori, P. (2016). *How to Measure Inequality of Opportunity: A Hands-On Guide.* Life Course Working Papers Series, No. 2016-04. May 2016. University of Queensland, Brisbane.

Burton K.R., Wong I.K. (2004). *A force to contend with: The gender gap closes in Canadian medical schools.* CMAJ. 2004 Apr 27;170(9):1385-6. doi: 10.1503/cmaj.1040354. PMID: 15111465; PMCID: PMC395806.

Canadian Pacific Railway Limited. (2015, May 14). *Notice of annual and special meeting of shareholders and management proxy circular.* Retrieved from http://s21.q4cdn.com/736796105/files/doc_financials/Annual-Report/cp-proxy-2015.pdf.

Canada Mortgage and Housing Corporation. (1987). *Housing in Canada 1945 to 1986 An Overview and Lessons Learned.* https://publications.gc.ca/collections/collection_2017/schl-cmhc/NH15-518-1987-eng.pdf.

Chen, K., Osberg, L., & Phipps, S. (2019). *Unequal opportunities and public policy: The impact of parental disability benefits on child postsecondary attendance.* Canadian Journal of Economics, 2019, vol. 52, issue 4, 1401–1432.

Chetty, R. (2008). *Moral hazard versus liquidity and optimal unemployment insurance.* Journal of Political Economy, 116(2), 173–234.

Chetty, R., Grusky, D., Hell, M., Hendren, N., Manduca, R., & Narang, J. (2016). *The fading American dream: Trends in absolute income mobility since 1940.* NBER Working Paper No. 22910. Retrieved from http://www.nber.org/papers/w22910.pdf.

Coldwell, M. J. (1948). *Am I my brother's keeper?* Ottawa, ON: CCF National Office.

Corak, M. (2004). *Generational income mobility in North America and Europe: An introduction in generational income mobility in North America and Europe.* Cambridge, UK: Cambridge University Press.

Corak, M. (2013). *Income inequality, equality of opportunity, and intergenerational mobility.* Journal of Economic Perspectives, 27(3), 79–102. Retrieved July 4, 2017, from http://pubs.aeaweb.org/doi/pdfplus/10.1257/jep.27.3.79.

Creedy, J. (1977). *Notes and memoranda: Pareto and the distribution of income.* Review of Income and Wealth, 23(4), 405–411.

Cross, P., & Sheik, M. A. (2015). *Caught in the middle: Some in Canada's middle class are doing well; others have good reason to worry.* SPP Research Papers, University of Calgary, School of Public Policy, 8(12).

Crow, J. W. (1988, January 18). *The work of monetary policy.* The Eric John Hanson Memorial Lecture Series II, Department of Economics, University of Alberta.

Cynamon, B. Z., & Fazzari, S. M. (2014). *Inequality, the Great Recession, and slow recovery.* http://dx.doi.org/10.2139/ssrn.2205524.

Davies, J. B. (2009). *Wealth and economic inequality.* In Salverda, W., NolanB., & Smeeding, T. (Eds.), The Oxford handbook of economic inequality (pp. 127–149). Oxford, UK: Oxford University Press.

Davies, J. B., Sandström, S., Shorrocks, A., & Wolff, E. N. (2008). *The level and distribution of global household wealth.* EPRI Working papers, University of Western Ontario. Retrieved from http://ir.lib.uwo.ca/economicsepri_wp/56/.

Diamond, P., & Saez, E. (2011). *The case for a progressive tax: From basic research to policy recommendations.* Journal of Economic Perspectives, 25, 165–190.

Djidel, S., Gustajtis, B., Heisz, A., Lam, K., & McDermott, S. (2019). *Towards an update of the Market Basket.* Catalogue no. 75F0002M. Release date: December 6, 2019. https://www150.statcan.gc.ca/n1/pub/75f0002m/75f0002m2019013-eng.html.

Doeringer, P. B., & Piore, M. J. (1971). *Internal labor markets and manpower analysis.* Lexington, MA: D. C. Heath.

Duclos, J., & Pellerin, M. (2016). *The evolution of hourly compensation in Canada between 1980 and 2010.* Canadian Public Policy, 42(3), 250.

Dynan, K. E., Skinner, J., & Zelkes, S. P. (2004). *Do the rich save more?* Journal of Political Economy, 112(2), 397–442.

Easterlin, R. A. (2013). *Happiness and economic growth: The evidence.* IZA DP No. 7187.

Fellegi, Ivan P. (1997). "*On poverty and low income.*" Chief Statistician of Canada. September 1997. https://www150.statcan.gc.ca/n1/pub/13f0027x/13f0027x1999001-eng.html.

Ferris, J. S., & Winer, S. L. (2007). *Just how much bigger is government in Canada? A comparative analysis of the size and structure of the public sectors in Canada and the United States, 1929–2004.* Canadian Public Policy, 33(2), 1–34.

Finance Canada. (2016). *Update of long-term economic and fiscal projections.* Ottawa Cat. No. F2-252/2016E-PDF.

Finance Canada. (2017). *Tax Planning Using Private Corporations.* Background Paper: https://www.canada.ca/content/dam/fin/migration/activty/consult/tppc-pfsp-eng.pdf).

Finance Canada. (2023*). Fall Economic Statement 2023.* https://www.budget.canada.ca/fes-eea/2023/report-rapport/FES-EEA-2023-en.pdf.

Finance Canada. (2024). *Budget 2024.* https://www.budget.canada.ca/2024/home-accueil-en.html#pdf.

Financial Times. (2012, May 31). *Interview: François Henri Pinault.* p. 3.

Förster, M., Llena-Nozal, A., & Nafilyan, V. (2014). *Trends in top incomes and their taxation in OECD countries.* OECD Social, Employment and Migration Working Papers, No. 159. http://dx.doi.org/10.1787/5jz43jhlz87f-en.

Fortin, P. (1996). *The Canadian fiscal problem: The macro-economic connection.* In L. Osberg & P. Fortin (Eds.), *Unnecessary debts.* Toronto, ON: James Lorimer Publishers.

Fortin, N., Green, D. A., Lemieux, T., & Milligan, K. (2012). *Canadian inequality: Recent developments and policy options.* Canadian Public Policy, 38(2), 121–145.

France, A. (1894). *Le lys rouge* [The red lily].

Frenette, M., Green, D. A., & Milligan, K. (2007). *The tale of the tails: Canadian income inequality in the 1980s and 1990s.* Canadian Journal of Economics, 40(3), 734–764.

Frenette, M., Green, D. A., & Milligan, K. (2009). *Taxes, transfers, and Canadian income inequality.* Canadian Public Policy, 35(4), 389–411.

Frey, B. S., & Stutzer, A. (2001). *Happiness and economics: How the economy and institutions effect human well-being.* Princeton, NJ: Princeton University Press.

Frey, C., & Osborne, M. A. (2013). *The future of employment: How susceptible are jobs to computerisation?* University of Oxford. Retrieved from http://www.oxfordmartin.ox.ac.uk/downloads/academic/The_Future_of_Employment.pdf.

Frydman, C., & Jenter, D. (2010). *CEO compensation.* NBER Working Paper No. 16585. Retrieved July 4, 2017, from www.nber.org/papers/w16585.

Gabaix, X., & Landier, A. (2006). *Why has CEO pay increased so much?* NBER Working Paper No. 12365.

Galarneau, D., & Sohn, T. (2013). *Long-term trends in unionization.* Ottawa, ON: Statistics Canada.

Gallup. (2011). *High gas prices cause lifestyle changes for many Americans: Slight majority report making major lifestyle changes, 67% experiencing hardship.* Retrieved from http://www.gallup.com/poll/147593/high-gas-prices-cause-lifestyle-changes-americans.aspx.

Georgieff, A. & R. Hyee. (2021). *"Artificial intelligence and employment : New cross-country evidence",* OECD Social, Employment and Migration Working Papers, No. 265. OECD Publishing, Paris, https://dx.doi.org/10.1787/c2c1d276-en.

Gillespie, W. I. (1996). *A brief history of government borrowing in Canada.* In L. Osberg & P. Fortin (Eds.), Unnecessary debts. Toronto, ON: James Lorimer Publishers.

Gordon, R. J. (2012). *Is U.S. economic growth over? Faltering innovation confronts the six headwinds.* NBER Working Paper No. 18315. Retrieved July 5, 2017, from http://www.nber.org/papers/w18315.

Gordon, R. J. (2016). *Beyond the rainbow: The American standard of living since the Civil War.* Princeton, NJ: Princeton University Press.

Gordon, R. J., & Dew-Becker, I. (2008). *Controversies about the rise of American inequality: A survey.* NBER Working Paper No. 13982.

Graves, F. (2014). *From the end of history to the end of progress: The shifting meaning of middle class.* Presentation to the Queen's 2014 International Institute on Social Policy. Retrieved July 5, 2017, from http://www.ekospolitics.com/wp-content/uploads/from_the_end_of_history_to_the_end_of_progress_august_19_2014.pdf.

Graves, F. (2017, April 27). *Canada 150: The end of progress.* Presentation to the Queen's Policy Review. Retrieved July 5, 2017, from http://www.ekospolitics.com/wp-content/uploads/presentation_by_frank_graves_april_27_2017.pdf.

Guvenen, F., Kaplan, G., Song, J., & Weidner, J. (2017). *Lifetime incomes in the United States over six decades.* NBER Working Paper No. 23371. Retrieved from http://www.nber.org/papers/w23371.

Guvenen, F., Kambourov, G., Kuruscu, B., & Ocampo-Diaz, S. (2024). "*Book-Value Wealth Taxation, Capital Income Taxation, and Innovation.*" NBER Working Paper No. 32585, June 2024, http://www.nber.org/papers/w32585.

Hays. (2014). *Oil & gas global salary guide 2013.* Retrieved from https://www.hays.com/cs/groups/hays_common/@og/@content/documents/promotionalcontent/hays_1269348.pdf.

Heckman, J. J. (1993). *What has been learned about labor supply in the last twenty years?* American Economic Review, 83(2), 116–121.

Heisz, Andrew (2019) Statistics Canada Income Research Paper Series *"An update on the Market Basket Measure comprehensive review."* Release date: July 18, 2019. https://www150.statcan.gc.ca/n1/pub/75f0002m/75f0002m2019009-eng.html.

Helliwell, J. F., & Huang, H. (2014). *New measures of the costs of unemployment: Evidence from the subjective well-being of 3.3 million Americans.* NBER Working Paper No. 16829.

Hester, A. (2007). *Canada as the "emerging energy superpower": Testing the case.* Canadian Defence & Foreign Affairs Institute. Retrieved from http://www.cdfai.org.previewmysite.com/PDF/Canada%20as%20The%20Emerging%20Superpower.pdf.

Hicks, J. R. (1946). *Income.* In R. H. Parker & G. C. Harcourt (Eds., 1969), *Readings in the concept and measurement of income* (pp. 74–82). Cambridge, UK: Cambridge University Press. (Original work published 1946)

Himmelstein, D. U., Lawless, R. M., Thorne, D., Foohey, P., Woolhandler, S. (2019). *Medical Bankruptcy: Still Common Despite the Affordable Care Act.* American Journal of Public Health. 2019 Mar;109(3):431-433. doi: 10.2105/AJPH.2018.304901. PMID: 30726124; PMCID: PMC6366487.

Hobson, J. A. (1900). *The economics of distribution.* New York, NY: Macmillan.

Hou, F., & Myles, J. (2007). *The changing role of education in the marriage market: Assortative marriage in Canada and the United States since the 1970s.* Statistics Canada Analytical Studies Branch Research Paper, Series 11F0019MIE — No. 299. Retrieved July 4, 2017, from www.statcan.gc.ca/pub/11f0019m/11f0019m2007299-eng.pdf.

International Monetary Fund. (2013). *Fiscal monitor.* Retrieved from http://www.imf.org/external/pubs/ft/fm/2013/02/pdf/fm1302.pdf.

Jäntti, M., Pirttilä, J., & Selin, H. (2014). *Estimating labour supply elasticities based on cross-country micro data: A bridge between micro and macro estimates?* CESIFO Working Paper No. 4994.

Jahoda, M. (1979). *The psychological meanings of unemployment.* New Society, 49(883), 492–495.

Jenkins, S. (1991). *The measurement of income inequality.* In L. Osberg (Ed.), *Economic inequality and poverty: International perspectives* (pp. 3–38). Armonk, NY: M. E. Sharpe.

Jenkins, S., & van Kerm, P. (2009). *The measurement of economic inequality.* In W. Salverda, B. Nolan, & T. Smeeding (Eds.), The Oxford handbook of economic inequality (pp. 127– 149). Oxford, UK: Oxford University Press.

Kahneman, D. (2011). *Thinking fast and slow.* New York, NY: Farrar, Straus and Giroux.

Kaissar, N. (2016, May 11). *Private equity's diminishing returns.* Bloomberg. Retrieved from https://www.bloomberg.com/gadfly/articles/2016-05-11/private-equity-has-diminishing-returns.

Keller, W., & Olney, W. W. (2017). *Globalization and executive compensation.* NBER Working Paper No. 23384. Retrieved from http://www.nber.org/papers/w23384.pdf.

Keynes, J. M. (1930). *Economic possibilities for our grandchildren.* In *Essays in persuasion* (pp. 358–374). New York, NY: Norton.

Killingsworth, M. (1983). Labor supply. New York, NY: Cambridge University Press.

Kindermann, F., & Krueger, D. (2014). *High marginal tax rates on the top 1%? Lessons from a life cycle model with idiosyncratic income risk.* NBER Working Paper No. 20601.

King, M., & Low, D. (2014). *Measuring the "world" real interest rate.* NBER Working Paper No. 19887. Retrieved July 5, 2017, from www.nber.org/papers/w19887.

Kneebone, R. (1996). *Four decades of deficits and debt.* In L. Osberg & P. Fortin (Eds.), *Unnecessary Debts.* Toronto, ON: James Lorimer Publishers.

Knight, F. H. (1933). *The economic organization.* Chicago, IL: University of Chicago Press.

Kocieniewski, D. (2012, September 11). *Whistle-blower awarded $104 million by I.R.S.* New York Times. Retrieved from https://www.nytimes.com/2012/09/12/business/whistle-blower-awarded-104-million-by-irs.html.

Korpi, W., & Shalev, M. (1979). *Strikes, industrial relations and class conflict in capitalist societies.* The British Journal of Sociology, 30(2), 164–187.

Krueger, D., & Perri, F. (2006). *Does income inequality lead to consumption inequality? Evidence and theory.* Review of Economic Studies, 73(1), 163–193.

Kumhof, M., Rancière, R., & Winant, P. (2013). *Inequality, leverage and crises: The case of endogenous default.* IMF Working Paper, Research Department, International Monetary Fund.

Kuznets, S. (1953). *Shares of upper income groups in income and savings.* Cambridge, MA: National Bureau of Economic Research.

Lapuente, V., & Rothstein, B. (2010). *Civil War Spain versus Swedish harmony: The quality of government factor.* QoG Working Paper, University of Gothenburg.

Leamer, E. E. (2007). *Housing is the business cycle.* NBER Working Paper No. 13428. Retrieved July 5, 2017, from www.nber.org/papers/w13428.

Leigh, A., Jencks, C., & Smeeding, T. (2009). *Health and economic inequality.* In W. Salverda, B. Nolan, & T. Smeeding (Eds.), *The Oxford handbook of economic inequality* (pp. 384–405). Oxford, UK: Oxford University Press.

Lemieux, T., & Riddell, C. (2016). *Who are Canada's top 1 percent?* In D. A. Green, W. C. Riddell, & F. St-Hilaire (Eds.), *Income inequality: The Canadian story.* Montreal, QC: Institute for Research on Public Policy.

Lu, Y., Morissette, R., & Schirle, T. (2011). *The growth of family earnings inequality in Canada 1980–2005.* Review of Income and Wealth, 57(1).

Luscombe, M. (2022). *A Historical Look at Estate and Gift Tax Rates.* Tax & Accounting March 09, 2022.

Lydall, H. F. (1959). *The distribution of employment incomes.* Econometrica, 27, 110–115.

Maddison, A. (2003) *The world economy: Historical statistics.* Paris: OECD Publishing.

Magnan, M. L., St-Onge, S., & Thorne, L. (1995). *A comparative analysis of the determinants of executive compensation between Canadian and U.S. firms.* Relations Industrielle, 50(2).

Mankiw, N. G. (2013). *Defending the one percent.* Journal of Economic Perspectives, 27(3), 21–34.

Marshall, A. (1913). *Principles of economics* (8th ed.). New York, NY: MacMillan and Co.

Marx, K. (1967). *Capital* (Vol.1 to 3). New York, NY: International Publishers. (Original work published 1894)

McCracken, M. C. (1996). *Recent Canadian monetary policy: Deficit and debt implications.* In Osberg, L., & Fortin, P. (Eds.). (1996). *Unnecessary debts.* Toronto, ON: James Lorimer Publishers.

Mendelson, M. (2005). *Measuring child benefits: Measuring child poverty.* The Caledon Institute of Social Policy, Ottawa, February 2005.

Morelli, S., Smeeding, T., & Thompson, J. (2014). *Post-1970 trends in within-country inequality and poverty: Rich and middle income countries.* CSEF Working Paper 156.

Milanovic, B. (2009, May 4). *Income inequality and speculative investment by the rich and poor in America led to the financial meltdown.* YaleGlobal. Retrieved from http://yaleglobal.yale.edu/content/two-views- cause-global-crisis-part-i.

Milanovic, B., Lindert, P. H., & Williamson, J. G. (2011). *Pre-industrial inequality.* The Economic Journal, 121, 255–272.

Milligan, K., & Smart, M. (2014). *Taxation and top incomes in Canada.* NBER Working Paper No. 20489.

Murphy, B., Michaud, S., & Wolfson, M. (2008). *Income trajectories of high income Canadians 1982–2005.* IARIW 30th General Conference, Portoroz, Slovenia, August 24–30. Retrieved from www.iariw.org/papers/2008/murphy2.pdf.

Murphy, B., Roberts, P., & Wolfson, M. (2007, September). *High-income Canadians.* Perspectives on Labour and Income, 5-17, Cat No. 75-001-XIE. Ottawa, ON: Statistics

Canada. Retrieved from www.statcan.gc.ca/pub/75-001-x/75-001-x2007109-eng.pdf.

Murphy, B., & Veall, M. R. (2016). *A tale of two cities? The surge of top incomes at the city level in Canada*. In K. G. Banting, R. Chaykowski, & S. F. Lehrer (Eds.), *Thinking outside the box: Essays in honour of Tom Courchene*. Montreal, QC: McGill-Queen's University Press.

Newman, P.C. (1975). *The Canadian Establishment*. Toronto, McClelland & Stewart.

Nolan, B. (Ed.). (2018)*Inequality and inclusive growth in Rich Countries: Shared Challenges and Contrasting Fortunes*. Oxford, UK: Oxford University Press.

OECD. (2011). *Divided we stand: Why inequality keeps rising*. Paris: OECD Publishing. http://dx.doi.org/10.1787/9789264119536-en.

OECD. (2015). *In it together: Why less inequality benefits all*. Paris: OECD Publishing.

OECD (2021), *Inheritance Taxation in OECD Countries*, OECD Tax Policy Studies, No. 28, OECD Publishing, Paris, https://doi.org/10.1787/e2879a7d-en.

Osberg, L. (1981). *Economic inequality in Canada*. Toronto, ON: Butterworths.

Osberg, L. (1984). *Economic inequality in the United States*. Armonk, NY: M. E. Sharpe.

Osberg, L. (Ed.). (1991). *Economic inequality and poverty: International perspectives*. Armonk, NY: M. E. Sharpe.

Osberg, L. (Ed.). (2003). *The economic implications of social cohesion*. Toronto, ON: University of Toronto Press.

Osberg, L. (2003a). "*Understanding Growth and Inequality Trends: The Role of Labour Supply in the US and Germany*," Canadian Public Policy Vol. XXIX, Supplement January 2003, p. S163–S184.

Osberg, L. (2007). *The Evolution of Poverty Measurement—With Special Reference to Canada*. Available from https://www.researchgate.net/publication/228750590_The_Evolution_of_Poverty_Measurement-With_Special_Reference_to_Canada#fullTextFileContent [accessed Feb 12, 2024].

Osberg, L. (2008). *A quarter century of economic inequality in Canada 1981–2006*. Canadian Centre for Policy Alternatives. Retrieved July 5, 2017, from www.policyalternatives.ca/documents/National_Office_Pubs/2008/Quarter_Century_of_Inequality.pdf.

Osberg, L. (2011). *Why Did Unemployment Disappear from Official Macro-Economic Policy Discourse in Canada*? (2011), pp. 127–165. In F. Gobert, & A. Sharpe (Eds.) (2011). *New Directions for Intelligent Government in Canada: Papers in Honour of Ian Stewart*. Centre for the Study of Living Standards, Ottawa, ON.

Osberg, L. (2013). *Instability implications of increasing inequality: Evidence from North America*. Economic Modelling, 35, 918–930.

Osberg, L. (2014). *Can increasing inequality be a steady state?* OECD Statistics Working Papers, 2014/01. http://dx.doi.org/10.1787/5jz2bxc80xq6-en.

Osberg, L. (2015a, October). *How much income tax could Canada's top 1% pay?* Ottawa, ON: Canadian Centre for Policy Alternatives. Retrieved from https://www.policyalternatives.ca/publications/reports/how-much-income-tax-could-canadas-top-1-pay.

Osberg, L. (2015b). *How should one measure economic insecurity?* OECD Statistics Working Papers 2015/01. http://dx.doi.org/10.1787/5js4t78q9lq7-en.

Osberg, L. (2015c). *The hunger of old women in rural Tanzania: Can subjective data improve poverty measurement?* Review of Income and Wealth, 61(4), 723–738.

Osberg, L. (2016). *"We all own the Air: Why a Carbon Fee and Dividend Makes Sense for Canada."* EcoFiscal Commission, Montreal, April 2016, pp. 5–23. In *Revenue Recycling: Six Position Papers on the Options for Recycling Carbon Pricing Revenue*. http://ecofiscal.ca/wp-content/uploads/2016/04/Ecofiscal-Commission-Position-Papers-Options-Recycling-Carbon-Pricing-Revenue-April-6-2016.pdf.

Osberg, L. (2017). *On the limitations of some current usages of the Gini index*. Review of Income and Wealth. http://dx.doi.org/10.1111/roiw.12256.

Osberg, L. (2018). *The Age of Increasing Inequality: The Astonishing Rise of Canada's 1%*. Toronto, ON: James Lorimer Publishers.

Osberg, L. (2022). Witness Statement Of Lars Spencer Osberg, The Competition Tribunal In The Matter Of The Competition Act, R.S.C. 1985, C. C-34; And In The Matter Of the proposed acquisition by Rogers Communications Inc. of Shaw Communications Inc.; https://decisions.ct-tc.gc.ca/ct-tc/cdo/en/521128/1/document.do.

Osberg, L., & Bechert, I. (2017). "Social values for equality and preferences for state intervention: Is the USA 'exceptional'?" Presentation at the 7th ECINEQ Meeting, New York, NY, July 17–19.

Osberg, L., & Fortin, P. (Eds.). (1996). *Unnecessary debts*. Toronto, ON: James Lorimer Publishers.

Osberg, L., & Sharpe, A. (2002). *An index of economic well-being for selected OECD countries*. Review of Income and Wealth, 48(3), 291–316.

Osberg, L., & Sharpe, A. (2014). *Measuring economic insecurity in rich and poor nations*. Review of Income and Wealth, 60, S53–S76

Osberg, L., Sharpe, A., & Thomas, J. (2016a). *How much do changing terms of trade matter for economic well-being in Canada?* Ottawa, ON: Canadian Economics Association.

Osberg, L., Sharpe, A., Thomas, J., & Murray, A. (2016b). *How much does commodity price volatility matter for economic well-being in rich countries?* Paper presented at IARIW 34th General Conference, Dresden, Germany, August 23.

Osberg, L., & Siddiq, F. K. (1988). *The inequality of wealth in Britain's North American colonies: The importance of the relatively poor*. Review of Income and Wealth, 34(2), 143–164.

Osberg, L., & Smeeding, T. (2006). *"Fair" inequality? Attitudes to pay differentials: The United States in comparative perspective*. American Sociological Review, 71, 450–473.

Osberg, L., & Xu, K. (2008). *How should we measure poverty in a changing world? Methodological issues and Chinese case study*. Review of Development Economics, 12(2), 419–441.

Ostrovsky, Y. (2017). *Doing as well as one's parents? Tracking recent changes in absolute income mobility in Canada*. Economic Insights, Catalogue no. 11-626-X — No. 073. Ottawa, ON: Statistics Canada.

Page, B., Bartels, I. L. M., & Seawright, J. (2013). *Democracy and the policy preferences of wealthy Americans*. Perspectives on Politics, 11(1), 51–73.

Pareto, V. (1896). *La courbe de la répartition de la richesse*. In Ecrits sur la courbe de la répartition de la richesse (1–15).

Pareto, V. (1966). *Manuel d'economie politique*. librarie Droz. (Original work published 1907)

Parliamentary Budget Office. (2021). "Estimating the top tail of the family wealth distribution in Canada." https://www.pbo-dpb.gc.ca/web/default/files/Documents/Reports/RP-2021-007-S/RP-2021-007-S_en.pdf.

Pérez-González, Francisco. (2006). "*Inherited Control and Firm Performance*." American Economic Review, 96 (5): 1559–88.

Phipps, S, Osberg, L., & Burton, P. (2001). *Time as a source of inequality within families: Are husbands more satisfied with time for themselves than wives?* Feminist Economics, 7(2), 1–21.

Pichette, L., St-Amant, P., Tomlin, B., & Anoma, K. (2015). *Measuring potential output at the Bank of Canada: The extended multivariate filter and the integrated framework*. Bank of Canada Discussion Paper 2015-1.

Piketty, T. (2014). *Capital in the twenty-first century*. Cambridge, MA: Harvard University Press.

Piketty, T., & Saez, E. (2012). *Optimal labor income taxation*. NBER Working Paper No. 18521.

Piketty, T., Saez, E., & Stantcheva, I. (2011). *Optimal taxation of top labor incomes: A tale of three elasticities*. NBER Working Paper No. 17616.

Piketty, T., Saez, E., & Stantcheva, I. (2014). *Optimal taxation of top labor incomes: A tale of three elasticities*. American Economic Journal: Economic Policy, 6(1), 230–271.

Podoluk, J. R. (1968). *Incomes of Canadians*. Ottawa, ON: Dominion Bureau of Statistics.

Pollara. (2014). *In search of "the middle class": Canadians under financial stress*. Pearson Centre for Progressive Policy. Retrieved from http://www.pollara.com/wp-content/uploads/2015/01/Report.pdf.

Ramos, X., & Van de Gaer, D. (2017). *Is inequality of opportunity robust to the measurement approach?* Paper presented at 7th ECINEQ Meeting, New York, NY, July 17–19. https://www.ecineq.org/milano/WP/ECINEQ2017-450.pdf.

Rawls, J. (1982). *Social unity and primary goods.* In A. Sen & B. Williams (Eds.). *Utilitarianism and beyond*, pp. 159–185. Cambridge, UK: Cambridge University Press.
Reich, M., Allegretto, S., & Godoey, A. (2017). Seattle's minimum wage experience 2015–16. Policy Brief. Center on Wage and Employment Dynamics, Institute for Research on Labor and Employment, University of California Berkeley.
Rohde, N., Osberg, L., Rao, P., & Tang, K. K. (2016). *The effect of economic insecurity on mental health: Recent evidence from Australian panel data.* Social Science & Medicine, 151, 250–258.
Rohde, N., Osberg, L., Rao, P., & Tang, K. K. (2017). *Is it vulnerability or Economic insecurity that matters for health?* Journal of Economic Behavior & Organization, 134, 307–319.
Rohde, N., Osberg, L., & Tang, K. K. (2016). *The self-reinforcing dynamics of economic insecurity and obesity.* Applied Economics, 49(17), 1668–1678. http://dx.doi.org/10.1080/00036846.2016.1223826.
Roosevelt, F. D. (1936, June 27). *A rendezvous with destiny.* Speech before the 1936 Democratic National Convention Philadelphia, Pennsylvania. Retrieved from http://www2.austincc.edu/lpatrick/his2341/fdr36acceptancespeech.htm.
Roosevelt, F. D. (1944, January 11). *State of the Union message to Congress.* The American Presidency Project. Retrieved from http://www.presidency.ucsb.edu/ws/?pid=16518.
Rowntree, B. S. (1922). *Poverty: A Study of Town Life.* London, UK: Longmans, Green & Co., 1922, p. 167.
Ruggles, P. (1991). *Short- and long-term poverty in the United States: Measuring the American underclass.* In L. Osberg (Ed.). *Economic inequality and poverty: International perspectives*, pp.157–192. Armonk, NY: M. E. Sharpe.
Saez, E., Slemrod, J., & Giertz, S. H. (2012). *The elasticity of taxable income with respect to marginal tax rates: A critical review.* Journal of Economic Literature, 50(1), 3–50.
Saez, E., & Veall, M. R. (2003*). The evolution of high incomes in Canada, 1920–2000.* NBER Working Paper No. 9607.
Salazar, A. R., & Raggiunti, J. (2014). *Why does executive greed prevail in the United States and Canada but not in Japan? The pattern of low CEO pay and high worker welfare in Japanese corporations.* Osgoode Legal Studies Research Paper Series, Paper 82. Retrieved from http://digitalcommons.osgoode.yorku.ca/olsrps/82.
Salverda, W., Nolan, B., & Smeeding, T. (Eds.). (2009). *The Oxford handbook of economic inequality.* Oxford, UK: Oxford University Press.
Samuelson, P. A. (1948). *Economics — An Introductory Analysis.* New York, NY: McGraw-Hill.
Saunders, P. (2010). *Beware false prophets: Equality the good society and the spirit level.* London, UK: Policy Exchange.
Sawyer, M. (1976). *Income distribution in OECD countries.* OECD Economic Outlook, Occasional Studies. Paris: OECD Publishing.
Sen, A. (1999). *Development as freedom*, New York, NY: A. A. Knopf.
Siklos, P. L. (2010). *Revisiting the Coyne Affair: A singular event that changed the course of Canadian monetary history.* Canadian Journal of Economics, 43(3), 994–1015. http://dx.doi.org/10.1111/j.1540-5982.2010.01603.x.
Simons, H. C. (1969). *The definition of income.* In R. H. Parker & G. C. Harcourt Readings (Eds.), *The concept and measurement of income* (pp. 63–73). Cambridge, UK: Cambridge University Press. (Original work published 1938)
Statistics Canada. (1998). *Income distribution by size in Canada.* Catalogue No. 13-207.
Sullivan, J. (2023). *Remarks by National Security Advisor Jake Sullivan on Renewing American Economic Leadership at the Brookings Institution.* April 27, 2023. https://www.whitehouse.gov/briefing-room/speeches-remarks/2023/04/27/remarks-by-national-security-advisor-jake-sullivan-on-renewing-american-economic-leadership-at-the-brookings-institution/.
Summers, L. (2013). *Why stagnation might prove to be the new normal.* Financial Times.
Summers, L. (2014, February 24). *Why austerity is counterproductive in the new economy.* Speech to the National Association for Business Economics (NABE). Retrieved from http://larrysummers.com/nabe-why-austerity-is-counterproductive-in-the-new-economy/.

Summers, L. (2016). *The age of secular stagnation: What it is and what to do about it.* Foreign Affairs. Retrieved from http://larrysummers.com/2016/02/17/the-age-of-secular-stagnation/.

Tanzania Food and Nutrition Centre. (2014). *National nutrition survey 2014: Final Report.* The United Republic of Tanzania, Ministry of Health and Social Welfare. Retrieved from https://www.unicef.org/media/files/Tanzania_National_Nutrition_Survey_2014_Final_Report_18012015.pdf.

Ton, Z. (2012). *Why "good jobs" are good for retailers.* Harvard Business Review.

Tweddle, A., Battle, K., & Torjman, S. (2017). Welfare in Canada, Canada Social Report, Caledon Institute of Social Policy. Retrieved from http://www.caledoninst.org/Publications/PDF/1086ENG.pdf.

United Nations Economic Commission for Europe. (2011). *Canberra group handbook on household income statistics* (2nd ed.). Geneva: United Nations. Retrieved from www.unece.org/fileadmin/DAM/stats/groups/cgh/Canbera_Handbook_2011_WEB.pdf.

Van Langendonck, J. (Ed.). (2007). *The right to social security.* Social Europe Series, 2. Oxford, UK: Intersentia Press.

Veall, M. (2012). *Top income shares in Canada: recent trends and policy implications.* Canadian Journal of Economics, 1247–1272.

Veblen, T. (1953). *The theory of the leisure class.* New York, NY: Mentor Books. (Original work published 1912)

Watson, B., Osberg, L., & Phipps, S. (2016). *Economic insecurity and the weight gain of Canadian adults: A natural experiment approach.* Canadian Public Policy, 115–131.

Western, B., & Rosenfeld, J. (2011). *Unions, norms and the rise in United States wage inequality.* American Sociological Review, 76, 513.

Wilkinson, R., & Pickett, K. (2006). *Income inequality and population health: A review and explanation of the evidence.* Social Science and Medicine, 62(7), 1768–1784. [Epub 2005].

Wilkinson, R., & Pickett, K. (2010). *The spirit level: Why equality is better for everyone.* London, UK: Penguin Books.

Wolfe, B., & Haveman, R. (2001). *Accounting for the social and non-market benefits of education.* In J. Helliwell (Ed.), *The contribution of human and social capital to sustained economic growth and well being,* pp. 221–250. Paris and Ottawa: OECD and Human Resource Development Canada.

Wolfson, M., Brooks, N., Murphy, B., & Veall, M. R. (2016). *Piercing the veil — Private corporations and the income of the affluent.* Canadian Tax Journal, 64(1), 1–30.

Wolfson, M., Veall, M., & Brooks, N. (2014). *Piercing the veil — Private corporations and the income of the affluent.* Montreal, QC: Institute for Governance of Private and Public Organizations. Retrieved from http://igopp.org/wp-content/uploads/2014/06/wolfson-brooks-veall_-_incomes_of_affluent.pdf.

World Bank. (n.d.). *Data indicators.* https://databank.worldbank.org/home.aspx.

World Bank. (2016). *Digital Dividends: World Development Report.* International Bank for Reconstruction and Development / The World Bank. Washington, DC. https://documents1.worldbank.org/curated/en/896971468194972881/pdf/102725-PUB-Replacement-PUBLIC.pdf.

Xuereb, S., Fisher, M., Delorme, F., Lajoie, C. (2023). "Income Inequality In Canada From 1982-2021: Evidence From Distributional National Accounts." Working Paper N°2023/27, World Inequality Lab, Paris School of Economics.

Yalnizyan, A. (2010). *The rise of Canada's richest 1%.* Ottawa, ON: Canadian Centre for Policy Alternatives.

Young, C., Varner, C., Lurie, I. Z., & Prisinzano, R. (2016). *Millionaire migration and taxation of the elite: Evidence from administrative data.* American Sociological Review, 81(3), 421–446.

Zawilski, V. (2010). *Inequality in Canada: A reader on the intersections of gender, race and class.* Oxford, UK: Oxford University Press.

INDEX